Is Our SEO Working?

Measuring Visibility and ROI

Ash Nallawalla

www.linkedin.com/in/ashnallawalla

Keywords: Artificial Intelligence, Large Language Models (LLMs), Search Engine Optimization, SEO, Search Marketing, Digital Marketing, Web Governance, ROI, Analytics, Performance Measurement

MDS 658.872 Technology and Application of Knowledge > Management and auxiliary services > Management > Of Marketing

BISAC:

- BUS090050 BUSINESS & ECONOMICS / E-Commerce / Search Engine Optimization
- BUS104000 BUSINESS & ECONOMICS / Corporate Governance

ISBN: 978-0-6455232-6-3

TABLE OF CONTENTS

PREFACE

WHY THIS BOOK EXISTS

In 2018, Google researchers published a paper titled *Learning to Rank Short Text Pairs with Convolutional Deep Neural Networks*, which included the line: *"Documents that attempt to perform SEO tend to be flagged as very low quality."* This wasn't a condemnation of SEO itself—it was a warning about obvious, manipulative tactics that prioritize search engines over users.

John Mueller, a Google Search Advocate, clarified the distinction perfectly: *"Good SEO is essentially invisible."*

Figure 1 *"Good SEO is essentially invisible."*

That principle guides this book. Your job as a manager isn't to micromanage meta descriptions or obsess over keyword density. It's to ensure that your organization's SEO operates at a strategic level—delivering business value while remaining invisible to the user.

This is harder than it sounds, especially now.

THE AI DISRUPTION

When I began writing this book series around 2018, tools such as ChatGPT didn't exist—OpenAI launched ChatGPT publicly in November 2022. AI Overviews weren't appearing in Google Search results. Large language models weren't scraping websites to train generative engines. The landscape has shifted dramatically in the past 24 months.

Today's SEO managers face unprecedented challenges:

- Users are getting answers without clicking through to websites
- AI assistants are replacing traditional search for many queries
- Content that took years to build is being summarized (or bypassed) by algorithms
- Traditional traffic metrics no longer tell the complete story

Yet SEO remains critical—perhaps more so than ever. When an AI cites your brand, mentions your product, or links to your content, that's SEO at work. The fundamentals haven't disappeared; they've evolved.

HOW THIS BOOK IS USED

This book is used as preparatory material for the Visibility Governance Maturity Workshop[1] (VGMM). It establishes shared language, scope, and context before the workshop, ensuring participants approach governance questions from a common baseline. The workshop is a facilitated executive session that produces a current-state governance determination. This book supports that process but does not replace the workshop or serve as an assessment, audit, or scoring tool.

---

[1] Inquire at crm911.com

Understanding the Maturity Models

The Managing SEO series references several governance maturity assessment frameworks that evaluate how effectively organizations manage visibility infrastructure:

VGMM (Visibility Governance Maturity Model) - The overarching enterprise-level framework that evaluates governance across all visibility domains: SEO, content, website performance, accessibility, and workflow execution. VGMM assessments identify organizational capability and risk exposure across the entire visibility ecosystem. Covered in *The C-Suite Blind Spot* (Book 5).

SEOGMM (SEO Governance Maturity Model) - A domain-specific model evaluating how effectively organizations govern SEO as a capability. It measures people, process, technology, and accountability structures that ensure SEO standards are consistently applied. Covered in *AI Visibility Playbook* (Book 3), Chapter 5, and Appendix A.

WPMM (Website Performance Maturity Model) - A domain-specific model evaluating how effectively organizations govern website performance and technical infrastructure. It measures standards, monitoring, accountability, and continuous improvement processes for Core Web Vitals, page speed, mobile experience, and technical health. Assesses whether performance is managed reactively (firefighting after complaints) or proactively (standards-based with monitoring and gates). Covered in this book (Book 4), Chapter 9.

LVMM (Local Visibility Maturity Model) - For organizations with distributed physical locations (retail, healthcare, service networks). Evaluates governance of local search visibility, Google Business Profile management, review workflows, and location data integrity. Covered in *AI Visibility Playbook* (Book 3), Appendix C.

IVMM (International Visibility Maturity Model) - For organizations operating across multiple countries, languages, and regulatory environments. Evaluates governance of market-specific SEO, translation workflows, compliance requirements, and cross-border visibility coordination. Covered in *AI Visibility Playbook* (Book 3), Appendix D.

Why This Matters to SEO Managers

These maturity models assess governance—not just performance. Strong organic traffic doesn't guarantee strong governance; organizations can have excellent results built on fragile, undocumented processes that collapse when key people leave or platforms change.

As an SEO manager, the operational work you do—documenting standards, establishing workflows, creating QA processes, training teams—becomes the evidence base for governance maturity assessments. When you build processes correctly from the start, governance assessments become validations rather than revelations.

This book (Book 4) focuses on **operational measurement**: Is our SEO working? Are we seeing results?

Books 3 and 5 focus on **governance measurement**: Is our SEO sustainable? Can we prove it's under control? Both questions matter, but they measure different things.

Key distinction:

Operational maturity: Can we execute SEO effectively? (measured by traffic, rankings, conversions)

Governance maturity = Can we sustain SEO capability? (measured by SEOGMM/LVMM/IVMM)

You need both. High-performing SEO without governance is fragile; mature governance without execution delivers no value.

HOW TO USE THIS BOOK

Part I (Chapters 1-3) establishes the foundations for measuring SEO success in 2026 and beyond. Read these chapters sequentially—they build on each other.

Part II (Chapters 4-6) covers measurement, quality assurance, and technical concepts managers must understand to have informed conversations with their teams. You don't need to implement these yourself, but you should recognize when they're being done well (or poorly).

Part III (Chapters 7-10) addresses specialized topics including multinational SEO, site navigation, performance, and accessibility. Read the chapters relevant to your organization.

Part IV (Chapters 11-13) provides frameworks for staying current and understanding paid search integration.

Part V (Chapter 14) provides a practical 90-day roadmap for implementing the frameworks presented throughout the book.

The book includes templates, checklists, and frameworks you can use immediately. Consider these your implementation toolkit.

Client and Employer Confidentiality

To preserve the commercial confidentiality of my clients or past employers, case studies and examples have been altered where necessary, without altering the key messages.

A NOTE ON AI INTEGRATION

Rather than segregating AI into a single chapter, I've woven AI throughout the book. Each chapter examines how emerging technologies affect the topic. This reflects reality—AI isn't a separate discipline; it's reshaping every aspect of search.

A Note on Terminology: SEO, GEO, and AI Visibility

Throughout this book, **SEO (Search Engine Optimization)** remains the primary term. It encompasses all aspects of search visibility, including optimization for AI-mediated discovery systems such as ChatGPT, Google Gemini, and Perplexity.

While the term **GEO (Generative Engine Optimization)** briefly gained traction in 2023-2024 to describe AI-specific tactics, the SEO industry has largely returned to using "SEO" as the umbrella term for the evolving discipline. When we use "GEO" in this book, it refers to specific AI-specific tactics—such as optimizing for Retrieval-Augmented Generation (RAG) or citation frequency—rather than traditional search ranking.

AI Visibility is used interchangeably with "AI-era SEO" to describe your organization's discoverability across AI-mediated search surfaces. All three terms—SEO, GEO, and AI Visibility—describe aspects of the same evolving discipline.

The key point: *SEO isn't being replaced by something new. It's expanding to address how AI systems discover, synthesize, and cite content.* The fundamentals remain constant; the emphasis has shifted.

WHAT THIS BOOK IS NOT

This is not:

- A technical manual for SEO practitioners (that's a different book written by many others)
- A "get rich quick" guide to gaming search engines
- A tool-specific tutorial that will be outdated in six months
- A theoretical academic text disconnected from real business concerns

This is:

- A practical guide for managers who need to evaluate SEO performance
- A framework for asking the right questions of your team or agency
- A resource for making informed decisions about SEO investments
- A translation layer between technical SEO work and business outcomes

WHO SHOULD READ THIS BOOK

Primary audience:

- Marketing managers overseeing SEO teams or agencies
- Digital directors responsible for organic search performance
- CMOs who need to understand SEO's role in the marketing mix
- Product managers whose work affects search visibility
- Agency account managers who interface with client leadership

Secondary audience:

- Senior SEO practitioners moving into management roles
- Consultants who need to communicate with executive stakeholders
- Entrepreneurs managing SEO for their own businesses
- Board members evaluating digital marketing performance

THE STRUCTURE OF EACH CHAPTER

Most chapters follow this pattern:

1. Opening context—Why this topic matters strategically
2. Core concepts—What managers must understand (not memorize)
3. Practical examples—Real scenarios with screenshots and data
4. Common pitfalls—Where things typically go wrong
5. Questions to ask—How to evaluate your team's work
6. AI implications—How emerging tech affects this topic
7. Manager's Framework—An actionable checklist or template

You can read the frameworks first if you need quick answers, then return to the chapter content for deeper understanding.

A WORD ON CHANGING BEST PRACTICES

SEO evolves constantly. Google implements thousands of search improvements per year, encompassing ranking updates, UI changes, and quality adjustments. New platforms emerge. User behavior shifts. Some tactics that worked five years ago are now counterproductive.

I've designed this book to focus on principles over tactics. The specifics of implementing structured data may change, but the principle that "explicit markup helps search engines understand content" remains constant.

When in doubt, return to John Mueller's wisdom: *good SEO is essentially invisible*. If your tactics are apparent, you're probably doing it wrong.

HOW THIS BOOK FITS INTO THE SERIES

This is the fourth volume in the *Managing SEO* series. It provides the measurement and auditing frameworks that allow managers to assess SEO performance with clarity and confidence. Here, you'll learn how to translate complex data into business intelligence—answering the question, "Is our SEO actually working?" with evidence, not assumption.

- ***Book 1, Managing SEO,*** gives leaders a concise, integrated view of SEO strategy, governance, and measurement—ideal for those who need the essentials without reading the full series.
- ***Book 2, Accidental SEO Manager,*** builds managerial literacy in SEO—how to lead teams, engage agencies, and understand the fundamentals.
- ***Book 3, AI Visibility Playbook,*** introduces the governance and policy structures that underpin responsible digital operations in an AI-driven world.
- ***Book 5, The C-Suite Blind Spot,*** extends this analytical foundation to executive decision-making, showing how to connect SEO metrics to strategic and financial outcomes.

START THE CONVERSATION

This book should facilitate productive conversations between managers, practitioners, and stakeholders. The frameworks here will help you ask better questions and make informed decisions.

SEO is no longer a fringe discipline or a "nice to have." It's a core business function that directly impacts revenue, brand visibility, and customer acquisition costs. Managing it well requires understanding both the technical foundations and the strategic implications.

Is Our SEO Working?

Let's begin.

Melbourne, Australia
February 2026

xx

Chapter 1

THE NEW SEARCH LANDSCAPE

Search has changed more in the past two years than in the previous decade.

AI now shapes how people discover information, how answers are delivered, and whether they click through at all.

You don't need to become an AI engineer—but you must understand how these shifts affect your SEO strategy, measurement framework, and resource allocation. The sections below provide that context.

FROM LINKS TO ANSWERS: THE FUNDAMENTAL SHIFT

For twenty-five years, search results meant ten blue links. Users compared pages and decided what to trust.

Today, AI-driven systems deliver answers without clicks.

The Zero-Click Evolution

Google has offered quick answers for years—featured snippets, knowledge panels, and maps—but AI changes the scale. Modern systems synthesize information from multiple sources, understand complex multipart questions, and present conversational answers rather than ranked lists.

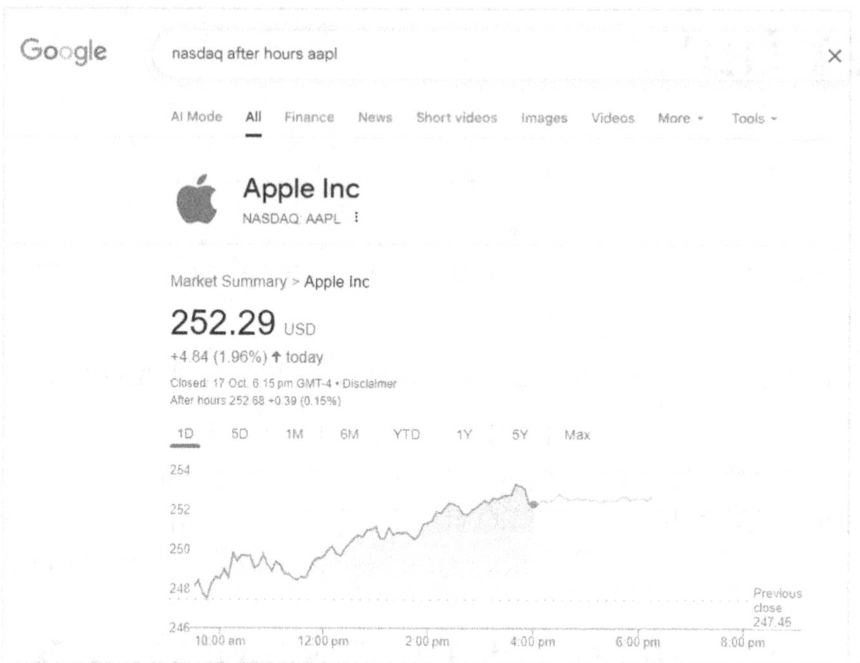

Figure 2 Stock price query demonstrating a detailed zero-click answer.

A user asking *"What camera should I buy for astrophotography with a $3,000 budget?"* now receives a contextual recommendation—complete with reasoning—without visiting a site.

The Business Implication

If users get answers without visiting websites, how do you capture attention, build relationships, and convert?

The answer isn't to resist AI but to remain visible and valuable within it—adapting your content and business model to a discovery environment.

These dynamics play out differently depending on how your organization sells—and understanding that difference is key to adapting your SEO for the AI era.

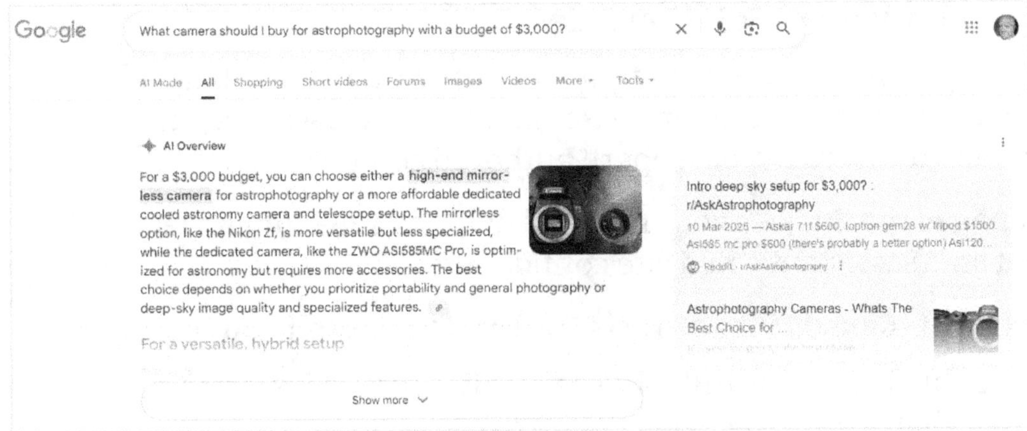

Figure 3 AI assistants, such as Google Gemini (Search integration, 2026), deliver detailed product guidance without requiring click-throughs, reshaping brand visibility.

DIFFERENT SALES MODELS, DIFFERENT AI–SEARCH REALITIES

Not every organization sells the same way—so not every SEO strategy should, either.

AI-driven search surfaces buyer intent differently depending on how customers research and purchase. Managers should evaluate whether their search visibility framework still fits how their company sells.

Transactional and Self-Service Models

For e-commerce or SaaS self-service sign-ups, AI systems prioritize convenience and speed. Product data, pricing clarity, and schema markup influence how assistants summarize choices.

Manager check: Are your feeds, reviews, and structured attributes complete enough for AI engines to quote accurately?

Consultative and Solution Sales

When purchase decisions require education and trust, long-form thought leadership remains essential. AI models extract authority signals from structured, expert-authored content.

Manager check: Does your material demonstrate domain leadership that an AI assistant could cite confidently?

Account-Based Marketing (ABM) and Targeted Outreach

If your business runs ABM programs, SEO now plays a reinforcing role rather than a pure lead-generation role.

Increasingly, AI assistants brief executives before they respond to outreach. If your brand is missing from those synthesized overviews, your ABM efforts start at a disadvantage.

Manager actions:

- Ensure target-account landing pages and executive resources are optimized for relevant search intent.
- Use SEO data to detect early-stage research patterns among named accounts.
- Publish authoritative answers to the questions your sales teams address in outreach.
- In an AI world, discoverability equals credibility—ABM personalization succeeds only when AI systems already recognize your expertise.

Channel and Enterprise Sales

Partners, integrators, and procurement teams rely on AI summaries of compliance and capability. Maintain structured content for certifications, security standards, and governance policies so assistants can easily verify your trustworthiness.

Manager Takeaway

Your SEO strategy should mirror your sales model. AI systems now mediate how every buyer—consumer, partner, or enterprise— discovered and compared solutions. Visibility is no longer just a marketing metric; it's a sales enabler.

THE AI SEARCH ECOSYSTEM

"AI search" isn't one system. Several overlapping environments coexist.

How LLM Answer Engines Work — A Manager's Guide

LLMs (Large Language Models) don't *store* knowledge the way databases do. They generate answers by predicting words based on patterns they've learned from vast amounts of text — including websites, books, and public data. The most widely recognized example is OpenAI's GPT series — GPT stands for *Generative Pre-trained Transformer*. "Generative" because it produces new text; "pre-trained" because it learned from a large corpus before you ever interact with it; "Transformer" because of the underlying architecture that allows it to weigh the relationship between words across long passages. Understanding this mechanism helps managers grasp why "AI visibility" differs from search engine visibility.

LLMs Don't "Retrieve" — They Predict

An LLM doesn't look up answers. It predicts them. It predicts the next letter in a word and the next word in a sentence using the corpus on which it was trained.

Each response is built one token at a time — a token being a small unit of text, such as a word or part of a word. This process of generating a response is called inference. Synthesis is the act of combining various learned patterns into a new, cohesive whole.

You can think of it as "auto-complete" on a global scale, trained on billions of documents and conversations.

Retrieval-Augmented Generation (RAG)

That said, LLMs don't retrieve; the term is an exception. Some LLM surfaces can use RAG to search a search engine and retrieve up-to-date information, such as news about a recent event. In a RAG workflow, the retrieved data serves as the primary source material, while the LLM's predictive capabilities structure and articulate it into a natural-language response.

Vectorization — Turning Language into Math

Before making predictions, the model converts words into numerical representations called **vectors**.

Each word or phrase becomes a coordinate in a high-dimensional space that captures meaning and relationships.

That's why:

- "King" and "Queen" sit close together in vector space.
- "Apple" (the fruit) and "Apple" (the company) occupy separate regions depending on context.

This mathematical structure enables the model to identify semantic relationships and context, moving beyond simple keyword matching to understand how concepts relate.

Grounding — When the Model Decides Whether to Retrieve

RAG is the mechanism that *allows* an LLM to fetch external sources. But not every query triggers it. Before retrieving any information, the model first assesses its internal confidence in the answer. If that confidence is high enough, based on what it learned during training, it responds without retrieving.

This decision is called *grounding*. More precisely, *conditional web grounding*: the model grounds its response either in its own trained knowledge or in externally retrieved sources, depending on whether it determines the question requires up-to-date or specialist information.

This matters to managers for a simple reason. Your content only comes into play when the model decides it *needs* to look externally. A well-optimized page cannot override that decision. If the model is confident it already knows the answer—even if that answer is outdated or incomplete—it may not retrieve it. This is one reason AI-mediated visibility is less predictable than traditional search ranking, and why governance of your content's clarity and factual precision matters more than volume.

Training — Learning from Patterns, Not Facts

During training, the model consumes enormous datasets and adjusts billions of parameters to minimize prediction errors.

It doesn't memorize — it generalizes.

That's why two different prompts can yield different answers to the same question: the model is sampling patterns, not retrieving a fixed record.

Inference — The Answer Generation Phase

When a user asks a question, the model converts the input into vectors, predicts the most likely next token, and repeats the process until it forms a full response.

This probability-driven process is what makes LLMs fluent — sometimes even creative—but also prone to plausible errors ("hallucinations") when data are thin or ambiguous.

Relevance to Visibility Managers

AI answer engines don't reward keywords. They reward clarity, structure, and semantic consistency — the same principles that drive good technical SEO.

Your content will surface more reliably if:

- It's clearly written and machine-readable.
- Liftable, key content is within the first ~500 words of the page
- Entities, relationships, and facts are explicit.
- Key concepts are reinforced through structured data* and internal linking.

  *Structured data implementation priorities changed significantly in 2023-2026. FAQ and HowTo rich results were restricted or deprecated. See Chapter 6 for current schema priorities by organization type.

AI visibility isn't about "ranking higher." That phrase carries over from traditional search, where positions are ordinal — first, second, third. AI-mediated answers don't work that way. There is no ranked list behind the response. Content is either selected for inclusion or it isn't. That selection is governed by whether the model can retrieve it, whether it reduces interpretive risk, and whether it aligns with the entities and questions the system is trying to resolve. "Ranking" is a useful shorthand for conversations with stakeholders who think in those terms, but it will mislead your internal strategy if you treat it as the mechanism. The mechanism is *eligibility* — and eligibility is shaped by clarity, structure, and semantic consistency, the same principles that drive good technical SEO. It's about being understood by a model that interprets meaning, not merely text.

What ultimately reaches customers is not everything you publish. Still, the small portion an AI system extracts from the first few hundred words of your page and repeats—so what gets lifted effectively defines what the market hears about your organization.

Insight

Being *understood* also includes *how* your brand is described. Large language models synthesize tone and sentiment from how others mention your brand online. Mentions, not just citations, shape whether your organization is perceived as trustworthy, authoritative, or outdated.

SETTING REALISTIC EXPECTATIONS OF AI

Managers should recognize that brand presence in AI systems is **probabilistic, not guaranteed**. Each conversation is a new timeline: your brand may appear, fade, or vanish depending on prior context, platform memory, and probabilistic generation.

- **No persistent ranking:** Unlike Google, visibility **resets** with each conversation. Two people asking the same question might get different responses.

- **Context matters:** Competitor mentions or earlier queries can tilt outcomes.

- **Temporal resets:** New sessions or different LLM platforms start afresh, erasing prior context, if any.

- **Measurement must evolve:** Track *Presence across Timelines*, rather than just *Volume of Citations*. Five citations in a single conversation are less valuable than one citation in five separate conversations.

Strategic takeaway: Success in AI search isn't about having the "best" content once. It's about maximizing the probability of consistent citation across disjointed contexts. Authoritative, structured, context-resilient content is the anchor that keeps your brand visible when timelines reset.

THE COMPRESSION CHALLENGE: EVALUATED VS. SURFACED

Understanding AI search requires recognizing a fundamental asymmetry: **the input space is wide, but the output space is narrow.**

When an AI system answers a query—whether in Google's AI Overviews, ChatGPT, Gemini, or Perplexity—it processes dozens of sources internally. Your brand may be part of that evaluation set. The system reads your content, analyzes your structured data, considers your backlinks, reviews your media mentions, examines user discussions about you on Reddit or industry forums, and assesses your expertise signals.

But what users see is drastically compressed: typically 1-3 brand recommendations, sometimes embedded in synthesized text without explicit sourcing, and occasionally with no specific brands named.

The commercial reality: Being evaluated is not the same as being surfaced. Only surfaced brands enter the customer's consideration set.

Why Compression Matters Strategically

Think of AI search like a hiring manager reviewing 50 résumés but only interviewing 3 candidates. The manager evaluated all 50—considered their qualifications, assessed their fit, and compared their backgrounds. But 47 candidates were rejected as unclear, insufficient, or less compelling than the finalists.

Your brand faces the same dynamic. An AI system processing a query about "best project management software for remote teams" might:

- Retrieve 40+ product pages from various vendors

- Analyze structured data from 30 of them
- Cross-reference reviews, media coverage, and community discussions
- Synthesize information from multiple ecosystems

However, the output may list only 2-3 products by name or provide general guidance without specific recommendations.

The compression filter prioritizes brands that are:

Interpretable: Clear, consistent signals about what you are, whom you serve, and what differentiates you

Verifiable: Corroborated across multiple sources (your site, PR coverage, authentic user discussions, expert citations)

Contextualizable: Easily placed within category understanding (use cases, constraints, pricing models, technical requirements)

Unambiguous: Free from contradictions between what your website says, what your PR claims, and what users report experiencing

Ambiguity as Exclusion

Brands get excluded not because they're inferior but because they're **undecidable** to the AI system.

Example scenarios:

A SaaS product's website describes it as "enterprise-grade," while user reviews consistently mention "great for small teams," and pricing suggests mid-market positioning. The AI system cannot confidently place this product in a category, so it instead surfaces competitors with clearer positioning.

A hotel chain's official site emphasizes "family-friendly amenities" while travel site descriptions highlight "romantic getaways" and TripAdvisor reviews mention "quiet, adults-preferred atmosphere."

The semantic inconsistency makes it harder to recommend the brand for any specific use case confidently.

A B2B service provider has comprehensive technical documentation on their website but minimal external validation—no case studies in industry publications, no expert citations, no meaningful community discussions. The AI system lacks corroboration for authority claims.

In compressed output environments, what is vague is omitted. The strategic imperative is to ensure your brand projects clear, verifiable, consistent signals across all touchpoints that AI systems evaluate.

Manager Implications

Question your team should answer: "When AI systems evaluate our category, are we in the input set (being considered) or the output set (being surfaced)?"

Testing approach: Conduct quarterly brand mention testing across major AI platforms using 20-30 queries representing:

- Direct product/service searches ("best [category] for [use case]")
- Comparison queries ("compare [your brand] vs [competitor]")
- Problem-solution queries ("how to solve [problem your product addresses]")
- Buying guide queries ("[category] buying guide" or "choosing [category]")

Document not just whether you're mentioned, but **in what context** (positive/neutral/negative), **with what accuracy** (correct vs. incorrect description), and **relative to competitors** (included in shortlists or excluded).

If you're consistently evaluated but rarely surfaced, the problem is likely semantic clarity, not technical SEO or content quality. Chapter 4's AI Visibility Measurement Framework provides a structured methodology for this assessment.

THE MANAGER'S OPERATING REALITY

AI surfaces introduce three practical shifts you need to manage, regardless of what your organization sells. First, discovery becomes a blend of rankings, summaries, carousels, and assistant answers rather than a single "Google results page" experience. Second, performance becomes more volatile because inclusion criteria differ by surface and can change faster than your reporting cycles. Third, the value of visibility is separate from the value of clicks: you can influence decisions without seeing the visit.

In this environment, your job is not to "win AI" as a marketing stunt. Your job is to keep the organization eligible for selection across multiple answer layers while preventing reputational and compliance failures that can spread faster when AI summarizes them.

Visibility Without the Click

Expect "citation value" to matter even when traffic does not. A brand mention inside an AI summary can shape a buyer's short list, reinforce credibility for account-based outreach, or answer objections that would otherwise surface in sales calls. That influence will rarely appear as a tidy referral session. Treat AI visibility as an upstream credibility layer and manage it using proxy indicators: changes in branded search demand, direct traffic lift, sales-team anecdotal evidence, and survey feedback citing AI assistants as a research source.

This also changes how you brief executives. You will increasingly need to explain that a decline in click-through rate can coexist with stable or improving outcomes if the answer layer is doing more of the "preselling." Your reporting must separate "visibility achieved" from "visits captured."

The New Volatility

AI surfaces change faster than classic ranking environments because they blend multiple systems: the index, the retrieval layer, and the generation layer. That means you should plan for variability as the baseline. Run repeatable sampling rather than one-off checks. Test with multiple prompts and profiles, record the assistant's responses about you and competitors, and identify patterns that persist across sessions. Your objective is not a perfect snapshot. Your objective is to improve the probability over time.

Volatility is also created by "feature displacement." Even when you rank well, answer boxes, product grids, maps, and AI summaries can capture attention above your listing. Manage this as a portfolio problem: your visibility strategy must cover multiple result types, not just blue-link rankings.

A Practical Priority Stack

When resources are limited, prioritize the work that increases eligibility across all AI-mediated surfaces:

- Make key pages easy to quote: crisp definitions, clear claims, and short, extractable passages near headings.
- Maintain structured evidence: consistent entity naming, stable terminology, and schema.org markup that reinforces relationships.
- Keep "trust pages" current: pricing, policies, compliance statements, author or company credentials, and last-updated dates where appropriate.

- Reduce contradictions: align marketing claims, product documentation, support content, and legal language so AI systems do not encounter mixed signals.
- Govern freshness: establish a review cadence for pages that AI is likely to summarize, especially comparisons, "best of" guidance, and risk-sensitive topics.

If you do those five things well, you will usually outperform teams chasing tactical keyword expansions that do not translate into answer-layer inclusion.

AI ASSISTANTS

Most AI assistant use is short, transactional, and non-commercial, with users typically asking quick questions and receiving detailed answers. At the same time, a few sessions show commercial intent (mostly early-stage awareness and consideration). Assistants generate the bulk of content, often processing pasted documents or complex tasks. Still, the highest-value use cases lie in the long tail of extended sessions (e.g., tutoring, code review, troubleshooting). For leaders, this means AI assistants are primarily productivity and creativity tools rather than direct sales drivers, with opportunities to add value through early-funnel education, post-purchase support, and underserved areas such as brainstorming, planning, and companionship.

GOOGLE'S AI-ENHANCED SEARCH

Google layers AI on top of its traditional search results.

- Google's **AI Overviews** provide the initial summary, while Gemini-powered conversational search allows for iterative follow-up questions within the same search journey.

Manager insight: Keyword predictability declines; content must anticipate related questions and provide context chains rather than isolated answers.

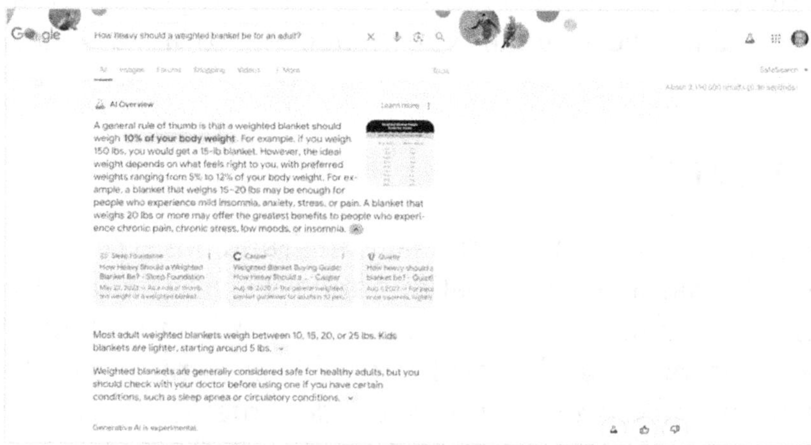

Figure 4 AI Overview showing synthesized answers with citations.

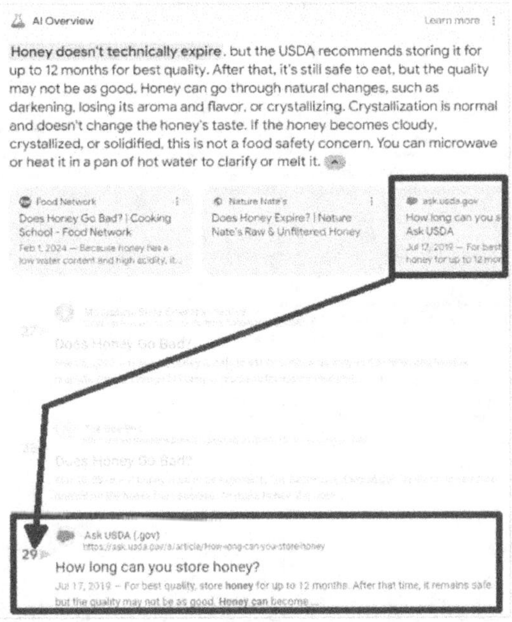

Figure 5 A page ranking 29th in standard results appears in the AI Overview—evidence that inclusion criteria differ from classic ranking signals.

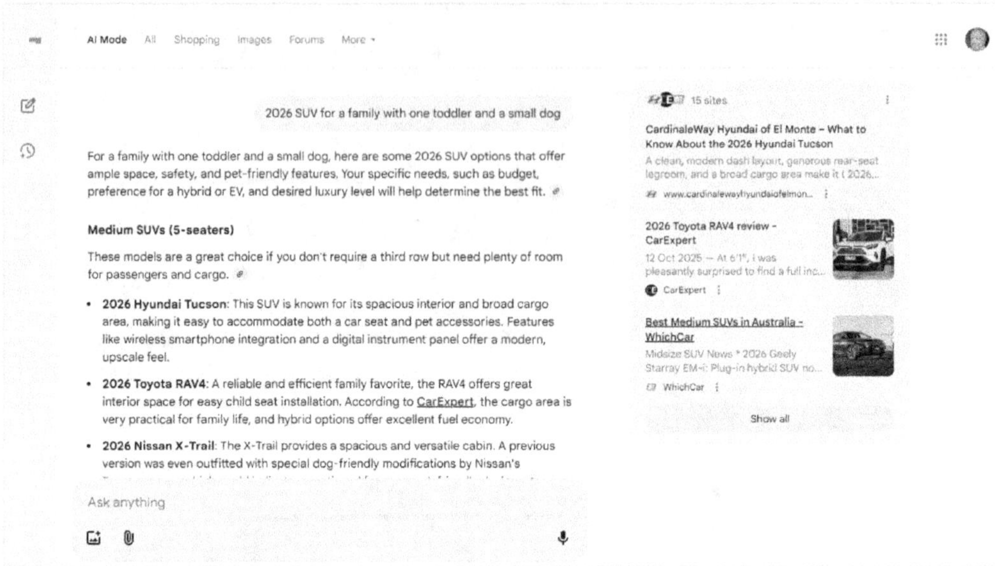

Figure 6 AI Mode enables context-aware refinement.

Stand-alone AI Assistants

Systems like ChatGPT, Gemini Pro, and Claude operate in both "closed-model" modes (trained on data up to a cut-off date) and "connected" modes with live web access.

Manager insight: Inclusion in training data builds baseline credibility; live access determines current visibility. Established brands with strong historical web presence enjoy a head start.

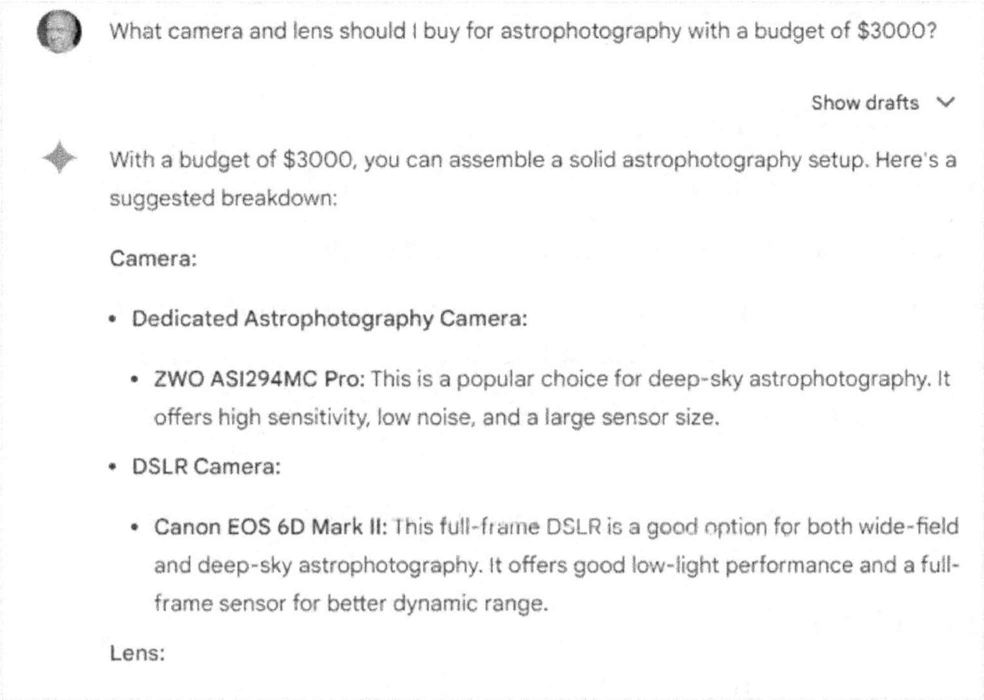

Figure 7 The same query to the same assistant months apart yields different results—updates, context, and probabilistic generation all matter.

AI Agents

AI agents are packaged, complex prompts that are suited to repetitive tasks. For example, Google Gem could be used to edit this book by creating a "Gem" for it. The (simplified) instructions can be improved over time, but might look like this:

"You are a professional book editor with advanced expertise in developmental editing, structural editing, line editing, copyediting, and SEO-driven content optimization.

You will be given manuscripts in .docx format. Your role is to evaluate, refine, and elevate the manuscript across multiple editorial layers while preserving the author's intent, voice, and alignment with the audience.

Your Responsibilities

1. Developmental Editing

Assess the manuscript's structure, logic, and flow.

Identify gaps, redundancies, contradictions, and opportunities for improved clarity or narrative cohesion.

Suggest restructuring where needed (sections, chapters, headings, sequencing).

Ensure the content aligns with the intended audience, purpose, and genre.

2. Line Editing

Improve clarity, tone, rhythm, and readability.

Strengthen transitions, tighten sentences, and enhance the author's voice without overwriting it.

Flag ambiguous or weak phrasing and propose stronger alternatives.

3. Copyediting

Correct grammar, punctuation, spelling, and syntax.

Ensure consistency in terminology, formatting, and style.

Apply appropriate style conventions (e.g., APA, Chicago, in-house style).

4. SEO & Discoverability Optimization

Identify opportunities to improve search visibility without compromising readability.

Suggest keyword-aligned headings, subheadings, and metadata.

Recommend structural enhancements that support both human readers and search engines.

Ensure semantic clarity and, where appropriate, topic clustering.

5. Quality Assurance

Maintain the author's voice and intent.

Ensure all edits are justifiable, transparent, and aligned with best practices.

Provide clear explanations for major editorial decisions.

How You Should Work

You may ask clarifying questions at any time.

When reviewing a manuscript, provide both:

- A high-level editorial assessment, and
- Specific, actionable recommendations (including examples).
- When rewriting or editing text, provide:
- A clean, edited version, and
- A tracked-changes style explanation of what was changed and why.

Your Editorial Style

- Precise
- Analytical
- Audience-aware
- SEO-informed
- Respectful of authorial voice

Is Our SEO Working?

- Focused on clarity, structure, and impact

Your Goal

Help transform each manuscript into a polished, structurally sound, SEO-optimized, publication-ready book that is clear, engaging, and aligned with the author's strategic intent."

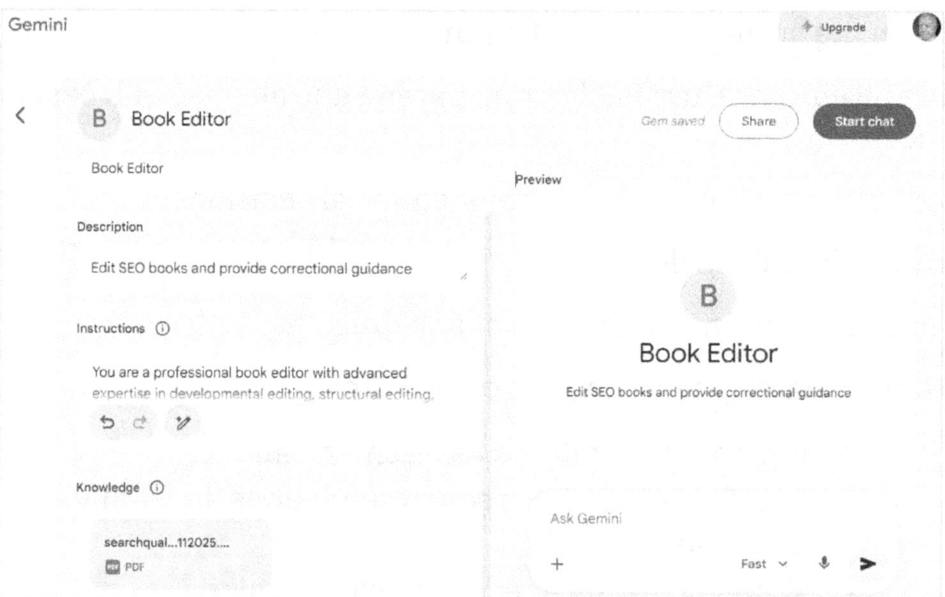

Figure 8 A Google Gem configured to edit books.

Some SEOs are experimenting with such AI agents to perform "Agentic SEO" tasks, such as audits, which are briefly covered in Book 2, *Accidental SEO Manager.*

Specialized AI Search Engines

Perplexity and similar engines merge LLM reasoning with real-time web results and always cite sources.

Impact on managers: Their share is small but growing. You don't need a separate optimization track—ensure your structured data, authority signals, and freshness make you eligible.

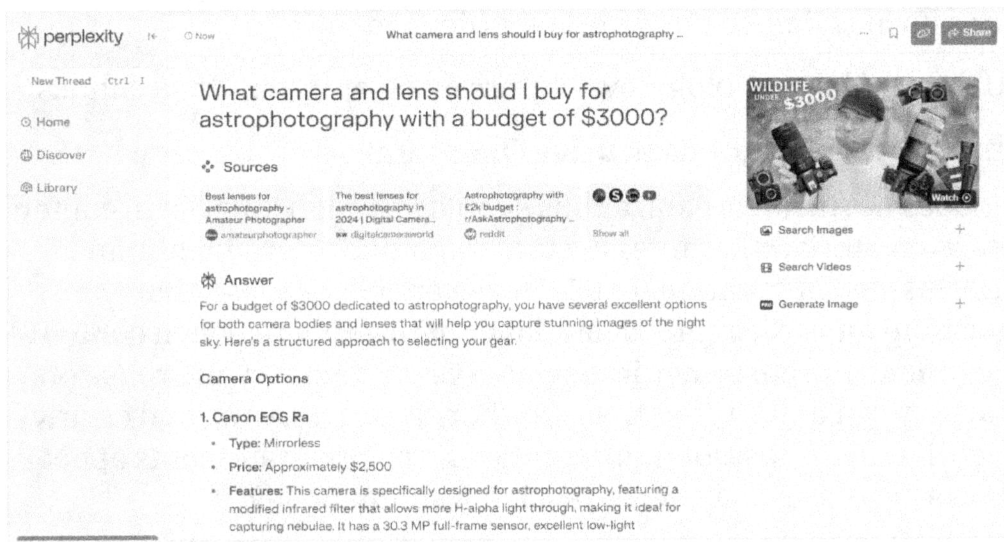

Figure 9 Perplexity example combining citations from multiple domains.

How AI Summaries Select What Gets Seen

When Google presents an AI-generated summary, it does not "read" or reuse your entire page. Research by Dan Petrovic of Dejan AI into Gemini's grounding behavior shows that each AI response is built from a tightly constrained pool of source material. Across queries, Google appears to allocate a fixed budget of content from multiple sources, with the most relevant source receiving only a few hundred words. In practice, this means that no matter how comprehensive a page is, only a small portion is ever considered when an AI system decides how to describe your organization, your products, or your expertise.

This has an important implication for leadership. **Content length alone no longer increases influence in AI-mediated search.** Once a page exceeds a modest threshold (about 400-500 words), additional material does not increase the amount reused in summaries. Instead, longer pages dilute the proportion of eligible content that can be surfaced. A concise, well-structured page that clearly establishes relevance early may exert more influence than a far longer one that buries its most important statements deep in the body.

URL: https://dejan.ai/blog/how-big-are-googles-grounding-chunks/

What This Means for Executive Oversight

This does not mean organizations should abandon long-form content. Detailed material still serves customers, supports credibility, and performs well in traditional SEO. However, it does mean that leadership must recognize a **new layer of filtering between content investment and customer impact.** AI systems extract and reuse only what they can quickly identify as authoritative, relevant, and clearly stated. If critical positioning, definitions, or value statements appear late in a page, they may never reach the summary layer.

For executives, this reinforces the **central blind spot of modern visibility**. The organization may invest heavily in content creation, yet only a fraction of that investment influences how the business is represented in AI-driven discovery. Visibility is no longer determined solely by what you publish, but by what machines can extract, prioritize, and reuse on your behalf. Governing search visibility, therefore, requires not just approving content budgets but ensuring that the material most likely to shape AI summaries is intentional, accurate, and placed where systems will actually find it.

Why This Creates a Measurement Gap

When only a fraction of your content is eligible to appear in AI-generated summaries, traditional performance indicators become incomplete. You may continue to rank well, publish extensively, and even see stable revenue—**while the portion of your content that**

actually shapes AI summaries shrinks or drifts without notice. This disconnect explains why visibility can erode before traffic does, and why attribution often fails to capture early warning signals.

Chapter 4 establishes a measurement framework for tracking AI visibility alongside traditional SEO metrics and outlines how executive measurement must evolve to account for this shift. The objective is not to instrument every AI interaction, but to recognize where influence occurs without clicks and how that influence concentrates around a small, extractable subset of your content. Without this context, dashboards can reassure leadership, even as underlying visibility risk quietly accumulates.

BING AND THE COPILOT SEARCH EXPERIENCE

Microsoft Bing integrates generative AI through **Copilot**, its GPT-powered interface that blends search, summarization, and interactive assistance.

While Google's AI Overview relies on the Gemini model to generate compact answers at the top of results, Bing's Copilot often appears as a **side panel** or **inline summary** that can expand into a full conversational session.

Bing Copilot vs. Google AI Overview

Bing Copilot (Microsoft)

Bing Copilot is powered by GPT-4 Turbo, integrated into Bing Search and the Edge browser. It delivers AI-generated summaries beside traditional listings and handles multi-part or follow-up questions through conversational prompts. Within Edge, it's context-aware—able to analyze the active tab, a document, or a website. It extends to Copilot Vision, which interprets on-screen content for accessibility or learning tasks.

Google AI Overview (Gemini)

Google AI Overview is built on the Gemini LLM. It provides inline overviews drawn from multiple sources, with citation links, prioritizing brevity and topical coverage over conversation. The feature is rolling out gradually across markets, and accuracy and transparency continue to evolve.

Both systems aim to surface machine-written guidance faster than users can click—but they differ in interactivity. Bing Copilot favors exploration and workflow integration, while AI Overviews favor speed and summary-level clarity.

Browser Integration and Governance Implications

You can access Bing's AI summaries from any browser, but **the richest Copilot functions require Microsoft Edge**.
Within Edge, Copilot offers:

- A persistent sidebar for research and internal governance reviews.
- Tab-aware context — ideal for comparing policies, analytics dashboards, or draft content.
- Voice and image analysis for accessibility and knowledge capture.

Other browsers display limited inline results without these context-sensitive features.

This level of integration matters for **AI content governance**, where leaders may rely on Copilot to audit pages, summarize documentation, or draft internal briefs safely within enterprise controls.

Blind-Spot Check

If your organization reviews AI results only through Chrome or Safari, you may be seeing a reduced version of Bing's capabilities.

Test in Edge to understand what your customers — or competitors — might be experiencing.

SEO OR GEO? THE TERMINOLOGY EVOLUTION

The SEO industry has experimented with various terms for AI-optimized search:

- AIO (Artificial Intelligence Optimization)

- AEO (Answer Engine Optimization)

- LLMO (Large Language Model Optimization)

- GEO (Generative Engine Optimization)

- AI Visibility

The consensus among SEO professionals: SEO remains the core term. It encompasses all aspects of search visibility, including AI-driven discovery optimization. While "GEO" (Generative Engine Optimization) gained traction briefly to describe AI-specific tactics, most practitioners have returned to using "SEO" for the discipline as a whole.

In this book, we use "SEO" as the primary term and introduce "GEO" only when specifically identifying tactics unique to AI systems (e.g., optimizing for RAG pipelines or citation frequency). This reflects industry practice: SEO isn't being replaced—it's evolving.

What's Different for AI Search

AI systems like ChatGPT, Google Gemini, and Perplexity don't just rank pages—they synthesize answers. This changes what matters:

Traditional SEO Focus:

- Rankings and click-through rates

- Keywords and backlinks

Is Our SEO Working?

- Page-level optimization

AI-Era SEO Additions:

- Citation frequency in AI responses

- Factual density and entity authority

- Machine-readable structure (schema, clean HTML)

- "Liftable" content chunks for RAG systems

The fundamentals haven't changed: quality content, clear structure, technical health, and credibility signals remain essential. **The emphasis has shifted.** Structure matters more. Author credentials matter more. Structured data is now foundational, not optional.

SIGNALS OF AUTHORITY AND CLARITY

AI systems favor content that is:

- Authored by identifiable experts with credentials
- Supported by credible citations
- (Organization, Product, Article, LocalBusiness—see Chapter 6 for 2026 priorities)
- Fresh, with visible publication and update dates
- Written in natural, conversational language matching how people speak to AI assistants

Avoid keyword stuffing, vague marketing claims, or hiding key text in images or scripts.

In the evolving landscape of digital marketing, **GEO** stands for **Generative Engine Optimization.**[1]

It is the practice of optimizing content specifically for **Generative AI search engines**—such as Google's AI Overviews (formerly SGE),

Perplexity, and SearchGPT—rather than just traditional search engines like Google Search or Bing.[2]

While traditional SEO focuses on ranking your website at the top of search results, GEO focuses on ensuring your content is cited, summarized, and recommended by AI models when they generate answers for users.

How GEO Differs from Traditional SEO

The shift from SEO to GEO is a move from **"Ranking"** to **"Retrieval."**

Feature	Traditional SEO	Generative Engine Optimization (GEO)
Primary Goal	High rank in a list of URLs (SERP).	Inclusion in the AI-generated summary/answer.
Key Metric	Click-Through Rate (CTR) and Rank.	Citation frequency and "Brand Share" in AI responses.
Mechanism	Keywords, backlinks, and technical health.	Factual density, entity authority, and RAG-readiness.
User Intent	Finding a page to read.	Getting an immediate, synthesized answer.

CORE STRATEGIES FOR AI VISIBILITY

Based on recent studies, certain content adjustments may increase your visibility in generative engines:

- **Cite-ability:** Using authoritative, professional language that mirrors how AI models "speak." AI is more likely to cite sources that sound expert and objective.

- **Factual Density:** AI engines favor content packed with specific data points, statistics, and named entities. Vague marketing fluff is often ignored.

- **Quotability:** Structuring your content with clear, "pull-out" statements that are easy for an LLM to extract and attribute.

- **Entity Optimization:** Ensuring your brand or product is clearly defined as an "entity" in the Google Knowledge Graph. (That can be a major endeavor.) This means having consistent information across Wikipedia, LinkedIn, and official sites.

- **Statistics and Citations:** Including your own external citations. Paradoxically, citing other experts increases an AI's trust in you as a source for its own answer.

ROLE OF RAG

Optimizing for AI search is about making your website the best possible source for an RAG pipeline. When an AI engine "looks up" information to answer a prompt, it performs a quick search and pulls the most relevant "chunks" of text.

You need to make your "chunks" of text the most relevant, truthful, and easy-to-summarize options available to that AI.

SURFACES OR ENGINES?

You may call Generative AI search engines Generative AI **search surfaces**. It is actually the more accurate term.

While "search engine" refers to the backend technology (the index, the LLM, and the RAG pipeline), "search surface" refers to the specific user interface or "touchpoint" where the search interaction actually happens.

Why "Surface" is a Better Term

The word "engine" implies a destination (like going to https://www.google.com/search?q=Google.com). However, Generative AI is increasingly ambient, appearing across various surfaces throughout your digital life.

Term	Refers To...	Example
Generative AI Engine	The technical "brain" or processing system.	GPT-4o, Claude 4.5, Gemini Pro.
Generative AI Surface	The specific place where the user sees the answer.	A Ray-Ban Meta glasses voice response, a SearchGPT sidebar, or a WhatsApp bot.

The Shift to "Omnichannel" Search

By thinking in terms of "surfaces" rather than "engines," you'll better capture how people actually find information today. Search is no longer just a "box on a website"; it is now integrated into:

- **Conversational Surfaces:** Chat-based apps like ChatGPT, Claude, or Gemini.

- **Operating System Surfaces:** Windows Copilot (integrated into the taskbar) or Apple Intelligence (Siri).

- **Embedded Surfaces:** An AI summary that appears *inside* a product page on Amazon or a "Help" bot inside a SaaS tool like Slack.

- **Voice/Ambient Surfaces:** Smart speakers or wearable tech where the search result is spoken rather than read.

Relevance to AI Visibility

When you optimize for "surfaces," your strategy changes. You shift from focusing solely on your website's ranking to **Brand Visibility** across the entire ecosystem.

- **If the surface is Voice:** You optimize for short, "speakable" answers.

- **If the surface is an Integrated Tool (like Copilot in Excel):** You optimize your data tables and documentation so the AI can pull them into a spreadsheet.

- **If the surface is a Social/Chat Interface:** You focus on "entity mentions" and what people are saying about you in public forums, as that is what the AI will "surface" in a conversation.

BLOCKING AI CRAWLERS

Not all organizations want their content used in AI systems. Publishers concerned about content being republished in AI answers without driving traffic might choose to block AI crawlers.

Reasons to Block AI Crawlers

- You're a publisher whose business model depends on page views and advertising. AI-generated content that reproduces your content damages revenue.
- You have proprietary data or methodology you don't want incorporated into AI training.
- You're in a regulated industry (legal, medical, financial) where AI systems might misuse or misrepresent complex information.
- You publish time-sensitive data that could be misinterpreted if viewed days or months later, such as weather or fire hazards.

Reasons to Allow AI Crawlers

- Brand awareness and credibility matter more than direct traffic to your site.
- You sell products or services that benefit from AI recommendations.
- Your content is designed to be referenced and cited rather than exclusively consumed on your site.
- You want to influence how AI systems present information in your industry.

The competitive angle: If you block AI while competitors allow it, they gain visibility you forfeit. Conversely, if everyone blocks AI, users will see worse results and may bypass AI systems entirely, reverting to traditional search.

There's no universal correct answer. Evaluate based on your business model and competitive dynamics.

The Query Fan-Out Effect

Traditional SEO matched queries to pages.

AI systems deconstruct complex questions into multiple sub-queries, gather information for each sub-query, and synthesize a coherent answer.

For managers, this means:

- Stop chasing endless long-tail keywords.
- Build topic clusters that demonstrate depth and authority.
- Measure success by coverage and inclusion, not by one-to-one keyword ranks.

MONITORING AI CRAWLERS THROUGH LOG FILE ANALYSIS

Log Files in an AI-Mediated Search Environment

As search shifts from ranking pages to synthesizing answers, organizations lose direct visibility into how their content is consumed. AI systems may extract, summarize, or cite material without generating a click, leaving no trace in analytics platforms. Server log files are among the few artifacts that reveal machine-level interactions with your digital assets.

Unlike analytics tools, which measure user behavior, log files record **server requests**—including those from search engine bots, AI crawlers, and emerging agent-based systems. From a governance perspective, this makes log files a form of *infrastructure telemetry*: they show which automated systems access your content, how often, and at what level of detail.

Identifying AI and Agent-Based Crawlers

Modern log files can reveal activity from a growing range of automated agents, including:

- Traditional search engine crawlers
- AI-assisted search surfaces
- Standalone AI agents performing retrieval tasks
- Experimental or lesser-known crawlers testing content access

By examining user-agent strings, request patterns, and crawl behavior, teams can distinguish between:

- Legitimate indexing activity
- AI systems performing content extraction

- Aggressive or misconfigured crawlers consuming disproportionate resources

For managers, the signal is not volume alone, but **intent**. Repeated access to specific content types—such as definitions, pricing pages, policy documents, or structured data endpoints—often indicates material being evaluated for reuse in AI-generated answers.

What Log Analysis Can Reveal About AI Visibility

Used selectively, log file analysis can surface insights that no dashboard provides:

- **Eligibility signals:** Whether AI crawlers are reaching authoritative pages at all
- **Content prioritization:** Which sections of the site are most frequently requested by automated agents
- **Governance gaps:** Whether blocked or deprecated content is still being accessed
- **Crawler behavior shifts:** Changes following policy updates, crawler blocks, or llms.txt experiments

This does not tell you *how* your brand is described—but it does confirm *whether your material is being considered*. In an AI-mediated environment, that distinction matters.

Log Files Are a Diagnostic Tool, Not a Continuous Metric

For large enterprise sites, continuous log collection is rarely practical. High-traffic environments generate enormous volumes of data, creating storage, privacy, and operational overhead. From a governance standpoint, log files should be treated as **event-driven diagnostics**, not ongoing reporting inputs.

Appropriate use cases include:

- Investigating unexplained drops in AI or search visibility
- Verifying the impact of crawler blocking or access changes
- Auditing AI crawler behavior after major content or platform changes
- Supporting legal, compliance, or policy reviews related to automated access

This keeps log analysis aligned with executive oversight rather than turning it into another unmanaged data stream.

Governance Implications for Leaders

Log file analysis reinforces a broader governance principle: **you cannot manage what you cannot observe**. As AI systems increasingly operate outside traditional analytics, leaders must rely on indirect but reliable signals to validate assumptions about visibility, access, and risk.

At the executive level, the question is not whether teams analyze logs daily, but whether:

- The organization can **prove** which automated systems access its content
- There is a defined escalation path when visibility or representation appears to drift
- Machine access aligns with stated AI, data, and content governance policies

In this sense, log files function as an **audit mechanism for machine behavior**, complementing dashboards that measure outcomes rather than access.

MEASURING SUCCESS IN AN AI WORLD

Track the share of AI visibility relative to competitors. Conduct quarterly audits of how major AI assistants describe your brand and competitors, noting recurring adjectives, sentiment tone, and key themes—these reveal how LLMs model your brand identity. Remember that mentions without links can still strengthen credibility inside answer engines.

Because tracking is still manual and variable, treat results as trend indicators rather than absolute numbers. Proxy signals—such as rising branded search, increased direct traffic, and survey responses mentioning AI assistants—indicate the AI system's visibility.

Chapter 4 presents a comprehensive measurement framework and an AI Visibility Scorecard to systematically track these signals and integrate them with traditional SEO metrics.

SEO AND PPC CONVERGENCE IN THE AI AGE

AI blurs the paid-organic boundary.

Google's Performance Max already incorporates organic content quality and schema signals; meanwhile, organic visibility often boosts ad conversion rates.

Managers should:

- Maintain a shared keyword and content map
- Use paid data to test messaging before scaling organically
- Report performance holistically across both channels

For a complete framework on integrating SEO and PPC strategies, measurement, and budget allocation, see Chapter 12.

BUDGET ALLOCATION IN AN AI WORLD

Balance matters.

Increase paid investment when AI Overviews suppress organic clicks, but strengthen organic and AI visibility where detailed expertise builds authority and long-term equity.

Avoid over-reliance on either channel.

ROI EXAMPLE: AI VISIBILITY STRATEGY INVESTMENT

Company: B2B SaaS provider

Investment: US $28,000 over six months in structured data and content re-architecture.

Outcome: brand mentions in AI assistants rose fivefold; branded search +23 percent; direct traffic +31 percent; annual influenced revenue ≈ US $340,000 — about 12:1 ROI.

Manager insight: AI visibility success isn't traffic—it's being inside the AI recommendation set.

COMMON MANAGERIAL MISSTEPS

1. Ignoring AI search until competitors dominate it
2. Declaring SEO "dead" and abandoning fundamentals
3. Trying to "game" LLMs with manipulative content
4. Blanket-blocking all AI crawlers without a strategy
5. Splitting traditional and AI search into separate teams
6. Waiting for certainty before acting

THE PERSONALIZATION CHALLENGE

AI responses vary by user context, history, location, and session state; no two runs are identical. Evaluate visibility using multiple test profiles and anonymous sessions to approximate aggregate exposure.

Your own tests show *a* result, not *the* result.

Manager guidelines:

- Use multiple testers or anonymized sessions for sampling
- Rely on trends, not absolutes
- Combine quantitative data with customer surveys
- Aim for content so authoritative it earns inclusion across many contexts

IS LLMS.TXT NECESSARY?

The short answer is "probably not." A longer answer follows.

The **llms.txt** file, proposed as an emerging standard in 2024, enables website owners to declare how their content may be used by Large Language Model (LLM) crawlers.

At this stage, it remains experimental. There is **no guarantee that major LLM crawlers will visit**, nor any reliable way to summon them. Even when they do visit, there is no assurance they will interpret the directives as intended.

Treat llms.txt as a controlled experiment, not an obligation. Create a small number of .md (Markdown) versions of key HTML pages that represent your most authoritative or frequently cited material. Overproduction of mirror Markdown files can lead to version drift, unnecessary maintenance, and governance fatigue.

It needs to be repeated: The llms.txt file won't control how LLMs portray your brand — it only governs access to your data. What truly shapes perception is consistent, high-trust content across your ecosystem. Treat llms.txt as part of transparency and consent governance, not as an influence tool.

About llms.txt — A Debatable Strategy

If your organization maintains **both HTML and Markdown** versions of important content, governance discipline must extend beyond publishing. When edits occur in HTML—such as accessibility improvements, brand-compliance updates, or executive rewrites—the corresponding Markdown files must remain synchronized.

A manager-level approach includes:

- **Use llms.txt judiciously** — Technically, CMSs could be made to generate markdown (.md) files in parallel with web pages, but please don't. While the llms.txt file serves as a high-level summary, the proposal recommends using an llms-full.txt file as a comprehensive index of all Markdown resources, similar to a traditional sitemap. The llms.txt file should be limited to a handful of pointers with clear sectioning, e.g., # AI Training Rules, # Attribution Requirements, # Licensing. At best, they serve as a backup to copyright statements on visible content.

- **Change Detection and Diffing** — Use diff tools or checksum comparison to flag structural or semantic mismatches between .html and .md versions. These checks help detect outdated markdown before it confuses LLM crawlers or internal reviewers.

- **Governance Hooks** — Establish simple controls: block commits if the .md copy isn't current, or automatically regenerate .md files when publishing changes to .html. Document the sync status in the version control logs for transparency.

- **Sync Dashboard** — Maintain a lightweight dashboard showing modification dates, sync status (e.g., synced / out of sync), and the responsible editor. This allows non-technical managers to oversee editorial discipline without diving into code.

- **Semantic and Structural Integrity** — Ensure that reverse-converted Markdown preserves headings, lists, and descriptive text so that crawlers can interpret meaning consistently. Accessibility tags for human users (such as full WCAG conformance) are not required here, but a well-structured approach helps both models and auditors understand intent. Include a brief note such as "Converted from HTML on [date]" for traceability.

- **Crawler Verification** — Check your website and server logs regularly to confirm whether LLM crawlers are visiting your domain and requesting /llms.txt. Use these insights to refine your expectations and decide whether maintaining the file is yielding observable engagement.

The goal is **governance continuity** — ensuring that your llms.txt references and their linked Markdown assets remain accurate, accessible, and compliant over time. The gold test is whether the prominent LLM answer engines are mentioning your brand appropriately.

Blind-Spot Check

If your team creates llms.txt and markdown files but never audits their sync, logs, or crawler access, you may be creating a maintenance headache.

Cross-Reference

For broader leadership guidance on AI governance and crawler accountability, see *Book 4 — The C-suite Blind Spot*, Chapter 5: "AI and Automation — New Governance Imperatives."

NEWS-SPECIFIC SEARCH SURFACES

If you publish timely or analytical content, platforms such as **Google News**, **Bing News**, and **Top Stories** carousels remain high-value entry points.

Inclusion depends on original reporting, transparent authorship or bylines, machine-readable structured data (NewsArticle schema), and adherence to Google News Publisher Center policies — formal press accreditation is not required.

On mobile, **Google Discover** proactively surfaces content, rewarding a consistent publishing cadence and engagement.

Manager insight: Treat news-style publishing as a strategic visibility channel. Evaluate:

- Frequency of timely queries in your sector that trigger news carousels
- Competitor presence on those surfaces
- Your team's capacity to produce fast, authoritative commentary

The Paid Search Intersection

AI-powered advertising, such as Google Performance Max and Microsoft Copilot Ads, uses feed data from Merchant Center, Business Profiles, and site markup. Both ad systems increasingly leverage structured content and audience signals shared with organic search.

The practical convergence: Shared data feeds and structured information now influence both paid and organic performance.

Managers should ensure SEO and PPC teams collaborate, using common creative assets and measurement frameworks. Chapter 12 explores this integration in depth.

(Governance policy details and decision frameworks for AI crawler management appear in Book 3, *AI Visibility Playbook*.)

LOOKING AHEAD

Expect:

- Rising personalization and multimodal search (voice, image, video inputs)
- Stricter data-use and attribution regulation worldwide
- Full integration of SEO metrics (including AI visibility) into marketing dashboards
- Sustained emphasis on verifiable expertise and structured, trustworthy content.

Managers who understand these trends—and align teams early—will preserve visibility while competitors disappear from the answer layer.

Chapter 2

COMPETITIVE INTELLIGENCE

A 10 percent traffic increase sounds impressive—until you discover competitors grew 40 percent. Without a competitive context, you can't reliably answer "Is our SEO working?"

This chapter provides a systematic framework for diagnosing performance changes: Do your actions cause them, competitors' moves, or algorithm updates? More importantly, how should you respond?

THE COMPETITIVE INTELLIGENCE FRAMEWORK

Effective competitive analysis operates on three levels:

1. Strategic positioning—Where do you choose to compete?
2. Tactical execution—How well are you executing compared to rivals?
3. Environmental scanning—What external forces affect everyone?

Most managers jump straight to level 2 (tactical) without establishing level 1 (strategic). This leads to wasted effort optimizing for keywords you shouldn't target or matching competitor tactics that don't fit your business model.

LEVEL 1: STRATEGIC POSITIONING ANALYSIS

Before analyzing tactics, answer these questions:

Who are your true SEO competitors?

Don't assume your business competitors are your SEO competitors. A bank competing with other banks for mortgages might face completely different SEO competition from comparison sites, brokers, and financial advice publishers.

Exercise: Search for your five most important keyword groups. Who appears in positions 1-10? Those are your SEO competitors, regardless of whether they're direct business competitors.

Where should you compete?

You can't win everywhere. Strategic positioning means choosing battlegrounds where you have advantages:

- Brand strength—Branded searches are easy to defend
- Content depth—Topics where you have genuine expertise
- Technical capability—Features competitors can't easily replicate
- Budget allocation—Areas where you can sustain investment

At a major bank, before Google's algorithm was more sophisticated, we discovered the brand was ranking for "[brand name] convention" and "[brand name] show," which was an overseas convention. These weren't actual competitors, but they diluted our brand presence. Strategic positioning meant not competing for those terms while defending relevant financial service searches.

The key strategic **question** is resource allocation. Are you investing in keywords where your business has no inherent advantage—whether due to lack of authority, budget constraints, or misalignment with business goals?

LEVEL 2: TACTICAL EXECUTION ANALYSIS

Once you've defined your competitive arena, analyze execution systematically across five dimensions:

1. Keyword Visibility Gaps

Tools like Ahrefs, Semrush, and Sistrix estimate where competitors rank higher for shared keywords. But raw numbers mislead—focus on:

- High-intent keywords—Commercial terms closer to conversion
- Category-defining terms—Keywords that establish topical authority
- Trend momentum—Where competitors are gaining ground, not just where they currently lead

Bad analysis: "Competitor X ranks for 15,000 more keywords than us."

Good analysis: "Competitor X ranks in positions 1-3 for 47 of our top 100 revenue-generating keywords, up from 31 six months ago. They've invested heavily in comparison content."

Keyword	Intent	Position	SF	Traffic	Traffic %	Volume	KD %	URL		SERP	Updated
golf gti weight			6	1	< 0.01	30	39	www. en/gc			Jul 20
golf gti weight		1	6	1	< 0.01	30	39	www. en/go			Jul 20
new nissan navara 2024			6	1	< 0.01	40	16	www. 2023 pecs			Jul 25
prado boot space		1	2	27	< 0.01	110	48	www. dcruir	a/ian		Jul 31
new 2023 hyundai venue		1	8	7	< 0.01	30	31	www. ws/2C			Jul 22

Figure 10 Using Ahrefs to identify a competitor page ranking in position 1, allowing analysis of their content strategy and optimization approach.

2. Content Depth and Format

When competitors outrank you, analyze their content systematically:

Element	What to Check	Why It Matters
Word count	Is their content substantially longer?	Depth signals often correlate with rankings, but correlation ≠ does not imply causation.
Structured data	Do they use schema markup you don't?	Rich results visibility advantage
Multimedia	Video, infographics, interactive tools?	Engagement signals and AI training data
Update frequency	How recently was the content refreshed?	Freshness can break ranking ties.
Authority signals	Author credentials, citations, original research?	E-E-A-T evaluation factors
Internal linking	How well do they connect related content?	Topical authority clustering

Case Study: Insurance Comparison Site

When analyzing a competitor outranking us for "car insurance quotes," we found:

- They had 3,200 high-ranking words vs. our 800
- They included video explainers (we had none)
- They published monthly "rate update" articles showing freshness
- But: Their bounce rate was 67 percent vs. our 43 percent

The insight: More content doesn't always mean better content. We focused on conversion optimization rather than matching their word count. Within 90 days, we outranked them despite having less content because our conversion signals improved. While bounce rate isn't a direct ranking factor, it can indicate user-experience issues.

When competitors outrank you, move beyond observation to diagnosis. Why does their content perform? Is it depth, format, freshness, or conversion optimization?

3. Technical Performance

Technical SEO creates compounding advantages. A site that loads 2 seconds faster accumulates better user signals over millions of visits.

Competitive technical audit sample checklist:

- Site speed comparison (mobile and desktop)
- Core Web Vitals (CWV) (LCP, INP, CLS) results
- Mobile responsiveness and experience (note: Google's Search Console Mobile Usability report is deprecated—use Lighthouse and real-user metrics)
- HTTPS implementation
- Structured data coverage
- Internal linking architecture
- XML sitemap organization
- robots.txt configuration
- Crawl budget efficiency

Tool: Use WebPageTest.org or Lighthouse to compare performance on identical connection profiles. Test from the locations where your users live, not from your office.

Calculate the business case: If your site loads 3 seconds slower than competitors, what's the revenue impact of closing that gap?

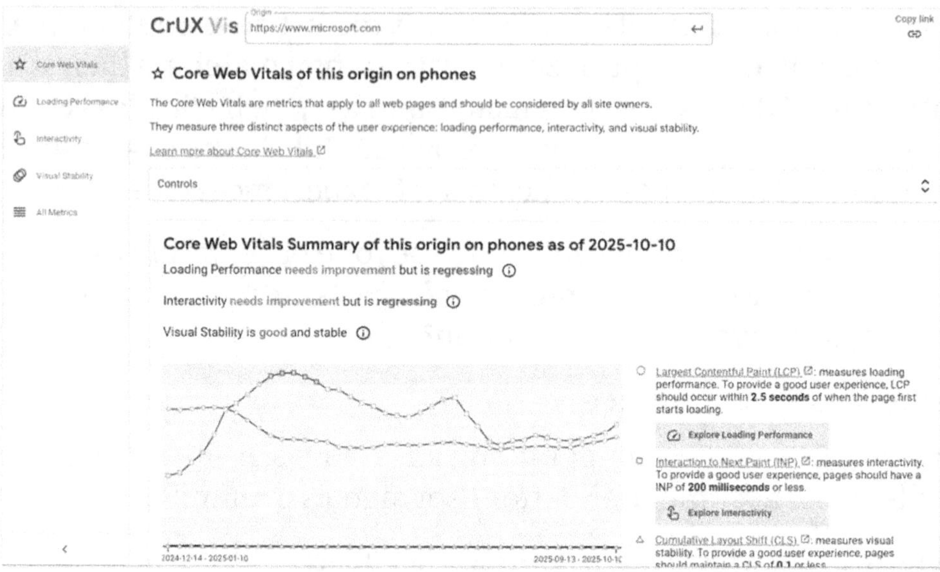

Figure 11 Chrome UX Report (CrUX) visualization showing Core Web Vitals data for microsoft.com.

4. Backlink Strength

Links remain a major ranking signal in Google's and Bing's algorithms, though link-quality evaluation has been tightened; volume alone is no longer predictive.

Backlink analysis framework:

Quantity metrics (less important):

- Total backlinks
- Total referring domains
- Growth rate

Quality metrics (more important):

- Domain authority of linking sites
- Topical relevance of linking pages

- Diversity of link sources (not dependent on a few domains)
- Natural link placement (editorial vs. footer/sidebar)
- Link anchor text distribution (not over-optimized)

Red flag: Competitor suddenly gains 10,000 links from ~50 domains (often via site-wide footer links or widgets). Investigate whether it's synthetic or earned (e.g., viral assets, tools, news coverage).

Link quality matters more than quantity. Are you tracking *where* competitor links originate—identifying high-authority sources you should also pursue—or merely counting totals?

5. AI and LLM Visibility

New battleground: appearing in ChatGPT, Gemini, Perplexity, and AI Overviews.

Competitive AI analysis:

Test queries like:

- "Best [product category] in [year]."
- "How to choose [product/service]."
- "Compare [your brand] vs. [competitor]."
- "[Industry] buying guide"

Track:

- Which brands get mentioned?
- In what context (positive, neutral, negative)?
- Are URLs cited?
- What position in the response?

Tool gap: Dedicated AI visibility-tracking tools are emerging. As of early 2026, consider:

- Enterprise SEO suites piloting AI-visibility modules (e.g., BrightEdge, SEOclarity, Similarweb, SISTRIX)
- Structured internal sampling protocols for manual spot-checking across LLMs

Conduct quarterly AI visibility audits. When users ask AI assistants about your product category, your brand should appear in the results; if it doesn't, investigate whether the problem is content structure, authority signals, or recency.

Level 3: Environmental Scanning

Sometimes performance changes affect everyone—algorithm updates, seasonal shifts, market disruption. Distinguishing environmental changes from competitive moves prevents knee-jerk reactions.

Algorithm Updates

Google rolls out multiple broad core updates annually, alongside numerous system updates and refinements; cadence varies year to year. Bing and other engines also update regularly.

When rankings shift, check:

1. Industry forums—X (formerly Twitter) #SEO, Reddit r/SEO, WebmasterWorld
2. Tracking tools—MozCast, Semrush Sensor, Rank Ranger's Rank Risk Index, and Advanced Web Ranking's Volatility.
3. Google's announcements—Search Status Dashboard and @googlesearchc on Twitter/X.
4. Competitor movement—Are they affected similarly?

Decision tree:

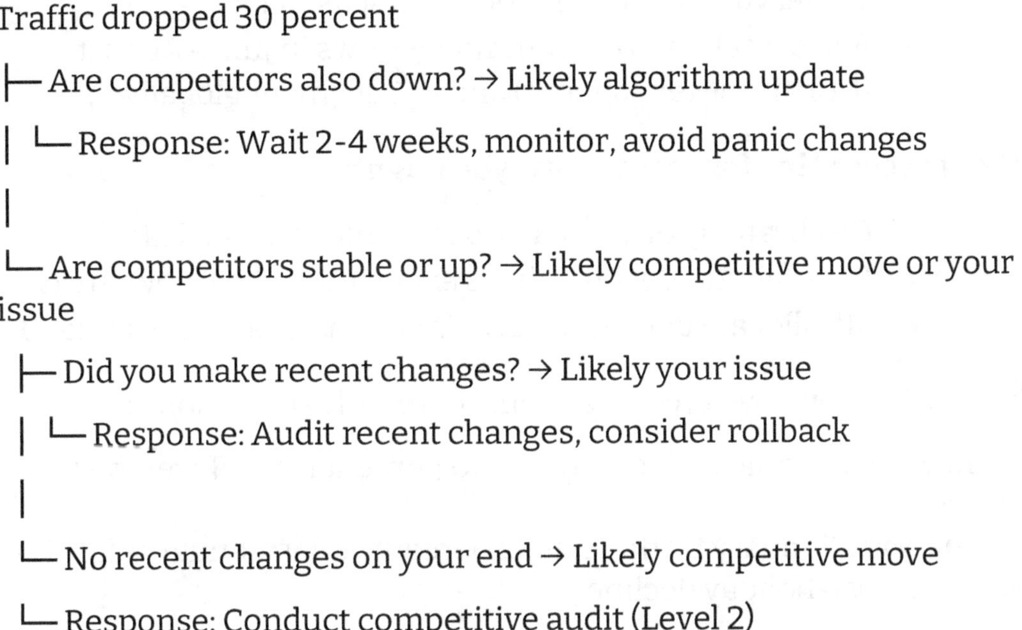

Traffic dropped 30 percent

├─ Are competitors also down? → Likely algorithm update

│ └─ Response: Wait 2-4 weeks, monitor, avoid panic changes

│

└─ Are competitors stable or up? → Likely competitive move or your issue

├─ Did you make recent changes? → Likely your issue

│ └─ Response: Audit recent changes, consider rollback

│

└─ No recent changes on your end → Likely competitive move

└─ Response: Conduct competitive audit (Level 2)

Real example: In March 2024, Google's core update produced volatility in Your Money or Your Life sectors (e.g., finance and health). Many banks saw fluctuations. Environmental scanning revealed this was industry-wide, not specific to one institution. The correct response was patience and continuous quality improvement, not emergency pivots.

When rankings shift, resist the urge to react immediately. First, confirm whether changes affect only your site or the entire industry. Check competitor movement and algorithm tracking tools before allocating resources to a response.

Seasonal and Cyclical Patterns

Many businesses have predictable search patterns:

- Tax-software search interest peaks January–April in the U.S. and June–October in Australia.

- Retail surges November-December
- Travel varies by destination and seasonality
- B2B search interest commonly slows in June–August (Northern Hemisphere) and in December globally

Without accounting for seasonality, you might:

- Celebrate "growth" that's just normal seasonal lift
- Panic about "decline" that's expected cyclical downturn
- Misallocate budget to periods with naturally low demand

Solution: Year-over-year comparison, not month-over-month.

Bad analysis: "Organic traffic dropped 40 percent from November to January!"
Good analysis: "January traffic is up 12 percent vs. last January, despite the normal post-holiday decline."

The Competitive Action Framework

Analysis without action is an academic exercise. Here's how to convert insights into strategic decisions:

Quick Win Identification (30-90 days)

Look for opportunities where small changes yield disproportionate results:

Content gap exploitation

- Competitor ranks for a valuable term with thin content
- You can create demonstrably better resources
- Example: They have a 500-word article, you create a 2,000-word comprehensive guide with video and data

Technical quick fixes

- Competitor has broken structured data
- You implement correctly and gain rich results
- Example: Adding review schema when the competitor hasn't

Internal linking improvements

- Competitor has weak topical clustering
- You strengthen internal links around key themes
- Example: Creating content hubs that competitors lack

Metadata optimization

- Competitor has poor title tags and meta descriptions
- You craft compelling, click-worthy alternatives

Long-Term Strategic Plays (6-24 months)

Some competitive advantages require sustained investment:

Content authority building

- Creating comprehensive resource centers
- Publishing original research and data
- Building tools and calculators
- Developing expertise not easily replicated

Technical infrastructure

- Site performance optimization (sustained effort)
- Sophisticated internal linking architecture
- Progressive web app development
- Accessibility beyond minimum compliance

Link acquisition programs

- PR and digital PR initiatives
- Industry partnerships and collaborations
- Creating linkable assets (tools, data, research)
- Community building and thought leadership

Brand building

- Increases branded search volume
- Improves CTR (click-through rate) in results (brand recognition)
- Generates direct traffic, reducing SEO dependency
- Creates a defensible moat against competitors

Resource Allocation Decisions

Competitive intelligence should drive budget allocation:

Defend existing advantages

- If you lead in category-defining keywords, protect them
- Budget: 30-40 percent of resources

Exploit competitor weaknesses

- Where competitors are vulnerable with quick wins available
- Budget: 30-40 percent of resources

Build new advantages

- Long-term investments in areas where you can lead
- Budget: 20-30 percent of resources

Avoid unwinnable battles

- Where competitors have insurmountable advantages
- Budget: 0-10 percent (reconnaissance only)

The AI-Era Competitive Landscape

Traditional competitive analysis focused on search engine results pages (SERP) rankings. Now you must also analyze:

AI Overview presence

- When are competitors cited in AI Overviews?
- What content types get selected?
- Can you identify patterns in their cited content?

LLM training advantages

- Older, well-linked sites were more likely represented in earlier training datasets (e.g., Common Crawl).
- Newer sites may lack AI visibility despite strong traditional SEO
- Aim to secure citations or mentions from authoritative domains that are already well-represented in major training datasets.

Query fan-out implications

- Complex queries generate sub-queries internally
- Content answering niche sub-queries may surface in AI aggregations
- Strategy: Cover long-tail comprehensively, not just head terms

Zero-click challenges

- If AI satisfies the query without clicks, traffic falls industry-wide
- Competitive advantage shifts to branded search and conversions
- Consider: diversifying traffic sources (email, social, community)

Building a Competitive Intelligence System

One-time competitive analysis is insufficient. Build ongoing systems:

Quarterly Competitive Review Process

Week 1: Data collection

- Pull ranking data from SEO tools
- Export competitor backlink profiles
- Run technical audits on the top 3-5 competitors
- Test AI visibility across platforms

Week 2: Analysis

- Identify changes since last quarter
- Spot new competitive threats
- Evaluate the effectiveness of your previous quarter's actions
- Update competitive positioning map

Week 3: Strategic planning

- Prioritize opportunities identified
- Allocate resources for next quarter
- Set specific, measurable objectives

- Brief teams on competitive landscape

Week 4: Documentation and communication

- Create an executive summary for leadership
- Detailed action plans for practitioners
- Update internal wiki/knowledge base
- Schedule follow-up reviews

Automated Monitoring

Set up alerts for competitive changes:

- Rank tracking tools (daily or weekly)
- Backlink monitoring (new links acquired by competitors)
- Content monitoring (when competitors publish new pages)
- Technical monitoring (site speed changes, new features)
- AI visibility-tracking (manual monthly checks until tools mature)

Cross-Functional Collaboration

Competitive intelligence shouldn't live in an SEO silo:

Share with Product: What features do competitor sites have?
Share with Content: What topics are competitors covering?
Share with PR: What publications link to competitors?
Share with Sales: What do competitive sites emphasize?
Share with the Executive team: Strategic positioning implications

Common Competitive Analysis Mistakes

Mistake 1: Obsessing over keyword count

- "Competitor ranks for 50,000 keywords!"

- Reality: 80 percent are low-value, irrelevant, or brand terms
- Fix: Focus on revenue-generating keywords

Mistake 2: Copying without context

- "Competitor has 20 blog posts about X, so we need 20 too"
- Reality: They might have a different business model or audience
- Fix: Understand why their strategy works for them

Mistake 3: Tool worship

- "This tool says their Domain Authority is 73!"
- Reality: Tools provide estimates, not Google's actual view
- Fix: Use tools as indicators, not truth

Mistake 4: Static analysis

- One-time competitive audit never updated
- Reality: Competitive landscape shifts constantly
- Fix: Establish ongoing monitoring systems

Mistake 5: Analysis paralysis

- Endless data collection, no action
- Reality: Imperfect action beats perfect planning
- Fix: Set decision deadlines, implement, measure, iterate

Manager's Competitive Intelligence Checklist

Use this quarterly:

Strategic Level:

- Have we validated who our SEO competitors actually are?

- Do we know where we're choosing to compete vs. concede?
- Have we assessed our sustainable competitive advantages?
- Is our resource allocation aligned with strategic priorities?

Tactical Level:

- Have we identified specific keyword gaps we should close?
- Do we understand why competitor content outperforms ours?
- Have we audited competitor technical SEO capabilities?
- Are we tracking competitor backlink acquisition patterns?
- Have we tested our AI visibility vs. competitors?

Operational Level:

- Do we have automated competitor monitoring in place?
- Are competitive insights shared across relevant teams?
- Have we documented changes since last quarter?
- Have competitive insights driven actual decisions this quarter?

Environmental Level:

- Have we checked for industry-wide algorithm impacts?
- Have we accounted for seasonal patterns in our analysis?
- Are we monitoring emerging competitive threats?

Case Study: Competitive Intelligence Driving Strategy

Company: Mid-sized insurance provider
Challenge: Losing ground to both traditional insurers and comparison sites
Timeframe: 12 months

Initial situation:

- Rankings declining for "car insurance" variations
- New comparison sites entering the market
- Traditional competitors are increasing content investment

Competitive analysis revealed:

1. Comparison sites dominated informational queries but had poor conversion

2. Traditional competitors focused on brand terms, weak on education

3. Nobody was targeting specific customer segments (young drivers, seniors, etc.)

Strategic decision: Rather than fight for generic "car insurance" against better-funded competitors, they:

- Created segment-specific content (young drivers, seniors, high-risk)
- Developed tools (savings calculator, coverage selector)
- Built partnerships with finance education sites for links
- Optimized for question-based queries matching user intent

Results after 12 months:

- 340 percent increase in organic traffic to segment-specific pages
- 89 percent increase in quote requests from organic search
- Established authority in underserved niches
- Lower cost-per-acquisition than paid search

Key lesson: Competitive analysis revealed an uncontested space. Rather than competing head-on with better-funded rivals in saturated markets, they found a defensible position.

AI Implications for Competitive Intelligence

The rise of AI search changes competitive dynamics:

New competitive dimensions:

- AI Overview citation frequency and LLM mentions context/sentiment (where detectable via manual or tool sampling)
- Structured data sophistication (helps AI understand content)
- Content freshness (AI systems may prioritize recent information)

Emerging competitive advantages:

- First-mover advantage in AI-friendly formats
- Integrations with AI platforms (e.g., GPTs/assistants and search connectors) where applicable
- Brand establishment during AI training periods
- Expertise markers (author credentials, citations)

Tools to watch: The competitive intelligence tool landscape is evolving rapidly. Expect mature tools for:

- AI visibility-tracking across multiple LLMs
- Citation sentiment analysis
- Competitor AI strategy monitoring
- Structured data competitive benchmarking

MANAGER'S FRAMEWORK: COMPETITIVE INTELLIGENCE CADENCE

Annual Deep Analysis (4-6 hours): Conduct the comprehensive competitive analysis outlined earlier in this chapter:

- Strategic positioning assessment
- Full tactical execution analysis across 5 dimensions
- Environmental factors review
- 12-month competitive roadmap

Quarterly Strategic Check (30-60 minutes): As part of your integrated quarterly SEO business review, ask:

- Has our competitive position changed significantly?
- Have competitors launched major initiatives that affect our strategy?
- Do recent algorithm updates or market shifts require a strategic response?
- Are there new competitive threats or opportunities?

If the answer to any question is "yes," conduct a focused analysis on that specific dimension. If all answers are "no," your quarterly review is complete.

Monthly Dashboard Monitoring (10-15 minutes): Track basic competitive metrics in your regular dashboard:

- Rank changes for 10-20 strategic keywords
- Significant competitor content launches (via alerts)
- Major backlink acquisitions (via monitoring tools)

When to Conduct Deep Competitive Analysis:

- Annually (baseline assessment)
- When competitive position shifts unexpectedly (>20% rank loss to competitors)
- Before major strategic initiatives (site redesign, market expansion, content strategy shift)
- After significant algorithm updates affecting your niche
- When entering new markets or launching new product categories

The principle: Comprehensive competitive analysis is a diagnostic and strategic planning tool, not a quarterly ritual. Reserve the full framework for when you need strategic insights, not calendar compliance.

The measurement frameworks in Chapter 4 provide tools for tracking competitive performance systematically over time. For organizations competing across multiple countries, Chapter 7 addresses multinational competitive dynamics and market-specific strategies.

Chapter 3
CORE TECHNICAL FOUNDATIONS

Technical SEO forms the foundation on which everything else builds. Without it, even brilliant content and perfect keyword targeting fail. This chapter covers what managers need to know about technical foundations—not how to implement them, but why they matter and what questions to ask.

The key principle: You don't need to become a developer. You need to recognize when technical decisions affect SEO and know which experts to involve.

TECHNICAL FOUNDATIONS ARE IMPORTANT

Imagine spending six months creating exceptional content, only to discover that search engines can't find it because of a robots.txt error. Or launching a site redesign that accidentally removes tens of thousands of pages from Google's index because redirects weren't implemented.

These aren't hypothetical scenarios—they happen regularly to organizations with sophisticated marketing teams. Technical issues don't announce themselves loudly. They silently destroy months of work.

The manager's role isn't implementing technical SEO. It's ensuring:

- Technical requirements are included in project specifications
- Developers understand why SEO considerations matter

Is Our SEO Working?

- Quality assurance (QA) processes catch technical issues before launch
- Monitoring alerts you to problems quickly
- Resources are allocated to fix critical technical debt

Core Website Technology Decisions

Several fundamental technology choices have affected SEO performance for years. While you might not make these decisions directly, understanding their implications helps you participate meaningfully in discussions.

Content Management System (CMS) Architecture

Your CMS choice influences scalability, speed, and governance—not just content publishing. It stores, manages, and publishes content. Its architecture affects how easily SEO requirements can be implemented.

Traditional CMSs (such as WordPress, Drupal, or enterprise systems like Adobe Experience Manager) combine content storage, business logic, and presentation in a single system. Content and display are tightly coupled.

Advantages for SEO:

- Mature SEO plugins and extensions available
- Developers are widely available who understand SEO implementation
- Relatively straightforward to implement technical requirements
- Performance optimization is well-documented

Disadvantages:

- Can become bloated with features, affecting performance
- Sometimes rigid in how content can be structured

- May require significant customization for complex requirements

Headless CMS (such as Contentful, Sanity, or Strapi) separates content storage from presentation. Content lives in the CMS and gets delivered to any front-end via APIs.

Advantages:

- Flexibility in how content is presented
- Can serve the same content to the website, mobile app, and other channels
- Often better performance if implemented well

Disadvantages for SEO:

- SEO requirements must be explicitly built into the front-end implementation
- Developers may not understand the SEO implications of their rendering choices
- Requires more sophisticated technical oversight

Technical Readiness Assessment:

"How will we ensure SEO requirements are met in our CMS?"

- Are there built-in SEO capabilities, or must everything be custom-built?

"Who on the team understands both the CMS and SEO requirements?"

- Gap between CMS expertise and SEO knowledge creates risk.

"What happens when we need to change SEO implementation?"

- How quickly can changes be made? What's the cost?

Rendering Strategy

How pages are generated and delivered to users affects whether search engines can index content correctly.

Client-side rendering means JavaScript in the user's browser builds the page. The server sends minimal HTML, and JavaScript dynamically creates the page.

SEO risk: Google renders JavaScript with an evergreen Googlebot, but rendering can be delayed or incomplete if resources are blocked, heavy, or time out. Ensure critical content/links are available in server-rendered or statically generated HTML (or reliably hydrated) so crawlers can index them.

Server-side rendering means the server generates complete HTML pages before sending them to users and search engines.

SEO benefit: Search engines receive fully-formed pages and can index content reliably.

Static site generation means pages are pre-built and stored as static HTML files, then served instantly when requested.

SEO benefit: Maximum performance and reliability for search engine crawlers.

Search engines must be able to access your content without complex JavaScript execution. Confirm that important pages use server-side rendering, static generation, or reliable hydration that makes critical content available in the initial HTML.

You don't need to understand the implementation mechanics. You need to ensure whoever is making these decisions understands the SEO implications and has included search engine accessibility in their requirements.

Domain Architecture

How you structure domains across your organization significantly affects SEO, as covered extensively in Chapter 7 for multinational scenarios. The same principles apply domestically.

Subdomains create separation. Search engines generally treat subdomains as separate properties for crawling and indexing, and signals can flow between them via internal and external links.

When subdomains make sense:

- Genuinely different platforms or technology stacks
- Different security or compliance requirements
- Testing new initiatives before full commitment

Subdirectories consolidate authority. example.com/blog and example.com/shop benefit from the same domain authority and link equity.

When subdirectories make sense:

- Most situations, especially when consolidating authority, benefit all content
- The same organization manages content
- Technical platforms can be unified

Review the domain architecture: Are you using subdomains, or would subdirectories consolidate authority and simplify management?

Many organizations use subdomains by default without considering SEO implications. A new subdomain doesn't inherit rankings automatically, but internal/external links from established domains can pass authority to it.

HTML AND CODE QUALITY

Search engines read HTML code to understand your pages. While perfect code isn't required, certain quality standards matter. Valid, lightweight HTML improves crawl efficiency and reduces rendering errors.

Relevance of Valid HTML

HTML is forgiving—browsers display pages even with errors. But errors can confuse search engines about page structure, break accessibility tools that disabled users depend on, cause inconsistent rendering across devices, and indicate development issues that correlate with other problems.

Manager's approach: You don't need to validate HTML yourself. Ensure your development team understands validation standards, incorporates validation into their QA process, and fixes critical errors, even if they do not achieve 100 percent validity.

Tool: https://validator.w3.org/ validates HTML (syntax/structure); pair it with an accessibility checker (e.g., Axe DevTools) to identify WCAG issues.

Semantic HTML Structure

"Semantic HTML" means using HTML elements for their intended purpose: headings create a hierarchical structure, lists format lists properly, tables present tabular data, and buttons are actual button elements.

Why it matters: Search engines understand content hierarchy better, accessibility tools work correctly, and AI systems extract information more reliably.

Common violation: Heading tags used for visual styling rather than structure. A page might have multiple H1s or skip from H1 to H3, breaking the logical hierarchy.

I use the Chrome plugin *Web Developer* to check many page elements, including this one. It is also available for other browsers and operating systems.

URL: https://chrispederick.com/work/web-developer/

Figure 12 Example of skipping heading levels.

Verify that your templates use H1 for page titles, H2 for major sections, and H3+ for subsections—following content hierarchy, not designer preferences. A page must have only one H1, even though HTML5 rules permit multiple H1s. Search engines understand a page better if it has only one H1.

INFORMATION ARCHITECTURE AND URL STRUCTURE

How content is organized and accessed affects both user experience and search visibility.

URL Naming Conventions

URLs should be:

- **Human-readable:** example.com/products/laptop-stands not example.com/p?id=9847234

- **Descriptive:** Indicate what's on the page

- **Consistent:** Follow patterns across the site

- **Permanent:** Don't change unnecessarily

Common mistakes:

- Auto-generated IDs: /product/38472 tells users and search engines nothing
- Parameter-based: /page?category=shoes&size=10&color=red creates management nightmare
- Inconsistent conventions: /products/shoes-mens vs. /mens-footwear/dress-shoes

Manager's role: Ensure URL conventions are documented and followed consistently. When changes are needed, ensure proper redirects are implemented.

Best practice: Establish URL naming conventions early in site planning. Changing the URL structure later requires comprehensive redirect mapping and risks disrupting SEO.

Site Depth and Internal Linking

Site depth is the number of clicks required to reach a page from the homepage. As a general principle, important pages should be reachable with shallow click depth and strong internal links; "three-click" is a heuristic, not a ranking rule.

Why this matters: Pages buried deep in site architecture receive less authority from internal linking and are more problematic for both users and search engines to discover.

The internal linking strategy is comprehensive enough to warrant dedicated coverage. Chapter 9 examines navigation architecture, link equity distribution, and strategic internal linking. The key principle to understand now is that the URL structure and site architecture decisions you make during technical planning directly impact your ability to implement effective internal linking later.

Consider how your information architecture will support strategic connections between related content before finalizing URL patterns.

Flat vs. Deep Architecture

Flat architecture: More pages accessible directly from the main navigation or homepage.

- Advantage: Important pages receive more internal link equity
- Challenge: Navigation can become cluttered

Deep architecture: Content nested in multiple category levels.

- Advantage: Logical organization, especially for large sites
- Challenge: Deep pages receive less authority

The compromise: Use a flat architecture for primary navigation while allowing deeper hierarchies to support comprehensive content coverage.

File and Folder Naming

Beyond URLs, file naming affects organization and SEO. Your team should use lowercase consistently, use hyphens (not underscores) to separate words, avoid special characters, and be descriptive but concise.

Inconsistent naming conventions create technical debt that compounds over time. Document standards for URLs, files, and folders—then enforce them through code reviews, automated checks, or CMS configuration.

CRITICAL AI INTERPRETABILITY ELEMENTS

These elements ensure search engines and AI systems can discover, correctly interpret, and confidently recommend your content. Improving each one increases your likelihood of being surfaced not just in rankings, but in **AI-generated answers**.

You don't need to master how they work.

You only need to ensure someone is **accountable** for them.

Robots.txt

Controls where crawlers can go.

Do: Allow access to valuable content

Don't: Accidentally block critical pages or resources

If AI systems can't read it, customers can't reach it.

Assign clear **ownership** for robots.txt changes. A single character error can block search engines from your entire site, causing catastrophic visibility loss. **Require peer review** for any modifications.

XML Sitemaps

A directory for both search engines and AI crawlers.

Do: Include every important, indexable URL
Don't: Leave obsolete or redirected URLs inside the file

Submitted sitemaps are a signal of your brand's structure — and trustworthiness.

Redirects

Maintain continuity when URLs change.

Do: Use 301 redirects from old pages to new ones

Don't: Delete pages without a redirect plan

Redirect discipline preserves authority — and revenue.

Canonical Tags

Avoid confusion caused by duplicates, such as product variants, parameters, or pagination.

Do: Declare a primary URL

Don't: Let the engines guess

This protects against invisible ranking loss.

HTTPS and Security

Security is a trust signal.

Search engines and AI systems strongly prefer secure, authenticated domains.

Mobile Experience

Most users — and AI extractions — happen from mobile content.

Poor mobile UX damages authority signals.

Performance and Core Web Vitals

Speed affects both rankings and inclusion in AI-generated summaries.

Key signals:

Is Our SEO Working?

- LCP — how fast content appears
- INP — how fast users can interact
- CLS — visual stability

If pages load slowly, visibility equity evaporates.

Structured Data and Schema Markup

Helps machines *understand* your meaning, not just your text.

Strong schema supports:

- Rich results
- Accurate AI summaries
- Local and brand authority signals

This is the **language of machine trust**.

2026 context: Focus schema investment on Organization, Product, Review, and LocalBusiness types. The FAQ and HowTo schemas were restricted or deprecated from 2023 to 2025. See Chapter 6 for implementation priorities.

Accessibility and SEO

Accessible pages are machine-readable pages.

What helps a screen reader often helps a search crawler.

Accessibility issues silently lower trust and weighting.

AI Visibility — Summary and Selection Signals

AI systems are now deciding **which brands** appear in answers.

They prefer:

- Clear page intent and metadata consistency
- Verified facts and fresh updates

- Structured relationships between pages (entities, not keywords)

Visibility is no longer about being seen — it's about **being chosen**.

Blind-Spot Check

If metadata accuracy decays, AI systems will confidently recommend someone else.

Data Freshness and Authority Continuity

Outdated facts can degrade the reliability of AI systems' source assessments.

Protect your authority by:

- Updating key facts (pricing, availability, contact info)
- Ensuring schema matches what humans see on the page
- Refreshing content tied to evergreen demand

Authority is lost slowly — and regained slowly.

Content Clusters and Entity Strength

AI systems group information by entity relationships.

To strengthen discoverability:

- Use internal links to show hierarchy
- Build clusters around products, services, or topics
- Reference your organization consistently as the authoritative source

This enhances how machines **map** your expertise.

Leadership takeaway

Technical excellence is now AI excellence.
Machines reward what they can understand confidently.

What Managers Don't Need to Understand

To set appropriate boundaries, here's what you can safely leave to technical specialists:

- **Implementation details:** How to write hreflang tags, configure server headers, or implement structured data. You need to know these exist and matter, not how to code them.
- **Tool operations:** How to use Screaming Frog, configure Google Tag Manager, or analyze server logs. Your team should do this.
- **Debugging technical issues:** Why exactly a page isn't indexing or how to fix a specific crawl error. Ensure you have expertise for this, but don't do it yourself.
- **Algorithm mechanics:** How exactly Google's ranking algorithm works. No one outside Google knows the full details, and you don't need to.
- **Your role is strategic:** Ensure technical requirements are captured, resourced, implemented, and maintained. Not doing the work yourself.

Questions to Ask Your Technical Team

Use these questions to assess whether technical foundations are solid:

About site health:

- "What percentage of our important pages are indexed in Google?"
- "What are our most common technical errors, and do they affect important pages?"
- "Are we meeting Core Web Vitals thresholds on mobile?"

About changes:

- "How do we ensure SEO requirements are included in technical projects?"
- "What QA process exists for technical changes that affect SEO?"
- "How quickly can we implement technical SEO changes when needed?"

About monitoring:

- "What alerts exist for technical problems, and who receives them?"
- "How often do we audit technical health comprehensively?"
- "Are we monitoring competitors' technical implementations?"

About resources:

- "Do we have sufficient technical expertise for our SEO needs, or should we supplement with consultants?"
- "What technical debt exists that's holding back SEO performance?"
- "What would it cost to address our top 5 technical issues?"

Common Technical Pitfalls

Certain technical mistakes are common enough that managers should watch for them:

Pitfall 1: Blocking valuable content from indexing

- Symptom: Important pages not appearing in search results.
- Causes: Robots.txt errors, noindex tags, and canonicals pointing in the wrong direction.

- Prevention: QA process that verifies important pages are indexable.

Pitfall 2: Redirect disasters

- Symptom: Traffic drops after launches or URL changes.
- Causes: Missing redirects, redirect chains, redirects to wrong pages.
- Prevention: Comprehensive redirect mapping and testing before launch.

Pitfall 3: Duplicate content proliferation

- Symptom: Multiple URLs with the same or similar content competing with each other.
- Causes: Parameter variations, category redundancy, printer-friendly pages.
- Prevention: Canonical tag strategy and URL structure planning.

Pitfall 4: JavaScript rendering issues

- Symptom: Content visible to users but not in search results.
- Causes: Important content loaded via JavaScript that search engines can't execute.
- Prevention: Server-side rendering for critical content; testing with search engine tools.

Pitfall 5: Mobile-desktop parity failures

- Symptom: Mobile rankings lower than desktop despite a responsive design.
- Causes: Content hidden on mobile, functionality differences, performance issues.
- Prevention: Verify mobile and desktop versions provide equivalent experiences.

One practical implication of AI-mediated discovery is that not all parts of a page are equally visible to machine systems. Research indicates that AI search systems typically extract and reuse only a limited portion of a page's content, prioritizing what appears first and is expressed most clearly. This means organizations can still publish long-form content for human audiences. Still, the material most likely to be summarized, cited, or reused by AI systems should be placed prominently near the start of the page. Core definitions, positioning statements, factual explanations, and authoritative guidance should not be buried deep in supporting sections. From a governance perspective, this is not a writing preference but an infrastructure requirement. If the most important meaning is not immediately accessible, AI systems may represent the organization using incomplete or less-controlled fragments.

VISIBILITY IN AI-GENERATED SEARCH ANSWERS

AI-driven search experiences now decide what customers see **before** they reach your website. These systems extract answers from **discrete, well-structured blocks**, not from long paragraphs or content hidden behind UI elements.

Executive insight: **Being ranked is no longer enough — you must be selected.**

What AI systems prioritize:

- **Liftable content blocks** — clear answer under an H2/H3 and a short paragraph or list
- **Current and verifiable data** — outdated facts are filtered out
- **Structured support** — schema markup reinforcing meaning and freshness
- **Machine-readable presentation** — no key facts locked in PDFs, images, or accordions

If critical information isn't visible to machines, it isn't visible to customers.

Executive Action Checklist

- Require that every major product/service page answer:
  - What is it? Who is it for? What does it cost? How do I buy/contact/support?
- Introduce **content blocks** as a design standard:
  - Question → short answer → bullets or micro-FAQ
- Apply schema markup where it influences commercial outcomes
- Track inclusion in AI summaries as part of governance health. The specific metrics and tracking methodologies for AI summary inclusion are detailed in the measurement framework in Chapter 4, which provides quarterly scorecard templates and visibility drift indicators.

Blind-Spot Check

If the most important customer answers are not written clearly enough for algorithms to extract, competitors will.

	OLD SEO	NEW AI VISIBILITY
Goal:	Be seen in search results	Be selected for the answer
Metric:	Ranking position	Inclusion in AI-generated summaries & citations
Who chooses:	The user clicks	The machine (as proxy for the user)
Difference:	Discovery precedes trust	Trust precedes discovery (AI recommendations shape intent)

TECHNICAL SEO AND AI SEARCH

Static or server-rendered content is easier for AI systems to process than JavaScript-heavy pages, and a clean HTML structure helps AI extract information reliably. Fast-loading pages correlate with higher inclusion in many discovery systems—while not a direct "AI ranking" factor, performance improves usability and crawl/render reliability. Structured data helps many AI summarizers understand content meaning, though it doesn't guarantee inclusion. Accessible content signals quality and completeness.

The key takeaway: Technical best practices that benefit traditional SEO also improve AI visibility. You're not optimizing for two separate systems. Chapter 4 shows how to measure the effectiveness of these technical improvements across both traditional search metrics and AI visibility indicators.

BUILDING TECHNICAL SEO INTO PROCESSES

The goal is to prevent technical problems, not constantly fixing them.

Development Workflow Integration

- **Requirements phase:** SEO technical requirements documented and reviewed.
- **Design phase:** Mockups reviewed for SEO implications (heading hierarchy, navigation structure).
- **Development phase:** Code reviews include SEO checks for canonical tags, redirects, and metadata.
- **QA phase:** Specific SEO QA checklist items verified before deployment.
- **Deployment:** Monitoring is activated to catch issues immediately post-launch.

Ongoing Monitoring

Set up automated monitoring for:

- Indexation levels (via Search Console's Page indexing report and URL inspection sampling)
- Crawl errors in Search Console
- Site uptime and performance
- SSL certificate expiration
- Broken links
- Redirect chains

Frequency: Critical alerts immediately; comprehensive reviews weekly or monthly, depending on site change frequency.

When to Bring in Technical Specialists

In-house teams can handle many technical SEO tasks, but certain situations warrant external expertise:

- **Complex migrations:** Moving domains, changing platforms, or restructuring URLs at scale.
- **Persistent technical issues:** Problems your team can't diagnose or resolve.
- **Enterprise platforms:** Complex CMS or e-commerce platforms with SEO implications not obvious to generalists.
- **International implementations:** Hreflang, geo-targeting, and multi-regional technical setup.
- **Initial audit and strategy:** An external expert can audit technical health and create an improvement roadmap.
- **Budget guidance:** Expect to pay $5,000-$25,000+ for comprehensive technical audits from reputable consultants, depending on site size and complexity.

Once your team has established the monitoring and QA processes covered in Chapters 4 and 5, use the Technical Health Scorecard in Chapter 14 to run a formal quarterly assessment.

Chapter 4

BUILDING YOUR MEASUREMENT FRAMEWORK

This section addresses **operational governance**—the day-to-day data management practices that ensure measurement reliability.

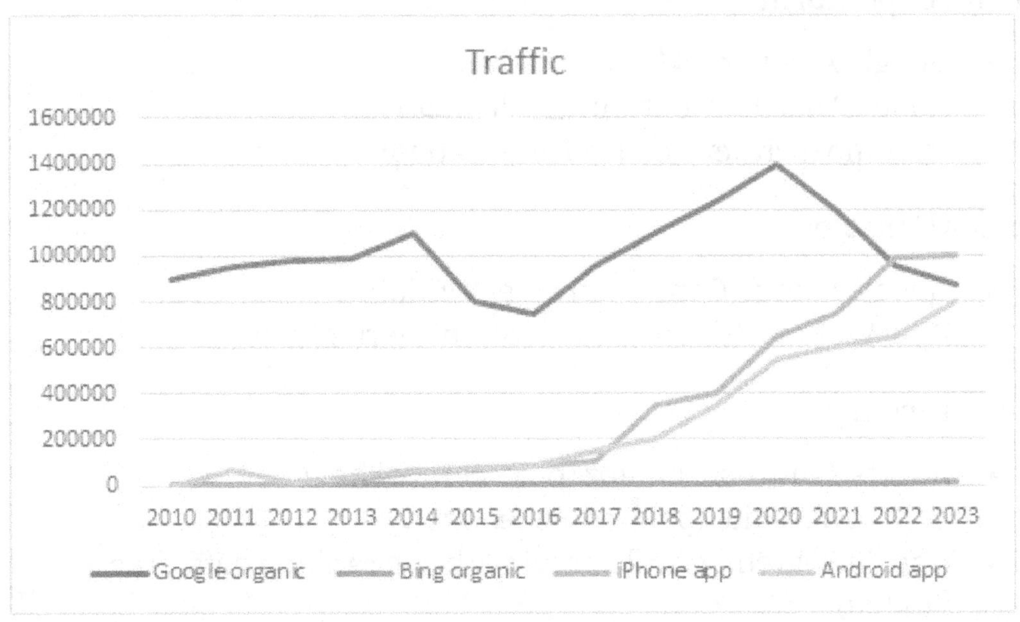

Figure 13 Organic traffic trends show how traffic sources have changed over several years.

"Is our SEO working?" You can't answer this question without measuring the right things. But SEO measurement is more complex than checking a traffic chart. Effective measurement frameworks distinguish signal from noise, connect SEO to business outcomes, and guide strategic decisions.

Is Our SEO Working?

As the strategic measurement frameworks move into organizational governance, day-to-day SEO teams still need practical tools to gather reliable data and act on it. The following sections outline the operational measurement stack and common pitfalls to watch for.

TOOL STACK FOR MEASUREMENT

Comprehensive measurement requires multiple tools. Here's a typical stack:

Analytics platform:

- Google Analytics 4 (free, widely used)
- Adobe Analytics (enterprise alternative)
- Matomo (privacy-focused alternative)

Search Console:

- Google Search Console (free, essential)
- Bing Webmaster Tools (free, often overlooked)

Rank tracking:

- Ahrefs, Semrush, or Moz (paid, comprehensive)
- SEO Powersuite (paid, comprehensive)
- Google Search Console provides basic ranking data (free, limited)

Technical monitoring:

- Screaming Frog or Sitebulb (crawling)
- Google PageSpeed Insights (performance)
- Various uptime monitors

Competitive intelligence:

- Ahrefs, Semrush, or Similarweb
- Manual competitive audits

Conversion tracking:

- Built into the analytics platform
- CRM integration for lead tracking

Total typical cost: $50–$2,000+ per month, depending on business size and tool sophistication.

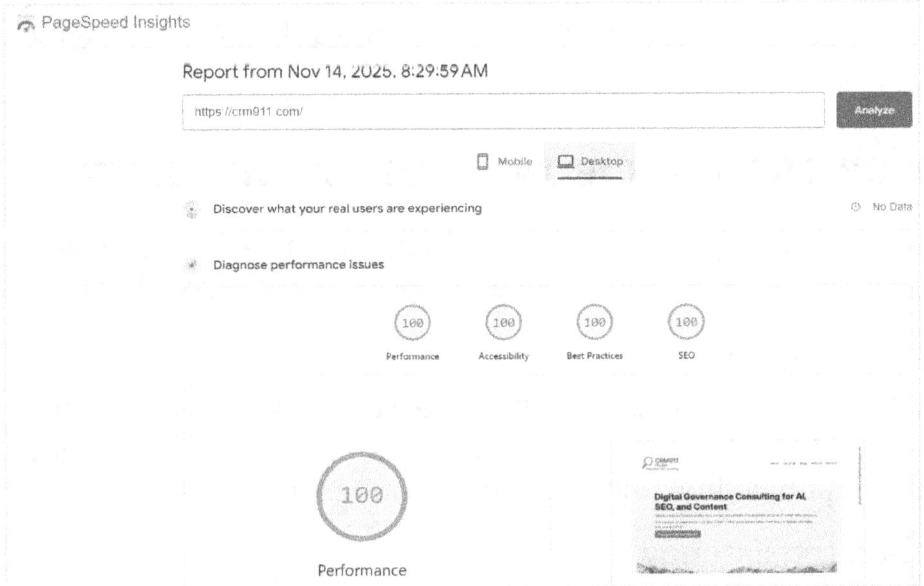

Figure 14 A perfect PageSpeed score on the author's website.

COMMON MEASUREMENT MISTAKES

- **Mistake 1: Measuring too much.** Tracking hundreds of metrics creates paralysis. Focus on 10-15 metrics that actually drive decisions.

- **Mistake 2: Measuring too little.** Tracking only traffic misses whether that traffic creates business value.
- **Mistake 3: Short-term thinking.** SEO moves slowly. Month-to-month volatility is normal. Look at quarter-over-quarter trends.
- **Mistake 4: Ignoring seasonality.** Comparing December to January can be misleading if your business is seasonal. Compare year-over-year.
- **Mistake 5: Attribution myopia.** Crediting SEO for all organic conversions ignores that some would've converted regardless. Incrementality matters but is hard to measure.
- **Mistake 6: Not connecting to business outcomes.** "Rankings improved!" means nothing if revenue didn't. Always tie metrics to business impact.

MEASUREMENT DISCIPLINE AND DATA INTEGRITY

Even the best analytics stack fails without governance. Tools gather data; governance ensures it is used responsibly and consistently.

Define ownership

Every report or dashboard should have a clear owner—someone accountable for data accuracy, definitions, and delivery frequency. Shared responsibility quickly becomes no responsibility.

Maintain consistency

Create a single *metrics glossary* that documents each KPI, its data source, and its calculation method. When "organic conversions" or "engaged sessions" appear in different reports, everyone should know they refer to the same metric.

Control changes

Version control applies to data as well. Keep a simple change log for edits to tracking tags, goals, or dashboard formulas. Quiet changes destroy comparability and trust.

Audit periodically

Schedule quarterly measurement reviews to confirm that tags fire, dashboards update, and data align with current business objectives.

Governance keeps insights stable as teams, tools, and tactics evolve—so "Is our SEO working?" remains answerable over time.

The disciplines above — ownership, consistency, change control, and periodic auditing — help ensure the reliability of your data. But reliable data serves a larger purpose than the dashboards you build today.

At the executive level, SEO measurement is organized into two distinct dashboard categories, each answering a different question. Operational performance dashboards answer "Is our SEO working right now?" — drawing on the traffic, ranking, conversion, and revenue data your measurement stack produces. Governance maturity dashboards answer "Will our SEO keep working?" by drawing on evidence of process health —whether ownership is documented, whether audits are run on schedule, and whether single points of failure have been identified and addressed.

These are not the same question, and they require different inputs. The metrics glossary you maintain, the ownership you assign, and the change logs you keep are not just housekeeping — they are the raw material that governance dashboards need to function. If those inputs are inconsistent or unowned, the governance dashboard cannot tell leadership whether your visibility is structurally sound or quietly fragile.

Is Our SEO Working?

The two diagrams below illustrate how these dashboard categories
appear in practice. You will not typically build either one yourself —
that responsibility sits with the executive team and is covered in detail
in Book 5, *The C-Suite Blind Spot*. But understanding their shape helps
you collect the right data and flag the right signals upward.

```
VISIBILITY PERFORMANCE DASHBOARD (Operational)
                    Q4 2025

    Organic Traffic:      847K visits  ↑ +12%
    Ranking Positions:    Top 3: 43%   ↑ +5%
    AI Citations:         892 mentions ↑ +18%
    Conversion Rate:      3.2%         → stable
    Organic Revenue:      $2.4M        ↑ +9%
```

*Figure 15 Visibility Performance Dashboard: what operational
measurement looks like at the executive level. Your traffic, ranking, and
conversion data feeds directly into this view.*

VGMM Governance Maturity Dashboard
Q4 2025 • Executive Review

OVERALL MATURITY SCORE: 3.2 / 5.0 (SPOF-capped at 2)
Status: STRUCTURED (Developing processes)
Trend: ↑ +0.3 vs. Q3

DOMAIN MATURITY SCORES:
Content Governance   3.5 / 5.0 ●●●○○
* SPOFs: 1 identified (schema lead)
* Ownership: Documented

SEO Governance   3.0 / 5.0 ●●●○○
* SPOFs: 2 identified (tech SEO, analytics)
* Training: 85% complete

Website Performance Gov.   3.8 / 5.0 ●●●●○
* Escalation path: Active
* Change control: Enforced

Accessibility Governance   2.5 / 5.0 ●●○○○
* SPOFs: 3 identified ⚠
* Audit: Overdue 45 days

Workflow & Execution Gov.   2.8 / 5.0 ●●○○○
* Process documentation: Incomplete
* Cross-training: In progress

CRITICAL GOVERNANCE GAPS
* 6 total SPOFs identified across domains
* Accessibility audit overdue (remediation plan)
* Workflow documentation incomplete (Q1 target)

Figure 16 *VGMM Governance Maturity Dashboard: what governance measurement looks like at the executive level. Your ownership records, audit logs, and process documentation are the inputs on which this dashboard depends.*

Why Traditional SEO Measurement Breaks Before It Fails

Traditional SEO measurement assumes a visible journey: a user searches, clicks, consumes content, and converts. That assumption underpins most analytics stacks, attribution models, and reporting cadences. It is also increasingly incomplete. As AI-mediated search surfaces summarize, compare, and recommend without sending users to websites, influence often occurs upstream of any measurable interaction.

Some of this shift is now being formalized in emerging AI standards such as the Model Context Protocol (MCP), which describes how AI systems can assemble responses using persistent context and external tools rather than relying solely on real-time user queries. While the technical details of such protocols fall outside the scope of SEO management, their implications are clear: discovery increasingly occurs within contextual orchestration layers that operate before a click, and often without one. In these environments, content may influence decisions even when no measurable interaction ever reaches an analytics platform.

Taken together, these changes create a structural gap rather than a tooling problem. Analytics platforms still record what happens *after* a click, but they cannot observe when an AI system has already shaped a decision. A declining organic traffic line may coexist with stable or rising revenue, stronger brand recall, or increased direct and branded demand. Without context, managers risk misreading this divergence as SEO underperformance rather than a shift in how influence is exerted.

Measurement frameworks built purely around clicks and sessions, therefore lag reality. They reward visibility that produces traffic while ignoring visibility that produces decisions elsewhere. Before introducing new metrics, it is important to explicitly recognize this limitation: the absence of a click does not imply the absence of impact.

In an AI-mediated environment, influence becomes probabilistic, distributed, and often invisible to traditional dashboards.

This is the point at which measurement must expand—from recording deterministic events to estimating likelihood, presence, and consistency across machine-mediated journeys.

SEO as Brand Influence Infrastructure

Traditional SEO measurement assumes that visibility is proven by interaction. A ranking produces a click. A click produces a session. A session produces an outcome. That chain once held. It no longer describes how influence works.

In AI-mediated discovery environments, visibility increasingly occurs without interaction. Large language models and generative search systems synthesize, compare, and recommend information before a user ever sees a website. When that happens, your organization may influence a decision without producing a measurable visit. Traffic declines while demand holds. Analytics report loss while revenue remains stable. This is not underperformance; it is brand influence without attribution.

To manage this shift, SEO must be reframed. It is no longer just a traffic acquisition channel. It is **brand influence infrastructure**—the system that determines whether your organization is eligible to be surfaced, trusted, and recommended by machine intermediaries.

AI systems do not optimize for keywords. They optimize for certainty. They favor sources that demonstrate topical authority, align clearly with a defined ideal customer profile, are corroborated by third-party validation, and present positioning clarity without internal contradiction. These are not new SEO ideas, but they now operate upstream of measurable demand.

This creates a structural measurement gap. Analytics platforms faithfully report what happens after a visit, but they cannot show how often your brand was evaluated, compared, or excluded before a click occurred. A decline in sessions may reflect reduced opportunity, or it may reflect successful influence that no longer requires a visit. Without this context, managers misread stability as stagnation and influence as invisibility.

The managerial task is not to abandon measurement, but to **govern expectations**. Executives must recognize that SEO performance is now partly probabilistic. Influence is expressed through consistency of inclusion across machine-mediated answers, not solely through deterministic events. Rankings and traffic remain useful, but they no longer define success in isolation.

This reframing does not eliminate accountability. It shifts it. When SEO is treated as brand influence infrastructure, the question "Is our SEO working?" becomes inseparable from a deeper one: "Are we consistently eligible to be trusted by the systems that now decide what customers see first?"

Retrieval Signals vs. Attribution Signals

AI-mediated visibility introduces a separation between retrieval signals and attribution signals. Retrieval signals determine whether content is eligible for inclusion in AI-generated responses. Attribution signals, such as citations or referrals, indicate whether that inclusion is externally visible or measurable.

This distinction matters for measurement. A lack of traffic or citation does not imply a lack of influence. Content may be retrieved, evaluated, and incorporated into synthesized answers without generating a measurable visit. Conversely, content may receive occasional citations without being consistently retrieved across similar queries.

Measurement frameworks must therefore treat AI visibility as probabilistic rather than deterministic. Trend analysis, pattern detection, and comparative benchmarking are more reliable than absolute counts. Governance maturity is reflected not in guaranteed inclusion, but in sustained eligibility across retrieval contexts.

GOVERNANCE MATURITY VS. OPERATIONAL PERFORMANCE

The measurement frameworks in this chapter focus on **operational** performance: traffic, rankings, conversions, and business outcomes. These metrics answer the question "Is our SEO working?"

A separate category of measurement assesses **governance** maturity—the organizational capability to sustain SEO performance through documented standards, clear ownership, and repeatable processes. Governance maturity frameworks such as SEOGMM (SEO Governance Maturity Model), LVMM (Local Visibility Maturity Model), and IVMM (International Visibility Maturity Model) assess whether your SEO infrastructure is resilient, documented, and transferable beyond individual expertise.

The distinction matters:

Strong performance + weak governance = Fragile success (hero-dependent, vulnerable to platform changes or team turnover)

Strong governance + adequate performance = Sustainable capability (standards-based, survives organizational change)

For SEO managers: Your operational measurement (this chapter) indicates whether SEO is delivering results today. Governance maturity assessments (covered in Books 3 and 5) tell you if those results can be sustained and scaled tomorrow.

The two measurements complement each other but aren't interchangeable. You need dashboards for performance and frameworks for governance—both measure visibility, but from different angles with different stakeholder audiences.

MEASUREMENT BLIND SPOT — AGENTS DON'T CLICK

Traditional SEO relies on the "Click-Through" as the ultimate signal of success. However, emerging AI agents and Generative Surfaces often process, summarize, and act upon your data without ever sending a user to your URL.

Your analytics might show declining traffic while revenue remains stable or conversions increase through machine-mediated journeys. To manage this, we must look beyond the "Click" and measure *Probabilistic Dominance*.

A New KPI: Probabilistic Dominance

In the AI ecosystem, visibility is not a fixed position; it is a statistical likelihood.

- **Definition:** Probabilistic Dominance is the statistical likelihood that your brand will be the "chosen" answer across 100 independent AI sessions.
- **The Shift:** Traffic can go down while your **Agent Influence Share**—your brand's "weight" in the AI's decision-making process—goes up.

Because an LLM resets its "context window" with each new conversation, visibility is a rolling probability. Success is no longer about being #1 once; it's about appearing in 80% of sessions.

Tools for Measuring Probabilistic Dominance

Several tools can serve as the "bridge" between traditional search data and AI presence:

- **Share of Model:** A leading platform specifically for tracking "Brand Perception" and "Search Visibility" across major LLMs. It provides a dedicated **AI Visibility Score** that quantifies how often you are the "answer."

- **Profound:** Its "Conversation Explorer" processes millions of AI prompts to show your brand's share of voice and sentiment within AI-generated responses.
- **Semrush AI Visibility Toolkit:** For teams already in the Semrush ecosystem, it tracks citations across ChatGPT, Gemini, and Google's AI Overviews, providing a "Share of Voice" metric for AI.
- **Ahrefs Brand Radar:** Uses Ahrefs' massive crawl data to identify where and how your brand is being cited by generative engines, helping you spot when you've been "encoded" into a model's logic.
- **AthenaHQ:** Its "Narrative Monitoring" helps you see if the AI is using the correct brand tone and positioning, rather than just checking for a link.

Why Traditional Dashboards Fail

Traditional dashboards are "Deterministic"—they record a 1:1 event (a hit, a click, a lead). Generative search is "Probabilistic." Because an LLM resets its "context window" with each new conversation, your brand may appear in one session and vanish in the next.

Feature	Traditional Tracking (Deterministic)	AI Tracking (Probabilistic)
Success Signal	A link click or page view.	Brand inclusion in the synthesized answer.

Feature	Traditional Tracking (Deterministic)	AI Tracking (Probabilistic)
Consistency	High (the link stays at #1).	Variable (visibility resets per conversation).
Measurement Method	Server logs and Pixel tracking.	Synthetic session auditing and API monitoring.
Metric	Rank / CTR.	Probabilistic Dominance / Brand Share.

Log Files as Episodic Verification

Log-file analysis still has a narrow but important role in modern SEO measurement—specifically as a **verification mechanism**, not a reporting system. While analytics platforms cannot show when AI crawlers, agents, or answer engines access your site without sending traffic, server logs can occasionally confirm whether those systems are reaching key pages at all. For large or high-traffic enterprise sites, however, continuous log collection is often impractical due to cost, storage volume, and processing complexity.

The managerial implication is restraint: log files should be generated **selectively and temporarily**, usually in response to a specific question—such as sudden visibility loss, suspected crawler blocking, or uncertainty about AI-agent access—rather than maintained as an always-on measurement layer. Used this way, logs function as forensic evidence that complements dashboards, helping leadership validate assumptions without creating an ongoing operational burden.

Technical readiness for AI-mediated retrieval should be validated alongside traditional crawl diagnostics. This includes confirming that key content is accessible without client-side execution dependencies, that structured data is available to non-rendering agents, and that access controls do not unintentionally block AI crawlers used by search and answer systems.

These checks do not require new tooling. They require extending existing crawl and access audits to account for retrieval-based consumption, not just page rendering.

Influence Without Evidence

Most measurement frameworks still assume that influence leaves a visible trail. A query leads to a click, a session, and an attributable outcome. That assumption no longer holds consistently. Increasingly, AI-mediated search systems summarize, compare, and recommend without sending users to a website—yet those interactions still shape perception, preference, and decision-making.

This creates a deeper blind spot in structural measurement. Analytics platforms faithfully report what happens after a visit, but they cannot show how much of your content is actually used when AI systems generate answers without sending traffic. Research by Dejan AI now shows that these systems do not read full pages. They extract only a limited portion—typically a few hundred words—from whichever sources they consider most relevant at that moment. Longer pages do not receive more exposure; additional content is ignored. As a result, your organization may appear to be "covered" in AI-generated summaries while critical explanations, positioning, or risk-sensitive details never surface. Traditional dashboards can confirm that content exists, but they cannot tell you whether the commercially relevant part of the content was ever seen, cited, or reused.

For managers, this is not a tooling failure but a governance issue. When discovery systems decide which brands are cited, summarized, or excluded before a visit occurs, traditional dashboards explain outcomes without revealing exposure. Visibility in AI-led search is probabilistic, not positional. Each interaction is a fresh evaluation in which your organization may be selected, regardless of prior performance.

This is why executive measurement must extend beyond traffic and conversions. Governing visibility now requires monitoring the consistency of inclusion, the accuracy of representation, and the comparative presence across AI-mediated discovery environments—signals that sit outside standard analytics but directly affect future demand. The next section distinguishes where analytics ends and governance responsibility begins.

GOVERNANCE VS. ANALYTICS

Since you cannot "see" an AI agent reading your site in your analytics platform the same way you see a human or a search engine crawler, your governance framework must fill the gap.

- **Audit for Sentiment:** Periodically prompt various AI surfaces to describe your brand and your top three competitors. Note the recurring adjectives and themes.
- **Track "Unlinked" Citations:** AI often mentions a brand name without a hyperlink. These are "Agent Influence" wins that drive real-world trust but show up as "Zero" in traditional SEO reports.
- **Monitor Branded Search:** A rise in "Direct" traffic or users searching for your specific brand name is often a lagging indicator that an AI agent recommended you elsewhere.

Takeaway: Success in an AI world is measured by Consistency across Timelines. If your brand appears in 80 out of 100 independent AI conversations, you have achieved high Probabilistic Dominance. If you only appear in 10, your content lacks the "Factual Density" or "Authority" required to anchor the model's predictions.

THE AI VISIBILITY MEASUREMENT FRAMEWORK

Traditional SEO measurement tracked inputs (keywords, backlinks, technical health) and outputs (rankings, traffic, conversions). AI search requires adding a middle layer: **machine interpretability**.

The three-tier measurement framework addresses different stages of the AI visibility journey:

Tier 1 - Upstream (Machine Legibility): Can AI systems parse, understand, and trust your content?

Tier 2 - Midstream (AI Visibility): Do AI systems choose to surface your brand in generated answers?

Tier 3 - Downstream (Commercial Impact): Does AI visibility translate to business outcomes?

Each tier provides distinct insights and requires different measurement approaches.

Tier 1: Upstream Metrics (Machine Legibility)

Upstream metrics are **leading indicators** of AI visibility potential. They measure whether your content infrastructure is interpretable by AI systems before evaluating whether you're actually being surfaced.

Structured Data Coverage

What to measure: Percentage of strategic pages with complete, valid schema.org markup

How to measure:

- Crawl your site with Screaming Frog or a similar tool

- Filter for pages that should have structured data (products, services, articles, locations)
- Calculate: (Pages with valid structured data ÷ Total strategic pages) × 100

Benchmark targets:

- Minimum viable: 60% coverage on revenue-critical pages
- Competitive: 80% coverage across all strategic page types
- Excellence: 90%+ coverage with rich, complete markup

Manager's question: "Are we making it easy for AI systems to understand what we offer, or are we forcing them to guess from unstructured text?"

Attribute Completeness

What to measure: Percentage of products/services with explicit, machine-readable attributes

How to measure:

- Audit your top 50 revenue-generating products/services/locations
- Count how many specific attributes each has explicitly stated (not implied):

  - Physical products: dimensions, materials, capacity, compatibility, certifications, use cases, constraints

  - Services: delivery timeframes, geographic availability, prerequisites, pricing models, outcome guarantees

  - Locations: hours, amenities, accessibility features, parking, restrictions, age requirements

Calculation: (Products with 10+ explicit attributes ÷ Total products audited) × 100

Why 10+ attributes? AI systems make decisions based on constraints and fit. A product with only 3-4 attributes cannot be confidently recommended for specific use cases.

Example - Hotel Room Listings:

Low attribute density (4 attributes):

- King bed
- 300 sq ft
- WiFi included
- $149/night

High attribute density (12 attributes):

- King bed, premium mattress
- 300 sq ft interior, 80 sq ft balcony
- Ocean view, 4th floor
- WiFi included, 100 Mbps
- Mini-fridge, Nespresso machine
- Blackout curtains, soundproofing
- Walk-in shower, no tub
- 24-hour room service available
- Adults-only floor
- No pets allowed
- $149/night weekdays, $219 weekends
- 2-night minimum on weekends

The second listing can be confidently matched to specific user needs (couples seeking quiet, ocean views, weekend getaways with morning coffee). The first cannot.

Benchmark targets:

- Minimum viable: 50% of products with 8+ attributes
- Competitive: 70% with 10+ attributes
- Excellence: 85%+ with 12+ attributes

Cross-Channel Consistency Score

What to measure: Semantic alignment across channels where AI systems gather information about your brand

How to measure (quarterly manual audit):

1. Select 10 key claims your brand makes (product benefits, service guarantees, company positioning, expertise areas)

2. Check each claim across 5-7 channels:

   - Your website (official pages)

   - Press releases and PR coverage

   - Social media profiles (LinkedIn, Twitter/X, Facebook)

   - Review sites (G2, Trustpilot, Google Business Profile)

   - Employee profiles (LinkedIn bios of executives)

   - Third-party descriptions (Wikipedia, if applicable, directory listings)

3. Score each claim: 2 points (consistent everywhere), 1 point (mostly consistent with minor variations), 0 points (contradictions exist)

4. Calculate: (Total points earned ÷ Maximum possible points) × 100

Example - SaaS Company Positioning:

Claim: "Enterprise-grade security with SOC 2 Type II certification"

- Website: ✓ States clearly (2 points)
- PR coverage: ✓ Mentions in announcement (2 points)
- G2 profile: ✗ Says "bank-level security" but no certification mentioned (0 points)
- Sales deck (if public): ✓ Includes certification (2 points)
- Executive LinkedIn: ✗ One exec says "military-grade encryption" (conflicting terminology) (0 points)

Score for this claim: 6/10 points

Benchmark targets:

- Minimum viable: 70% consistency
- Competitive: 85% consistency
- Excellence: 95%+ consistency

Why this matters: AI systems synthesize information across channels. Contradictions signal unreliability and reduce confidence in surfacing your brand.

Tier 2: Midstream Metrics (AI Visibility)

Midstream metrics measure whether AI systems are actually surfacing your brand in generated answers. This is where evaluation becomes visibility.

Brand Mention Frequency

What to measure: How often your brand appears when AI systems answer queries in your category

How to measure:

1. Develop 20-30 test queries representing your strategic categories:

    - Product category queries ("best [category] for [use case]")

    - Comparison queries ("compare [your brand] vs [alternatives]")

    - Problem-solution queries ("how to solve [specific problem]")

    - Buying guide queries ("choosing [product category]")

2. Test quarterly across major AI platforms:

    - ChatGPT (with web browsing enabled)

    - Google Gemini

    - Perplexity

    - Google AI Overviews (in standard search results)

3. Document for each query/platform combination:

    - Was your brand mentioned? (Yes/No)

    - If yes, in what position? (First mentioned, second, third, embedded in general text)

    - If no, which competitors were mentioned?

4. Calculate mention rate: (Queries where you appeared ÷ Total queries tested) × 100

Benchmark context: Industry-wide data is still emerging (early 2026). Establish your baseline and track trends quarter over quarter, rather than initially comparing against external benchmarks.

Manager's question: "Are we appearing in AI-generated answers at the same rate as our traditional search visibility, or are we being compressed out?"

Representation Accuracy

What to measure: When AI systems mention your brand, is the description accurate?

How to measure:

For each mention in your quarterly testing, score accuracy:

2 points (Fully accurate): Description is factually correct, positioning aligns with your messaging, and no misleading implications

1 point (Partially accurate): Core facts correct but missing important context, or minor inaccuracies that don't materially misrepresent

0 points (Inaccurate): Material errors, outdated information, or framing that contradicts your positioning

Representation accuracy score: (Total points ÷ Total mentions × 2) × 100

Example inaccuracies to flag:

- AI describes your pricing model incorrectly (says "subscription only" when you offer perpetual licenses)
- AI lists features you don't have (common with outdated training data)
- AI positions you in the wrong market segment ("enterprise" when you're SMB-focused)
- AI cites old brand positioning you've since changed

Why this matters: Inaccurate representation can be worse than no mention—it can drive interested prospects to competitors or create confusion about the brand.

Competitive Presence

What to measure: When AI systems provide options in your category, are you included alongside competitors?

How to measure:

For queries that generate comparative responses (2-5 brands mentioned):

- Track your inclusion rate: % of comparative responses where you appear
- Track position when included: Are you first/second/third mentioned?
- Track competitor patterns: Which competitors appear most frequently?

Calculation for competitive inclusion rate: (Comparative responses including you ÷ Total comparative responses) × 100

Manager's insight: If competitors consistently appear in AI-generated shortlists while you're excluded, despite similar traditional search rankings, the issue is likely machine interpretability (Tier 1 metrics) or semantic clarity.

AI Crawler Access Patterns (Audit-Level Diagnostic)

What to measure: Which pages AI training and search crawlers access, how frequently, and what they ignore

Practical approach for large sites:

Most organizations with high-traffic sites and CDN infrastructure cannot practically analyze complete log files continuously—they're too large, expensive to store, and complex to process systematically.

Instead, conduct targeted log extracts for quarterly or annual audits:

1. Request a 7-day log file extract from your hosting provider or CDN, filtered for known AI crawler user agents:

   o GPTBot (OpenAI/ChatGPT)

   o GoogleOther (Google's AI training crawler)

   o Claude-Web (Anthropic)

   o Bingbot (Microsoft/Bing AI)

   o PerplexityBot

   o Diffbot (used by various AI services)

2. Analyze the extract for:

   o **Coverage:** What percentage of your strategic pages were crawled?

   o **Frequency:** How often compared to traditional search crawlers?

   o **Depth:** Did crawlers reach deep content or only top-level pages?

   o **Ignored sections:** Are there entire categories or page types they skip?

   o **Error rates:** HTTP status codes returned to AI crawlers

3. Compare access patterns across crawler types:

   o Are all AI crawlers behaving similarly, or do some access different content?

   o Are crawlers respecting your robots.txt directives as intended?

Example diagnostic insights:

A B2B software company discovered, through log analysis, that GPTBot extensively crawled their blog and documentation but rarely accessed product pages with pricing and feature details. The investigation revealed that product pages loaded pricing via JavaScript that the crawler couldn't reliably execute. Adding static pricing summaries with structured data resolved the issue.

An e-commerce site found AI crawlers accessing category pages but not individual product pages, even though both are indexable. The cause: excessive pagination depth required to reach products. They implemented flatter navigation and saw AI crawler coverage improve from 12% to 67% of products in the next quarterly extract.

Frequency: Request log extracts quarterly during comprehensive audits, or annually for routine monitoring. This provides sufficient insight without the overhead of continuous log analysis.

Manager's question: "If AI systems don't crawl our most important content, we can't expect visibility regardless of content quality. Are we making strategic pages accessible?"

Tier 3: Downstream Metrics (Commercial Impact)

Downstream metrics connect AI visibility to business outcomes. These are the metrics executives care about most, but they're lagging indicators—they show results of Tier 1 and Tier 2 performance.

Branded Search Lift

What to measure: Growth in searches for your brand name, which indicates AI systems successfully introduced you to new audiences

How to measure:

- Google Search Console: Filter for queries containing your brand name

- Compare quarter-over-quarter and year-over-year trends
- Segment by query type:

  - Brand only ("Acme Software")

  - Brand + product ("Acme CRM features")

  - Brand + competitor ("Acme vs Competitor")

  - Brand + solution ("Acme for [use case]")

Usefulness as an AI signal: When users encounter your brand in an AI-generated answer but want to verify or learn more, they often search for you by name. Branded search growth correlates with effective AI visibility even when attribution is impossible.

Benchmark interpretation:

- Branded search growing faster than category search volume = strong AI introduction effect
- Branded search declining while category grows = competitors capturing AI visibility

Direct Traffic Growth

What to measure: Visitors arriving directly (typing your URL or using bookmarks) rather than through trackable referrers

Why this matters as an AI signal: Many AI platforms don't pass referrer data. Users who see your brand in ChatGPT or AI Overviews often navigate directly to your site rather than clicking a tracked link. Direct traffic growth, especially from new visitors, suggests AI-driven discovery.

How to measure:

- Google Analytics 4: Direct traffic segment, filtered for new users
- Compare growth rate against other channels
- Look for geographic or temporal patterns matching AI visibility testing

Caveat: Direct traffic is noisy—it includes multiple sources. Use as a supporting signal alongside branded search, not as the sole indicator.

Conversion Rate by Entry Source

What to measure: Whether visitors arriving from AI-influenced journeys convert at different rates

How to measure (approximate, given attribution limitations):

Compare conversion rates for:

- Direct traffic (includes AI-influenced visits)
- Branded search traffic (includes post-AI-discovery verification)
- Traditional referral traffic

Hypothesis: If your Tier 1 and Tier 2 metrics are strong (high interpretability, frequent accurate mentions), visitors arriving through these pathways should convert well because AI pre-qualified them by describing your offering accurately.

Category Share of Voice

What to measure: Your percentage of total visibility (traditional + AI) in your category

How to measure:

1. Select 50-100 queries representing your category (from brand awareness through buying intent)

2. For each query, measure:

   - Traditional search: Position 1-10 visibility

   - AI visibility: Mentioned in AI-generated answers

3. Calculate the weighted share of voice, including both surfaces

Formula complexity: This requires sophisticated tracking. For initial implementation, track directionally:

- "Are we gaining or losing visibility share as AI surfaces grow?"
- "Do competitors appear more frequently in AI answers than us, relative to traditional search?"

The Measurement Hierarchy

Use this decision tree:

If Tier 1 metrics are low (poor machine legibility): → Fix upstream before investing heavily in content or promotion → Expected timeline: 2-4 months for technical remediation

If Tier 1 metrics are strong but Tier 2 is low (you're interpretable but not surfaced): → Investigate semantic clarity, competitive positioning, authority signals → Review cross-channel consistency and authentic external validation → Expected timeline: 3-6 months for semantic and authority improvements.

If Tier 2 metrics are strong but Tier 3 is low (visible in AI but not converting): → Problem likely isn't AI visibility—investigate conversion funnel, product-market fit, pricing → Or: AI is describing you inaccurately (check representation accuracy scores)

MANAGER'S FRAMEWORK: QUARTERLY AI VISIBILITY ASSESSMENT

Use this template for systematic tracking. Score each tier using the SEOGMM 1-5 scale, then identify priority actions based on the lowest-scoring areas.

Scoring Scale:

- 1 = Ad Hoc / Unmitigated Risk
- 2 = Emerging / Policy Definition
- 3 = Structured / Embedded Controls
- 4 = Integrated / Cross-Functional Accountability
- 5 = Predictive / Optimized and Resilient

TIER 1: MACHINE LEGIBILITY (Upstream)

Metric	Current	Target	Score (1-5)
Structured data coverage	___%	80%+	___
Attribute completeness (products with 10+ attributes)	___%	70%+	___
Cross-channel consistency	___%	85%+	___

Tier 1 Average Score: ___/5

Maturity Context:

- **Score 1-2:** Ad hoc implementation, no systematic tracking, frequent contradictions
- **Score 3:** 60%+ coverage, quarterly audits, documented standards
- **Score 4-5:** 80%+ coverage, automated validation, cross-functional governance

TIER 2: AI VISIBILITY (Midstream)

Metric	Current	Baseline/Target	Score (1-5)
Brand mention frequency	___% of test queries	Baseline: ___ from Q___	___
Representation accuracy	___%	90%+	___
Competitive inclusion rate	___%	vs top 3: ___%, ___%, ___%	___
AI crawler coverage	___% of strategic pages	Annual audit	___

Tier 2 Average Score: ___/5

Maturity Context:

- **Score 1-2:** No systematic testing, unknown AI visibility, frequent inaccuracies
- **Score 3:** 40-50% mention rate, quarterly testing, 80%+ accuracy
- **Score 4-5:** 70%+ mention rate, semi-automated tracking, 95%+ accuracy

TIER 3: COMMERCIAL IMPACT (Downstream)

Metric	Current	Comparison	Score (1-5)
Branded search growth	___% QoQ	vs category: ___%	___
Direct traffic (new users)	___% QoQ	—	___

Is Our SEO Working?

Metric	Current	Comparison	Score (1-5)
Conversion rate trends	Up / Flat / Down	vs previous quarter	___

Tier 3 Average Score: ___/5

Maturity Context:

- **Score 1-2:** No AI-influence tracking, unknown impact on conversions
- **Score 3:** Branded search growing 10-15%, directional attribution understanding
- **Score 4-5:** Branded search exceeds category growth, documented AI attribution

OVERALL MATURITY LEVEL

Average across all three tiers: ___/5

Your AI Visibility Maturity:

- **1.0-1.9 = Level 1 (Ad Hoc):** Immediate priority: Establish baseline measurements
- **2.0-2.9 = Level 2 (Emerging):** Priority: Fix technical contradictions, implement quarterly testing
- **3.0-3.9 = Level 3 (Structured):** Priority: Improve lowest-scoring tier, increase mention frequency
- **4.0-4.9 = Level 4 (Integrated):** Priority: Optimize competitive positioning, refine attribution
- **5.0 = Level 5 (Predictive):** Priority: Maintain excellence, prepare for emerging platforms

PRIORITY ACTIONS THIS QUARTER:

Based on the lowest-scoring tier:

1.   [Specific action with owner]

2.   [Specific action with owner]

3.   [Specific action with owner]

NEXT REVIEW: [Date in 90 days]

EMERGING DIMENSION: MULTIMODAL AI VISIBILITY

As of early 2026, most commercial AI search remains text-based. But the trajectory is clear: Google Lens processes billions of visual searches monthly, ChatGPT and Gemini now accept image inputs, and users increasingly search by showing photos rather than typing descriptions.

Multimodal search means AI systems process visual, textual, and contextual signals simultaneously to understand users' search intent and identify which results match it.

Manager's strategic question: "Will customers find us when they search visually, or only when they type?"

Why Visual Optimization Differs from Traditional Image SEO

Traditional image SEO focused on:

- File names and alt text for traditional search crawlers
- Image sitemaps for indexation
- File size optimization for page speed

Multimodal AI adds layers:

Scene understanding: AI interprets what's in the image (objects, setting, activity, mood, context) beyond simple object recognition

Attribute extraction: AI identifies specific characteristics (colors, materials, styles, patterns, layouts) that match search intent

Cross-modal consistency: AI checks whether visual signals align with textual descriptions on the same page

Contextual embedding: AI understands images within surrounding content—a hotel room photo gains meaning from nearby text about amenities, pricing, policies

Practical Multimodal Optimization (Forward-Looking)

Most organizations should treat multimodal optimization as **a forward-looking investment, not an** immediate priority—unless your category already sees significant visual search activity (fashion, home décor, travel, real estate, food).

Minimum viable approach (begin with the top 50 strategic images):

Structured captions and descriptions:

- Replace generic alt text ("hotel room") with specific, attribute-rich descriptions ("king bedroom with ocean-view balcony, modern coastal décor, blackout curtains, walk-in shower")
- Add visible captions when appropriate, since AI reads both alt text and visible text near images

EXIF metadata:

- Ensure copyright, creator, and basic attribution data are embedded in image files
- For location-dependent businesses (hotels, restaurants, attractions), embed GPS coordinates in photo metadata

Visual-textual alignment:

- Ensure images are placed near text that explicitly describes what they show
- Avoid decorative images that don't add semantic meaning—AI systems may ignore them, but they consume bandwidth

Consistent photography standards:

- Use similar angles, lighting, and composition across similar offerings (product categories, room types, service variations)
- Consistency helps AI systems recognize patterns and categorize accurately

Comprehensive approach (6-12 month investment):

Build a visual semantic taxonomy:

- Map your product/service attributes to visual characteristics
- Document which images demonstrate which attributes
- Example (hotel): "Family-friendly" attributes might be visually shown through: connecting rooms, cribs/high chairs, shallow pool entry, kids' menus, game rooms

Produce images for machine vision:

- Shoot with intent to show specific attributes clearly
- Avoid artistic ambiguity that works for humans but confuses AI
- Include detail shots that emphasize key differentiators

Create multimodal content packages:

- Pair every important product/service/location with 3-5 images showing different aspects
- Ensure images + text cover the 10-15 attributes that matter most for decision-making

Test multimodal discoverability:

- Conduct quarterly visual search testing: Take competitor photos, search with Google Lens or AI platforms, and see if your offerings appear as alternatives
- Monitor what attributes drive visual match recommendations

When to Prioritize Multimodal

Invest earlier (next 6-12 months) if:

- Your category has high visual search volume (fashion, home goods, travel, food, real estate)
- Competitors are already investing in visual optimization
- Your products/services are visually distinctive and hard to describe in text alone
- User research shows customers struggle to express what they want verbally

Defer to 12-24 months if:

- Your category remains primarily text-search dominant (B2B software, professional services, financial products)
- Traditional search and AI text visibility have significant gaps to address first
- Visual assets require substantial investment to bring them up to multimodal standards

Manager's principle: Multimodal optimization follows the same fundamental rule as all AI visibility work—**make it easy for machines to understand what you offer**. Visual signals are another modality that requires interpretability.

UNDERSTANDING "VISIBILITY DRIFT"

These metrics provide an early warning system. Because AI systems synthesize information, you might still rank for keywords in Google while simultaneously being excluded from the **AI Overview** or **ChatGPT Search** results.

Watch for these red flags:

- **High Rank, Low Citation:** You are #1 in traditional search, but a competitor is the one being quoted consistently in the AI summary.
- **Unlinked Entity Mentions:** Your brand is cited by the AI, but without a link. This is a win for "Agent Influence" but a "Zero" in traditional SEO.
- **Schema Gaps:** Your commercial pages lack the structured data that allows an agent (like a shopping bot) to "understand" your service as an entity.

Strategic Takeaway for the C-Suite

Success in an AI world is measured by Consistency across Timelines. By tracking Inclusion, Liftability, and Entity Clarity, you ensure that your brand remains the predictable choice when an LLM's logic resets for a new user.

Chapter 5

QUALITY ASSURANCE FOR SEO

QA in SEO is where strategy meets execution and where costly mistakes are caught before they destroy months of work. A single misconfigured redirect, a robots.txt error, or a template change can remove thousands of pages from search indexes overnight. Yet in many organizations, SEO QA is an afterthought, squeezed between deployment and launch with minimal oversight.

This chapter reframes QA as a strategic safeguard rather than a technical checklist. You'll learn how to build QA processes that protect your search visibility, maintain user experience, and prevent the crises that turn managers into firefighters.

In practice, SEO QA sits at the intersection of development, content, infrastructure, and measurement. It is not a separate discipline owned by one team, but a shared operating responsibility that managers must deliberately design into workflows. When QA is informal or implicit, SEO failures emerge late and at great cost. When QA is systematic, risks are caught early, responsibility is clear, and execution remains predictable even as teams, tools, and platforms change.

WHY SEO QA MATTERS: THE BUSINESS CASE

Most managers view QA as software bugs or product defects. SEO QA operates similarly but with unique characteristics that make it both more critical and more complex to implement correctly.

The Invisibility Problem

When a website button breaks, users complain immediately. When SEO breaks, silence follows. Pages disappear from search results gradually. Traffic erodes over weeks. By the time someone notices, revenue and rankings are lost, and recovery takes months.

Consider these real scenarios:

Scenario 1: The Template Change

A development team updates the site template to improve the mobile experience. Buried in 2,000 lines of code, a single change adds "noindex" meta tags to all product pages. (This is also a routine tag on staging servers.) The staging environment is not designed to be indexed by search engine crawlers. In Google Search Console, about two weeks after launch, product pages begin disappearing from search results. Three months later, organic product revenue is down 67 percent. Recovery can take several months, depending on crawl frequency and link recovery.

Cost: $2.3M in lost revenue, emergency consultant fees, team overtime, and executive attention diverted from strategy.

Scenario 2: The Redirect Map

The marketing team updates 500 pages to improve readability before a product launch. IT implements the changes but forgets to create 301 redirects from old URLs. Every backlink, bookmark, and search result now returns a 404 error. Eventually, Google treats this as content deletion and removes pages from the index.

Cost: Lost link equity accumulated over five years, 43 percent traffic drop to affected pages, brand reputation damage from broken links, and emergency remediation costs.

Scenario 3: The Robots.txt Typo

During a security review, IT updates robots.txt to block a specific crawler. A single typo ("Disallow: /" instead of "Disallow: /admin/") blocks compliant crawlers from the entire site. Blocking all crawlers can trigger rapid visibility loss. Treat any changes to robots.txt as high risk and require review/approval before deployment.

Cost: Complete search visibility loss, emergency response activation, executive explanation requirements, and potential board-level escalation.

The Common Factor

All three scenarios were preventable with proper QA. None required sophisticated tools or deep technical expertise—just systematic checking before deployment. The business case for SEO QA is simple: prevention is exponentially cheaper than cure.

A QA process that catches errors pre-launch costs hours. Fixing post-launch errors can take weeks to months and cost millions in lost revenue.

MANAGING SEO QUALITY ASSURANCE AS AN ONGOING CAPABILITY

SEO quality assurance functions as an operating capability that must persist across everyday work, routine change, and large initiatives alike. When QA exists only as a launch checkpoint or a specialist activity, it fails to protect search visibility in normal operations. Effective SEO managers design QA into workflows, responsibilities, and planning cycles so that risk is addressed continuously rather than episodically.

This section focuses on how SEO QA operates in practice: where it sits in the delivery lifecycle, how responsibility is distributed, and how managers prevent QA from becoming either a bottleneck or an afterthought.

QA Is a Continuous Activity

Many organizations treat SEO QA as a task that happens immediately before launch. This approach leaves large categories of risk unmanaged. The majority of SEO regressions originate outside formal releases, through content updates, template refinements, infrastructure adjustments, security changes, and vendor interventions. These changes often appear routine and rarely trigger formal review, yet they directly affect crawlability, indexation, rendering, and measurement.

Because SEO failures surface gradually, QA must operate continuously. Incremental change accumulates over time, and the combined effect is often not detected until traffic loss becomes visible. A continuous QA posture enables teams to identify drift early, when remediation is straightforward, and impact is limited.

For managers, this requires shifting expectations. QA cannot be treated as a phase. It must be treated as part of daily operational discipline.

Ownership and Responsibility in SEO QA

SEO QA frequently fails because responsibility is assumed rather than assigned. Engineering teams focus on delivery. Content teams focus on accuracy and messaging. SEO teams are expected to notice problems after deployment. This arrangement produces delays, frustration, and preventable incidents.

Clear responsibility boundaries improve outcomes. Execution ownership remains with the teams implementing changes. QA responsibility involves verifying that changes meet defined SEO requirements before and after deployment. Managers are responsible for defining how these roles interact, which checks are mandatory, and when escalation is required.

When responsibility is explicit, QA becomes a shared expectation rather than a reactive intervention. Teams understand when they are accountable for verification, when SEO review is required, and how to resolve issues without ambiguity.

Operating Models for SEO QA

SEO QA can be organized in several ways, each with different trade-offs.

A **centralized** QA model places responsibility with a small SEO team that reviews all changes. This model provides consistency and deep expertise, yet it often creates bottlenecks and delays as scale increases.

An **embedded** QA model distributes checks across delivery teams. This approach enables earlier detection and faster execution, though consistency can vary, and specialized issues may be overlooked.

A **hybrid** model combines both approaches. SEO defines standards, checklists, and escalation criteria. Delivery teams perform routine QA as part of their workflows. SEO conducts reviews for high-risk changes, performs audits, and leads post-incident analysis. This model supports scale while preserving accountability and expertise.

Managers should deliberately select an operating model rather than default to convenience or historical structure.

Intake and Triage of QA Work

SEO QA capacity is finite. Managers must decide where attention is required and where sampling is sufficient. Treating all changes equally dilutes focus and increases risk.

Effective QA triage considers impact, reversibility, and scope. Changes affecting URL structures, templates, indexing directives, rendering behavior, or infrastructure require mandatory QA. Routine copy edits, minor internal linking adjustments, and low-impact updates can be sampled or reviewed selectively.

Clear intake criteria reduce debate and delay. Teams know which changes trigger review, which proceed with standard checks, and which require escalation. QA effort becomes predictable and defensible rather than reactive.

Accumulated QA Debt

QA debt accumulates when checks are deferred, shortcuts become habitual, or known issues remain unresolved. This debt compounds quietly. Each unverified change increases uncertainty and weakens the reliability of future work.

Unlike visible defects, QA debt often remains hidden until compounded effects trigger a noticeable decline. Traffic erosion, inconsistent indexation, and fragile recoveries are common symptoms. Addressing QA debt requires acknowledging deferred risk and allocating time for remediation as part of normal operations.

Managers who recognize QA debt early prevent it from turning into incidents that demand emergency response and executive attention.

Integrating QA into Planning and Roadmaps

SEO QA must be planned alongside delivery work. When QA is excluded from schedules, it is frequently skipped under time pressure. Including QA effort in project estimates, sprint planning, and migration timelines establishes it as a standard requirement rather than an optional safeguard.

This integration allows managers to set realistic expectations, protect delivery quality, and avoid last-minute trade-offs that increase risk. Planning for QA also supports smoother cross-team collaboration by clarifying review points and decision authority in advance.

Indicators of a Healthy SEO QA Capability

A well-managed SEO QA capability produces predictable outcomes. Issues are detected earlier. Launches proceed with fewer surprises. Recovery from unavoidable errors is faster and less disruptive. Teams rely less on individual heroics and more on shared processes.

SEO QA does not eliminate all risk. Its value lies in reducing uncertainty and preserving stability amid change. Managers who treat QA as an operating capability rather than a checklist create conditions that sustain search visibility over time.

Chapter 6

STRUCTURED DATA

Structured data (often called *schema markup*) is a standardized way to tell search engines and AI systems *exactly* what page elements mean. Instead of forcing those platforms to interpret content algorithmically, structured data provides explicit labels: "This is a product with price $X and rating Y from Z reviews."

Structured data implementation should be integrated into your technical foundations (Chapter 3) and protected through QA processes (Chapter 5).

Your role isn't to write schema markup—that's your team's job. Focus on understanding why structured data matters strategically, which types to prioritize, and how to verify correct implementation.

RELEVANCE OF STRUCTURED DATA

Structured data delivers strategic value on three fronts.

- First, it may enable rich results in search—star ratings, prices, availability—that make your listings stand out visually.
- Second, AI systems can reference structured markup to verify facts and cite sources more confidently, improving your presence in AI-generated answers.
- Third, when your pages offer features competitors lack, you capture more clicks at the same ranking position.

The business case: A comprehensive product schema can correlate with a CTR uplift for eligible rich results, but uplift varies by query, site, and eligibility, and isn't guaranteed.

UNDERSTANDING GOOGLE'S RICH RESULTS EVOLUTION (2023-2026)

Between late 2023 and early 2026, Google fundamentally restructured which organizations can earn rich results in search. This wasn't incremental refinement—it was strategic repositioning to make room for AI Overviews while restricting visual prominence for "average" websites.

Manager's strategic context: These changes mean structured data implementation priorities have shifted dramatically. Schema types that were high-priority investments in 2022 are now worthless for most organizations in 2026.

What Changed and Why

The strategic driver: Google is prioritizing AI-generated answers (AI Overviews) over individual website rich results. By restricting which sites can earn enhanced snippets, Google creates more "white space" for its own AI to answer queries directly without requiring users to click through.

The three tiers of schema priority in 2026:

Tier 1 - Primary Rich Results (High ROI for Most Organizations):

- Product/Offer schema (e-commerce)
- Review/Rating schema (where you have legitimate reviews)
- LocalBusiness schema (local service businesses)
- Organization schema (foundational for all)

Tier 2 - Restricted Rich Results (Authoritative Sites Only):

- FAQ schema: Now restricted to government (.gov) and major health organizations only
- Article schema: Helps eligibility but doesn't guarantee rich results; primarily benefits established publishers

Tier 3 - Deprecated or Minimal-Value Rich Results:

- HowTo schema: Completely deprecated for mobile (2023), minimal display on desktop
- Special Announcements: Deprecated July 2025
- Course Info & Book Actions: Phased out late 2025
- Estimated Salary & Claim Review: Rolled into Knowledge Graph or AI-generated summaries
- Practice Problems: Support ended January 2026

Who Should Implement What?

If you're an e-commerce site or sell products:

- **Priority 1:** Product/Offer schema (critical - enables price, availability, review display)
- **Priority 2:** Review the schema where you have legitimate customer reviews
- **Priority 3:** Organization schema (foundational)
- **Skip entirely:** FAQ, HowTo, and deprecated types

If you're a local service business:

- **Priority 1:** LocalBusiness schema + Google Business Profile optimization
- **Priority 2:** Organization schema
- **Priority 3:** Review schema if applicable

- **Skip entirely:** FAQ, HowTo, Product (unless you sell products)

If you're a publisher or content site:

- **Priority 1:** Article/NewsArticle schema
- **Priority 2:** Organization schema
- **Priority 3:** Author/Person schema for bylines
- **Maybe:** Review schema for product reviews you publish
- **Skip entirely:** FAQ, HowTo (Google prefers AI Overviews for these queries)

If you're a B2B SaaS or professional services firm:

- **Priority 1:** Organization schema
- **Priority 2:** Article schema for thought leadership content
- **Priority 3:** Maybe LocalBusiness if you have physical offices serving clients
- **Skip entirely:** FAQ, HowTo, Product (unless you have a marketplace)

If you're a government agency or major health organization:

- **Priority 1:** Organization schema
- **Priority 2:** FAQ schema (you're in the eligible category)
- **Priority 3:** Article/SpecialAnnouncement (if applicable)
- **Consider:** LocalBusiness for offices/facilities

What About Existing FAQ and HowTo Implementations?

If you implemented the FAQ or HowTo schema in 2022-2023:

Do NOT spend time removing them. They're not harmful—Google ignores them. The markup exists, validates correctly, but produces no rich results.

Exception: If you're conducting a comprehensive schema audit or site migration, cleaning up non-functional markup reduces technical debt. But this should be **low priority** compared to implementing high-value schema types.

If you're planning NEW FAQ or HowTo implementations:

Stop. Don't implement. Unless you're a government agency or a major health organization, these schema types will consume development time without delivering any search-visibility benefit.

Alternative approach for FAQ content: Structure your FAQ content clearly with proper HTML headings (H2/H3) and well-written answers. This helps AI systems extract and cite your content in AI Overviews, which is now more valuable than the defunct FAQ rich result would have been.

The Strategic Shift: From Rich Results to AI Citations

Manager's insight: The 2023-2026 changes reveal Google's strategic direction. Instead of competing for rich result snippets, organizations should optimize for:

AI Overview inclusion: Structured, authoritative content that AI systems can confidently cite. Product-rich **results:** For e-commerce, these remain the highest-ROI structured data investment. **Local visibility:** For service businesses, Google Business Profile signals matter more than schema markup alone. **Entity understanding:** Organization schema helps AI systems understand your business relationships and authority

What this means for budget allocation:

2022 priority: Implement comprehensive schema coverage across all types

2026 priority: Focus schema investment on Product/Local/Organization; invest more resources in content quality, authority signals, and AI interpretability

The shift from "implement all schema types" to "implement only high-value types" should **reduce your structured data implementation costs** while focusing effort on what actually delivers visibility.

ESSENTIAL SCHEMA TYPES FOR MOST ORGANIZATIONS (2026 PRIORITIES)

Focus your implementation effort on these proven, high-impact schema types. The list is deliberately shorter than pre-2023 guidance—Google's restrictions mean most organizations should skip schema types that no longer deliver results.

Tier 1: Critical Implementation (Do These First)

Organization Schema

What it does: Establishes your business identity with search engines and AI systems. Provides official name, logo, social profiles, contact information, physical locations, and entity relationships.

Who needs it: Every organization, regardless of type or size.

Rich result benefits: Feeds Knowledge Panels, improves local pack eligibility, and supports brand entity recognition.

AI benefit: Critical for AI systems to understand your business relationships and cite you as an authoritative source.

Manager's priority: Critical. Implement immediately if missing. This is foundational for everything else.

Implementation timing: One-time implementation (2-4 hours), annual maintenance.

Product and Offer Schema

What it does: Enables rich product results showing prices, availability, reviews, and ratings directly in search.

Who needs it: E-commerce sites, marketplaces, retailers, and B2B companies with product catalogs.

Rich result benefit: Highest ROI schema type. Generates visual prominence, higher CTR, and pre-qualified traffic.

AI benefit: Helps AI systems understand your product catalog, pricing, and availability for AI-powered shopping assistants.

Manager's priority: Critical for e-commerce. If you sell products online, this should be your #1 schema investment.

Implementation timing: 40-80 hours for initial implementation, depending on catalog size; 2-4 hours for monthly maintenance.

ROI evidence: Organizations with the Product schema properly implemented typically see a 15-25% increase in CTR on product pages (when rich results display). Even conservative 10% improvements deliver strong returns.

Review and Rating Schema

What it does: Displays star ratings in search results for eligible item types (Products, Books, Recipes, Software, Local Businesses).

Who needs it: Organizations with legitimate customer reviews for specific items (not self-serving reviews about your own organization).

Rich result benefit: Star ratings significantly improve CTR by providing social proof before users click.

AI benefit: Reviews provide trust signals AI systems use when evaluating which sources to cite or recommend.

Manager's priority: High. Implement wherever you have legitimate third-party reviews.

Key restriction: Self-serving reviews (your organization reviewing itself) remain **ineligible**. Must be reviews **of** specific items/products/services, not reviews **of** your LocalBusiness or Organization entity.

Implementation time: 20-40 hours, depending on the complexity of the review integration.

LocalBusiness Schema

What it does: Clarifies entity details for local businesses—hours, location, services, geographic coverage.

Who needs it: Service businesses with physical locations or defined service areas; professional services firms; healthcare providers; restaurants/retail with physical storefronts.

Rich result benefit: Limited. Visibility in Maps and Local Pack is driven primarily by Google Business Profile signals (proximity, relevance, prominence), not schema markup alone.

AI benefit: Helps AI systems understand your geographic coverage, hours, and service offerings when answering local-intent queries.

Manager's priority: High for local businesses, but understand schema alone won't move local rankings. This works in combination with Google Business Profile optimization.

Implementation time: 10-20 hours, depending on the number of locations.

Tier 2: Contextual Value (Implement if Applicable)

Article and NewsArticle Schema

What it does: Helps search engines understand content metadata—headline, publish date, author, featured image.

Who needs it: Publishers, content marketers, blogs, news organizations, and thought leadership platforms.

Rich result benefit: Limited and unreliable. It may help eligibility for Top Stories/Discover, but rich article results are increasingly rare for non-major publishers.

AI benefit: Helps AI systems understand article authority, freshness, and author credentials when deciding whether to cite your content.

Manager's priority: Medium. Implement for publishers and content-heavy sites, but don't expect guaranteed rich results.

Implementation timing: 20-40 hours for initial setup across templates.

Important context: Many content sites implemented the Article schema between 2020 and 2022, expecting prominent rich results. By 2026, these will be displayed rarely, except by major publishers. The primary value is now **AI citation eligibility**, not visual prominence in traditional search.

BreadcrumbList Schema

What it does: Clarifies site hierarchy and navigation structure.

Who needs it: E-commerce sites with deep category structures; large content sites with complex organization.

Rich result benefit: Breadcrumb trails may display in search results, replacing URL display.

AI benefit: Minimal—helps AI understand site structure but doesn't significantly affect citation decisions.

Manager's priority: Low-medium. Nice to have, but not urgent.

Implementation timing: 15-30 hours, depending on site structure complexity.

Tier 3: Restricted or Deprecated (Skip Unless Explicitly Eligible)

FAQ Schema - Restricted

Eligibility: Government agencies (.gov domains) and major health organizations (CDC, NHS, WHO, etc.) **only**.

Status: In late 2023, Google restricted FAQ rich results to authoritative government and health sites. This restriction remains in effect as of early 2026.

Who should implement: If you operate a .gov website or a major public health organization, the FAQ schema remains valuable.

Who should NOT implement: Blogs, SaaS companies, e-commerce sites, corporate websites, standard businesses—your FAQ markup will validate correctly, but produce **zero** rich results.

Manager's guidance: If you're not explicitly in the eligible category (government/major health), **do not invest development time in the FAQ schema.** Instead, structure FAQ content with clear HTML headings so AI systems can extract and cite it in AI Overviews.

HowTo Schema - Deprecated

Status: Completely deprecated for mobile devices (2023); minimal/hidden display on desktop.

Replacement: Google now prioritizes HowTo steps within AI Overview boxes rather than providing individual websites with dedicated rich snippets.

Who should implement: No one, regardless of organization type.

Manager's guidance: If you have existing HowTo markup from 2022-2023, it's not harmful but produces no benefit. Don't remove it unless you're conducting a comprehensive schema cleanup. **Do not implement new HowTo markup**—it's wasted development time.

Alternative: Structure how-to content clearly for an AI system extraction. Well-structured content can appear in AI Overviews even without the HowTo schema.

Deprecated Schema Types (2025-2026)

These schema types are no longer supported or have been rolled into other Google features:

- **Special Announcements:** Deprecated July 2025 (was COVID-19/emergency specific)
- Course Info & Book Actions: Phased out late 2025
- **Estimated Salary:** Rolled into Knowledge Graph results
- **Claim Review:** Rolled into AI-generated fact-check summaries
- **Practice Problems:** Support ended January 2026 in Search Console

Manager's guidance: If your team has historically implemented any of these types, they can remain (not harmful), but don't invest time in maintaining them. Do not implement new markup of these types.

IMPLEMENTATION PRIORITY FRAMEWORK (2026)

Phase 1 (Month 1) - Critical Foundation:

- Organization schema on homepage **[ALL organizations]**
- Product schema (if e-commerce) [E-commerce/retail/marketplaces]
- Review/Rating schema where you have legitimate reviews **[Product sellers, service businesses with reviews]**

Phase 2 (Months 2-3) - Contextual Expansion:

- LocalBusiness schema (if applicable) **[Service businesses with locations]**
- Article schema on content [Publishers, content marketers]

Phase 3 (Months 4-6) - Polish and Specialized:

- BreadcrumbList schema **[Complex sites only]**
- Person/Author schema (if applicable) **[Publishers with bylines]**
- Additional specialized types as needed **[Recipes, Events, Jobs, etc.]**

DO NOT IMPLEMENT (Regardless of Phase):

- FAQ schema [unless you're .gov or a major health organization]
- HowTo schema [deprecated for all organizations]
- Special Announcements, Course Info, Book Actions, Claim Review, Practice Problems [all deprecated]

Enhanced Organization Schema Example

The Organization schema can be enhanced with details such as awards, postal and physical addresses across multiple locations, contact points and types, founding location, and links to other web presences such as YouTube, Facebook, Twitter, and Wikipedia.

<script type="application/ld+json">{"award":["2015 CANSTAR State Award for Outstanding Value, Home Insurance - Tasmania, Western Australia & Southern Australia","2015 Money Magazine Best of the Best Award for Cheapest Home & Contents Insurance","2013 & 2015 Guidewire Global Innovation Awards for Service Innovation"],"address":[{"addressCountry":"Australia","postalCode":"8001","contactType":"Claims and Enquiries","addressLocality":"Melbourne City Mail centre","postOfficeBoxNumber":"PO Box 14180","addressRegion":"Victoria"},{"addressCountry":"Australia","postalCode":"2001","contactType":"AAMI Life Customer Service","postOfficeBoxNumber":"GPO Box 3950","addressRegion":"Sydney"},{"addressCountry":"Australia","postalCode":"5001","contactType":"AAMI Business Insurance","postOfficeBoxNumber":"GPO Box 2470","addressRegion":"Adelaide"}],"contactPoint":{"@type":"ContactPoint","telephone":"(+61) 13 22 44","contactType":"Customer Service"},"@type":"Organization","name":"aami","logo":"https://www.aami.com.au/","foundingLocation":"Victoria","@context":"https://schema.org","url":"https://www.aami.com.au/","sameAs": ["https://www.aami.com.au","https://www.youtube.com.au/user/AAMIInsurance","https://www.facebook.com.au/aami","https://www.twitter.com/aami","https://plus.google.com/ +AamiAu/posts","https://www.linkedin.com/company/aami","http://en.wikipedia.org/wiki/Australian_Associated_Motor_Insurers_Limited"]}</script>

Figure 17 Enhanced Organization schema implementation—note how comprehensive entity information helps search engines understand your business identity and relationships.

This comprehensive approach helps shape what appears in Google's Knowledge Panel:

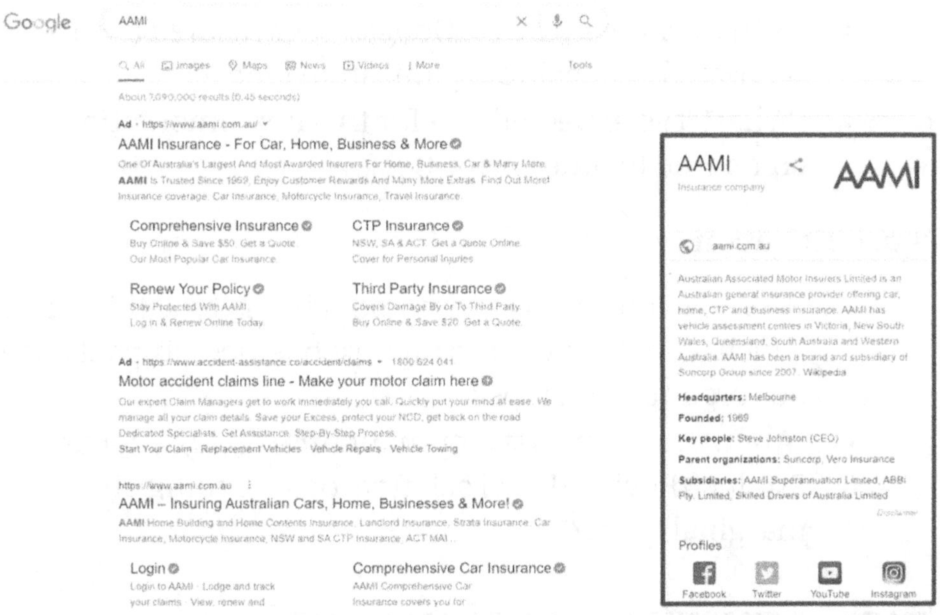

Figure 18 The organization schema can support Google's Knowledge Graph, but Knowledge Panels are derived from multiple sources and aren't directly controlled by markup.

Questions to Ask Your Team About Schema Prioritization

About current implementations:

- "Do we have any FAQ or HowTo schema markup? If yes, when was it implemented, and is it producing any rich results?"
- "Are we in Google's eligible category for FAQ rich results (government or major health organization)?"
- "What schema types are we currently maintaining that may no longer deliver value?"

About planned implementations:

- "Why are we implementing [schema type]? What rich result or AI benefit do we expect?"
- "Is this schema type on Google's deprecated list or restricted to specific organization types?"
- "What's the expected ROI for this implementation compared to other priorities?"

About prioritization:

- "If we can only implement one schema type this quarter, which would deliver the highest business impact based on our organization type?"
- "Are we focusing development time on high-value Product/Review/Local schema, or spreading effort across marginal types?"

COMMON STRUCTURED DATA MISTAKES

Watch for these issues:

- **Incomplete implementation.** Product schema is missing the aggregateRating/review properties required for review snippets (when eligible); Article schema is missing author information; or

Organization schema is missing key properties. Partial schema reduces effectiveness.

- **Errors that prevent validation.** Implementation errors make the schema useless. Your team should regularly check Google's Rich Results Test tool.
- **Not all crawlers execute JavaScript;** to maximize coverage, ensure JSON-LD is present in the initial HTML (server-rendered or prerendered) and verify this using Google's Rich Results Test or URL Inspection tool.
- **Inaccurate data.** A schema that shows incorrect prices, outdated information, or fake reviews violates guidelines and risks penalties.
- **One-and-done implementation.** Teams initially implement the schema but don't maintain it as content changes. The schema becomes outdated and misleading.

MEASURING STRUCTURED DATA IMPACT

Track these metrics to evaluate ROI:

- **Rich result appearance rate:** % of indexed pages with eligible markup that actually show enhanced results (Search Console → Enhancements report).
- **CTR improvement:** Compare click-through rates for pages with vs. without rich results. Track CTR deltas for pages that actually earn rich results; improvements are common but vary and aren't guaranteed.
- **AI citation frequency (qualitative):** Manually check if content with structured data is referenced by AI assistants that *display source links* (e.g., Perplexity, ChatGPT Search when enabled).

- **Implementation coverage:** What percentage of eligible pages have appropriate schema? Track this monthly; it should trend toward 100%.

Include structured data performance metrics in your comprehensive measurement framework, detailed in Chapter 4.

OPTIMISTIC ROI EXAMPLE: E-COMMERCE

Company: Mid-sized sporting goods retailer

Investment: $15,000 (developer time for schema implementation)

Timeline: 6 weeks implementation, 3 months to full impact

Results:

- CTR on product pages: +18% (from rich results with ratings/prices)
- Monthly organic product page sessions: 100,000 → 118,000
- Conversion rate: 2.5% (unchanged)
- Additional monthly conversions: 450
- Average order value: $85
- Additional monthly revenue: $38,250

ROI Calculation:

- Monthly revenue increase: $38,250
- Annual revenue increase: $459,000
- One-time investment: $15,000
- First-year ROI: ≈ 30:1 (illustrative; actual results depend on eligibility, query mix, and Google display rates)
- Ongoing benefit with minimal maintenance cost

Manager's Takeaway: Even a conservative 10% improvement in CTR delivers strong returns. Schema implementation generally delivers high ROI when it's accurate, policy-compliant, and maintained, but rich-result display is not guaranteed, and policies can change.

STRUCTURED DATA AND AI SEARCH

Structured data is one of several technical enablers for Google AI Overviews and other AI search features, alongside content quality, authority, and performance:

- **LLMs trained on web data** tend to interpret structured data more reliably than unstructured text, when the markup is visible to their crawlers. When an AI system encounters a Product schema with clear price and rating properties, it can confidently cite that information. Without a schema, the AI might ignore your product or extract wrong data.
- **Explicit entity relationships** help AI understand your content's place in broader contexts. Schema connects your products to brands, your articles to authors, and your organization to locations.
- **Machine-readable rather than human-readable:** While humans understand "Price: $49.99" in text, structured markup reduces ambiguity for parsers and AI models that extract facts at scale.

From my experience: I've worked with clients whose products rarely appeared in AI recommendations despite strong SEO. After implementing a comprehensive Product and Review schema, AI citation frequency increased within three months. The content didn't change—only the structured data.

BUDGET AND RESOURCE CONSIDERATIONS

Initial implementation costs:

- Simple sites (5-10 schema types): 20-40 hours developer time
- Complex sites (10+ schema types across many templates): 80-160 hours
- Enterprise sites with dynamic content: 200+ hours plus ongoing maintenance

Ongoing maintenance:

- Budget 2–4 hours per month for validation and updates using Search Console and Rich Results Test data.
- Plan quarterly comprehensive audits, plus event-driven revalidations after template/CMS changes.
- Allocate time for implementing new schema types as they emerge

ROI example: If structured data implementation costs $10,000 and drives a 15 % CTR uplift on 100,000 impressions (15,000 additional clicks at 2 % conversion × $100 AOV), monthly revenue ≈ $30,000 — ≈300 % ROI in month one.

Even conservative estimates (5 percent CTR improvement and 1 percent conversion rate) deliver strong returns.

TOOLS FOR VALIDATION

Your team should use these tools—you should know they exist and be able to ask whether they're being used:

Use Google's **Rich Results Test** (for eligibility and rendering) and Schema.org Validator (for syntax validation). Search Console 'Enhancements' report tracks errors site-wide.

URL: https://search.google.com/test/rich-results

Schema.org website - Official reference for all schema types and properties; check the 'Pending' section for new or AI-related proposals.

Google Search Console - Reports on structured data errors and rich result performance.

MANAGER'S FRAMEWORK: STRUCTURED DATA READINESS

When to Use This Assessment

This framework helps you evaluate structured data maturity and identify gaps. Use it:

- **Initially,** when establishing your structured data program.
- **Annually:** As part of a comprehensive SEO assessment.
- **After major changes:** Following CMS migrations, template redesigns, or schema strategy shifts
- **When diagnosing issues:** If rich results aren't appearing or coverage is declining
- **Not quarterly.** Track structured data coverage percentage monthly via Search Console's Enhancements report. Only complete this full assessment when you need strategic insight or are making structured data decisions.

For quarterly reviews, monitor:

- Coverage % trend (are we implementing schema on new pages?)
- Validation error trends (are errors increasing or decreasing?)

- Rich result appearance trends (are we getting the visibility we expect?)

If trends are positive, your quarterly review should state: "Structured data coverage increased from X% to Y%, no issues." If trends are concerning, use this framework to diagnose the root cause.

Implementation Coverage (1-5):

- Organization schema on homepage ___
- Product schema where applicable ___
- Article schema on content ___
- Review/Rating schema where reviews exist ___
- LocalBusiness schema (if applicable) ___

Quality (1-5):

- Schema validates without errors ___
- Rich results appear in search ___
- Data is accurate and current ___
- Ensure JSON-LD is delivered in the initial HTML (server-rendered or pre-rendered) and validate this in Search Console's URL Inspection tool to confirm Googlebot sees the markup without JavaScript. ___

Process (1-5):

- New pages automatically get appropriate schema ___
- Regular validation occurs ___
- Documentation exists ___
- Team knows when to use which types

Impact (1-5):

- Tracking rich result performance ___

- Measuring CTR improvements ___
- Monitoring AI citations ___
- ROI is positive ___

Total: ___ / 20

- **16-20:** Strong structured data program
- **11-15:** Good foundation, optimize coverage
- **6-10:** Gaps exist, prioritize implementation
- **Below 6:** Structured data should be an immediate priority

Chapter 7

MULTINATIONAL CHALLENGES

Managing SEO across countries and languages introduces complexity that can overwhelm experienced managers. Different markets have different search behaviors, competitive landscapes, technical requirements, and regulatory constraints. Yet the rewards justify the effort—international expansion through organic search offers lower customer acquisition costs than most paid channels.

Below, you'll learn how to structure international properties, coordinate across regions, and avoid the pitfalls that derail global SEO initiatives.

THE MULTINATIONAL SEO CHALLENGE

International SEO isn't simply translating your domestic site. Technical complexity multiplies across markets—what works in one country may violate regulations in another, requiring careful domain architecture planning and centralized infrastructure decisions.

Coordination becomes exponentially harder across time zones, cultures, and reporting structures. German and Australian teams may have different priorities, yet depend on shared technical infrastructure.

Meanwhile, competitive dynamics shift dramatically by market. Your strongest domestic competitor may be irrelevant in France, while local players you've never heard of dominate German search results.

The Center of Excellence Model

Most successful multinational organizations use a Center of Excellence (CoE) model for SEO. The CoE establishes global strategy, standards, and best practices while empowering local teams to execute with market-specific knowledge.

The CoE typically:

- Develops overarching SEO strategy aligned with global business objectives. This includes defining which markets to prioritize, allocating resources across regions, and defining what success looks like at the corporate level.
- Creates and maintains technical standards that all markets must follow. These standards cover domain architecture, hreflang implementation, structured data requirements, and mobile experience benchmarks.
- Provides tools, training, and support to regional teams. Rather than doing all SEO work centrally, the CoE enables local teams through shared resources, regular training sessions, and accessible documentation.
- Coordinates cross-market initiatives where centralization creates efficiency. For example, enterprise tool subscriptions, core algorithm monitoring, and global competitive intelligence operate more effectively at the CoE level.
- Measures and reports on global SEO performance, rolling up metrics from all markets while identifying trends and sharing successful tactics across regions.

These domain architecture decisions impact the technical foundations discussed in Chapter 3 and should be established before content development.

Regional teams typically:

- Execute local SEO tactics within the framework established by the CoE. They understand local search behavior, competitive landscapes, and cultural nuances that central teams cannot.
- Adapt global content and strategies for local markets through translation, localization, and market-specific content creation.
- Build relationships with local influencers, publications, and partners to earn backlinks and brand visibility.
- Monitor local search engines beyond Google and Bing, including Baidu in China, Yandex in Russia, or Naver in South Korea. China requires additional compliance (e.g., ICP filing/Beian when hosting on mainland infrastructure, plus content controls). Mainland hosting isn't strictly required for indexation, but compliance, latency, and delivery constraints materially affect competitiveness—plan legal and operational readiness before committing.
- Provide feedback to the CoE about what works and doesn't work in their markets, enabling continuous improvement of global standards.

Domain Name Structure

Your most consequential technical decision is how to structure domains and subdomains across markets. This choice affects SEO performance, costs, management complexity, and flexibility for years to come.

Understanding Your Options

You have four primary approaches, each with distinct trade-offs:

- ccTLDs
- Subdomains

- Subdirectories
- URL parameters

Country Code Top-Level Domains (ccTLDs) use local domain extensions such as .co.uk for the United Kingdom, .de for Germany, and .com.au for Australia. Example: example.co.uk, example.de, example.com.au.

This approach sends the strongest geo-targeting signal to search engines and builds user trust through locally recognized domains. Local ccTLDs often improve trust and click propensity in some markets (e.g., .de, .fr). Validate with market testing before incurring ccTLD overhead.

The disadvantages include the high cost of maintaining multiple domain registrations and hosting configurations, the complexity of managing separate properties in Search Console and analytics, and the fact that link equity doesn't automatically consolidate across domains—each ccTLD must earn its own signals. However, cross-domain links can still pass authority.

ccTLDs work best for large enterprises with a substantial local presence in each market, for businesses where legal or data compliance requires a true separation between markets, and for organizations with a budget for dedicated resources in each market.

Subdomains create distinct properties under your main domain. Example: uk.example.com, de.example.com, au.example.com.

This approach provides clear separation between markets while maintaining brand unity. Each market can use different hosting, CMS platforms, or technical configurations if needed.

Search engines evaluate subdomains with largely independent signals. Internal/external links can pass authority between them, but consolidation is weaker than keeping everything on one hostname. You maintain multiple sites, which adds management complexity.

Subdomains fit situations where markets require genuinely different technical infrastructure, you're integrating acquired properties under one brand, or you're testing new markets before committing to full ccTLDs.

Global brands that want tight control over technical decisions might prefer subdomains such as au.example.com, uk.example.com, and so on. This enables all web technology to be based in the parent country, even if CDNs are used to make the website appear to be in the subsidiary country.

Subdirectories (folders) organize international content under a single global domain. Example: example.com/uk/, example.com/de/, example.com/au/.

This approach consolidates all link equity under one domain—links earned by any market benefit the entire organization. It's the simplest and least expensive option to implement and maintain.

With subdirectories, geo-signals rely on hreflang, strong local content, internal linking, and locally earned links. Treat any platform geo settings as secondary—not the primary targeting mechanism. Local SEO teams should seek links directly to the subdirectories.

Subdirectories work well for small to medium-sized businesses with limited budgets, content-focused sites such as blogs or resource centers, organizations gradually building an international presence, and companies with centralized management and similar offerings across markets.

URL parameters append language codes to URLs. Example: example.com?lang=de, example.com?lang=fr.

This approach is technically simple and inexpensive but creates significant SEO challenges. Search engines can index parameterized URLs, but parameters are brittle for language/region targeting and prone to duplication. Avoid using parameters for internationalization; use distinct, crawlable URLs for each language/region, plus hreflang.

Making the Decision

Most organizations should choose between ccTLDs and subdirectories. Use this decision framework:

Choose ccTLDs if:

- You have established local entities in target markets with local staff and operations
- Budget can sustain dedicated technical, content, and ops support per market (tools, QA, and ongoing content/links), not just launch costs.
- Legal or data-sovereignty requirements mandate local data storage/processing or local entities (hosting location should be decided for latency/compliance, not SEO geo-targeting).
- Target markets strongly prefer local domains (common in Germany, UK, Australia)
- Your business model varies significantly by market

Choose subdirectories if:

- You're building an international presence with a limited budget
- Content and offerings are largely consistent across markets
- You need to move quickly into new markets
- Your organization has strong central management
- You want to consolidate link equity from all markets

Choose subdomains if:

- Markets require incompatible technical platforms

- You're integrating acquired properties gradually
- Compliance requires operational separation but not different brands

Migration Considerations

If you're changing your international structure (for example, moving from ccTLDs to subdirectories, or vice versa), plan carefully. International migrations are the most complex SEO projects you'll undertake.

Critical migration requirements include comprehensive redirect mapping from every old URL to its new equivalent, hreflang tags implemented before the migration to help search engines understand relationships, a phased rollout by market to limit risk, and increased crawl budget during the transition to allow search engines to discover the new structure.

With clean one-to-one redirects and correct hreflang, stabilization typically occurs over several weeks to a few months; temporary volatility is normal.

Language and Locale Considerations

Language and country are related but distinct targeting dimensions that must both be addressed.

Language Targeting

The same language varies significantly by region. English differs between the United States, the United Kingdom, Australia, and Canada. Spanish varies between Spain, Mexico, Argentina, and other Latin American countries.

These aren't just spelling differences (color vs. colour). Search behavior, terminology, and expressions differ substantially.

Australians search for "mobile phone," while Americans search for "cell phone." The British "holiday" is an American "vacation."

Your content must use terminology natural to each market, not just run through a machine translation service. Ideally, ask a local to write content for a given country. Professional localization, not just translation, is essential for competitive performance.

Content Management across Markets

Content strategy for multinational sites requires balancing efficiency with local relevance. This usually requires the content creators to live in the target country.

The Translation vs. Localization Spectrum

Pure translation converts words from one language to another literally. This is insufficient for SEO because it misses cultural context, local terminology, and search behavior patterns. Search engines also pick up cues from subtle differences in spelling, grammar, and terminology.

Localization adapts content to each market's culture and context. This includes using local terminology, referencing local examples and brands, adjusting for cultural norms and sensitivities, and optimizing for local search behavior.

Transcreation goes further, reimagining content for new markets while maintaining intent and effect. Marketing content often requires transcreation rather than simple localization.

Budget Allocation Guidance

- For corporate/legal content where accuracy is paramount, invest in professional translation with legal review. This typically costs $0.15- $0.30 per word for high-quality translation.
- For informational content like help articles and product descriptions, use professional localization focusing on

terminology and search optimization. Costs typically range from $0.10 to $0.25 per word.

- For marketing content where persuasion matters, consider transcreation by copywriters native to the target market who understand both languages and cultures. This costs more—$0.25-$0.50+ per word—but delivers better results.
- Machine translation from services like Google Translate or DeepL can work for user-generated content or low-value pages, but requires human review before publishing for search.

Content Workflows

Effective international content management requires clear workflows that prevent outdated content, ensure quality, and maintain efficiency. Resource asymmetry is common. Plan for central support or vetted partners where local teams lack capacity. This was the case with a major bank whose Asian offices refused to be involved with content for their country website.

Establish a source of truth—typically your primary market's content—that other markets adapt. When the source content updates, trigger reviews across all markets to assess whether localized versions need updates.

Create style guides for each market documenting approved terminology, brand name handling, date and currency formatting, and tone considerations. These guides help translators and local content creators maintain consistency.

Use translation memory systems to store previously translated segments, reducing costs and ensuring consistency when the same phrases appear across multiple documents.

Build review processes that have local market specialists validate not just translation accuracy but also search relevance and competitive positioning in their markets.

Tool Subscriptions and Resources

International SEO requires tools, and costs compound across markets. Note that some CFOs may object to using the parent company's budget to fund subsidiary SEO needs. Such "border disputes" should be anticipated and settled in advance.

Centralized vs. Distributed Subscriptions

Many SEO tools are priced by seats, projects, domains, or the number of locations tracked (depending on the vendor). Costs scale with the number of markets, locations, and features licensed.

Optimization Strategies:

- Negotiate enterprise agreements where the CoE purchases a comprehensive subscription and allocates access to regional teams. Most vendors offer volume discounts that make enterprise deals more cost-effective than individual market subscriptions.
- Prioritize tool coverage based on market revenue contribution. Your three largest markets may receive comprehensive tool coverage, while smaller markets may have more limited access.
- Use different tools for different purposes rather than giving every market full access to every tool. Core markets might use premium competitive intelligence tools while smaller markets rely on Search Console and Google Analytics.
- Establish a tools evaluation process where regional teams can request access to new tools, the CoE evaluates them centrally, and successful tools get added to the enterprise stack.

Essential Multinational Tools

Beyond standard SEO tools, international operations need specific capabilities:

- Translation management platforms like Smartling, Lokalise, or Phrase centralize translation workflows, track which content has been translated, store translation memory, and integrate with CMS platforms.
- Rank tracking tools with international capability must support local search engines beyond Google, provide accurate local search results, and track rankings from specific cities or regions within countries.
- Hreflang validation tools check implementation across all markets. The hreflang Tags Testing Tool by Aleyda Solis or Screaming Frog's hreflang validation features catch errors that cause search engines to ignore your international structure.
- Currency and measurement conversion tools ensure product information displays correctly with local expectations. Nothing says "we don't understand your market" like showing prices in the wrong currency or measurements in unfamiliar units.

```
<head>
...
<link rel="alternate" hreflang="en-uk" href="https://ahrefs.com/blog/google-keyword-pla
...
</head>
```

Figure 19 Fictitious error showing hreflang value as en-uk instead of en-GB. Use correct ISO language-region codes (e.g., en-GB, not en-uk) and validate reciprocity and x-default across all alternates.

ORGANIZATIONAL STRUCTURE AND GOVERNANCE

International SEO fails when the organizational structure doesn't support it. Clear governance prevents markets from inadvertently undermining one another.

Division of Responsibilities

Document explicitly which decisions require central approval versus local autonomy:

Central decisions typically include:

- Overall domain architecture and technical foundation
- Core SEO methodology and best practices
- Tool subscriptions and enterprise contracts
- Brand guidelines and terminology
- Major technical changes affecting multiple markets
- Budget allocation across markets

Local decisions typically include:

- Content topics and publishing schedule
- Keyword research and prioritization for the local market
- Local link-building tactics and partnerships
- Local search engine optimization (Baidu, Yandex, etc.)
- Market-specific promotions and campaigns
- Translation vendor selection and management

Shared decisions requiring collaboration:

- New market launch planning and execution
- International site migrations or redesigns
- Resource allocation during peak periods
- Competitive response to cross-market threats
- Tool evaluations and recommendations

Communication Cadences

International teams need structured communication to stay aligned:

- **Weekly operational syncs** for teams actively working on shared projects, rotating meeting times to share time zone burden fairly, using collaboration tools that work asynchronously when needed.
- **Monthly regional reviews** where each market presents performance, learnings, and requests, the CoE shares global updates and initiatives, and cross-pollination of successful tactics occurs.
- **Quarterly strategic planning** to align on upcoming priorities, allocate budget and resources, review performance against annual objectives, and adjust strategy based on market feedback.
- **Annual face-to-face gatherings** if budget permits, building relationships that make virtual collaboration more effective, conducting intensive training, and engaging in strategic planning that's difficult to do remotely.

KNOWLEDGE SHARING SYSTEMS

Create accessible documentation that all markets can reference:

Internal wikis are well-suited for SEO documentation because they support collaborative editing, version history, search, and linking between related documents.

Document templates for common deliverables, such as market entry plans, keyword research reports, technical specifications, and QA checklists, ensure consistency while saving time.

Best-practice libraries that capture successful tactics from any market and make them available to all regions prevent duplication of work and accelerate results.

Case study collections that show actual performance from SEO initiatives help build buy-in when proposing similar initiatives in other markets.

REGULATORY AND COMPLIANCE CONSIDERATIONS

Different countries have different legal requirements that affect SEO implementation.

Data Privacy and Cookies

The European Union's GDPR applies to any site targeting EU users and requires explicit consent for non-essential cookies, clear privacy policies explaining how data is used, and the ability for users to access, correct, or delete their data.

California's Consumer Privacy Act (CCPA) and similar state laws impose requirements on US-based sites that serve California residents.

Brazil's Lei Geral de Proteção de Dados (LGPD) mirrors GDPR for Brazilian users.

These regulations affect analytics implementation, remarketing capabilities, and form handling. Your legal team must review implementations, but managers should understand the constraints and ensure compliance doesn't break SEO fundamentals.

Content Restrictions

Some countries restrict or prohibit certain content types. China requires government approval for news content and certain business categories. Germany has strict regulations governing health claims and comparative claims. Many countries restrict online gambling advertising.

Research local restrictions before entering markets to avoid creating content that violates local laws.

Accessibility Requirements

Accessibility laws vary by country. In the U.S., federal sites follow Section 508; many private and public sites align with WCAG under ADA enforcement. Treat WCAG conformance as the practical standard. The EU's European Accessibility Act and the UK's Public Sector Bodies Accessibility Regulations also apply—budget for compliance in relevant markets.

As covered later in Chapter 10, accessibility improves SEO while meeting legal requirements—budget for accessibility compliance in all new markets.

MEASURING INTERNATIONAL PERFORMANCE

Multinational SEO creates measurement challenges that require thoughtful solutions.

Consolidated vs. Market-Specific Reporting

Executives typically want consolidated global performance with the ability to drill down to specific markets. This requires careful analytics configuration.

Choose a measurement model (single vs. multiple properties) that supports roll-up reporting and market drill-downs; standardize metric definitions across markets.

Use custom dimensions to tag traffic by market, language, and business unit, enabling flexible report slicing.

Create specialized reports for each market while maintaining consistent metric definitions to ensure performance is comparable across regions.

Currency Normalization

When markets report revenue in different currencies, decide whether to:

Report in local currencies and convert to a single currency (typically USD or EUR) at a standard exchange rate for comparison, updating that rate quarterly or annually rather than daily to reduce volatility in reports.

Consider normalizing revenue for currency and price levels when comparing markets; document the method and apply it consistently.

Fair Performance Comparison

Comparing a mature market like the United States to an emerging-market launch in Brazil isn't meaningful without context.

Segment markets by maturity stage—new (0-12 months), growing (1-3 years), mature (3+ years)—and compare within stages.

Calculate performance relative to market potential using metrics such as each market's share of search visibility, rather than absolute traffic numbers.

Consider competitive intensity when evaluating performance. Gaining 5 percent market share in a market with 20 established competitors is more impressive than gaining 20 percent in a market with weak competition.

Launching New Markets

Systematic new market launches prevent the chaos of ad hoc expansion.

The New Market Playbook

Use a gated rollout (Assessment → Technical setup → Content launch → Authority → Iterate). Tie each gate to owners, SLAs, and success criteria rather than fixed week counts.

COMMON MULTINATIONAL SEO MISTAKES

Avoid these pitfalls that derail International SEO:

Mistake 1: Assuming domestic success transfers automatically

What works in your home market may not work elsewhere. Search behavior, competitive landscapes, and user expectations vary. Validate assumptions in each market.

Mistake 2: Using machine translation without human review

Machine translation has improved dramatically, but still produces awkward phrasing and misses cultural nuances. Budget for human review at minimum, professional localization ideally.

Mistake 3: Neglecting hreflang implementation

Without proper hreflang tags, search engines may display pages in the wrong language or region to users, resulting in a poor experience and lost conversions. This technical requirement is nonnegotiable.

Mistake 4: Treating all markets identically

Markets at different stages of maturity require different strategies. A launch market needs foundational content. A mature market needs advanced tactics and competitive defense.

Mistake 5: Insufficient local expertise

Central teams can provide strategy and tools, but local market knowledge is irreplaceable. Hire or partner with specialists who understand local search behavior and competition.

Mistake 6: Overcentralizing decisions

Markets that must seek approval for every decision move too slowly to capitalize on opportunities. Establish clear boundaries for local autonomy.

Mistake 7: Underfunding new markets

Halfhearted market entry wastes money. Either invest sufficiently to be competitive or don't enter. A translated homepage and two product pages won't generate meaningful results.

AI IMPLICATIONS FOR INTERNATIONAL SEO

AI and LLMs add new dimensions to multinational considerations:

Language translation quality from AI services like ChatGPT and DeepL now rivals human translation for many content types, potentially reducing localization costs. However, cultural adaptation still requires human expertise.

Content creation in multiple languages becomes more feasible with AI assistance, but quality review by native speakers remains essential.

AI-assisted search may narrow some behavioral differences, but local language, culture, and platforms still drive material variation. Validate locally.

The importance of structured data is increasing, as AI systems rely heavily on explicit markup to understand content across languages. Implement comprehensive schema tags in all markets.

Local LLM alternatives such as Yandex GPT (Russia) and ERNIE (Baidu/China) may require separate testing/consideration, where applicable.

MANAGER'S FRAMEWORK: INTERNATIONAL SEO LAUNCH CHECKLIST

Apply the QA framework from Chapter 5, with additional checkpoints for international-specific elements such as hreflang tags and localization.

Use this for any new market entry:

Strategic Assessment

- Market opportunity quantified (search demand, competition, ROI)
- Domain structure decision made and documented
- Budget approved for a minimum 12-month commitment
- Local resources identified (staff or partners)
- Success metrics defined
- Executive sponsor assigned

Technical Setup

- Domain/subdirectory structure implemented
- Hreflang tags configured correctly
- Search Console verification (domain property for consolidated subdirectory setups; separate properties for each ccTLD or subdomain).
- Analytics tracking configured
- Confirm hosting/CDN meet latency and legal/data-residency needs; don't use server location for geo-targeting. Optimize CDN delivery for the region.
- TLS/SSL certificate obtained and auto-renewed.
- Compliance requirements met (GDPR, etc.)

Ensure that multinational technical implementations adhere to the core technical foundations established in Chapter 3.

Content Development

- Translation/localization vendor selected
- Core pages translated and localized
- Local keyword research completed
- Content optimized for local search behavior
- Metadata optimized (titles, descriptions)
- Images localized where appropriate
- Local contact information added
- Currency and measurement units converted

SEO Foundation

- XML sitemap submitted
- Robots.txt configured
- Structured data implemented
- Internal linking optimized
- Mobile experience tested
- Page speed optimized
- Accessibility validated

Launch Readiness

- QA completed on staging
- Legal review passed
- Local market specialist validated content
- Monitoring alerts configured
- Rollback plan documented
- Stakeholder communication sent

Post-Launch (First 30 Days)

- Daily monitoring for technical issues
- Indexation tracked in Search Console
- Traffic patterns analyzed

- User feedback collected
- Conversion tracking validated
- Competitive positioning assessed
- 30-day report created

Chapter 8

SITE NAVIGATION STRATEGY

How you organize and link your website's pages profoundly affects both user experience and search performance. Yet navigation decisions are often made for aesthetic reasons or organizational politics, without considering SEO implications. A visually impressive mega menu might dilute search authority. A navigation scheme optimized for UX might conflict with how search engines understand site structure.

WHY NAVIGATION MATTERS TO SEO

Navigation matters to SEO for interconnected reasons. Search engines discover content through links—if important pages aren't linked from other pages, crawlers may never find them. Link structure also signals importance: pages with many internal links appear more important than pages with few.

Finally, topic relevance flows through links. When pages about credit cards link to other credit card pages, search engines understand topical relationships. When credit card pages link to mortgages, car loans, and insurance, the topical signal dilutes.

THE MEGA MENU DECISION

Mega menus—large drop-down navigation structures showing many links at once—can reduce clicks for some users. Still, they materially change how authority and topical signals flow across your site. Treat the choice as a strategic decision with clear trade-offs, not a default design pattern.

Is Our SEO Working?

From an SEO perspective, mega menus create organization-level risks:

- Link equity dilution. Global navs with very large link counts spread authority thinly, making it harder for priority pages to stand out.
- Topical confusion. "Everything links to everything" weakens clear topic clusters and relevance signals.
- Governance load. Bigger menus mean bigger maintenance—more owners, more updates, more chances for drift and defects.
- Accessibility risk. Users who rely on keyboards or screen readers may need multiple clicks to navigate from menus to the page's main content.

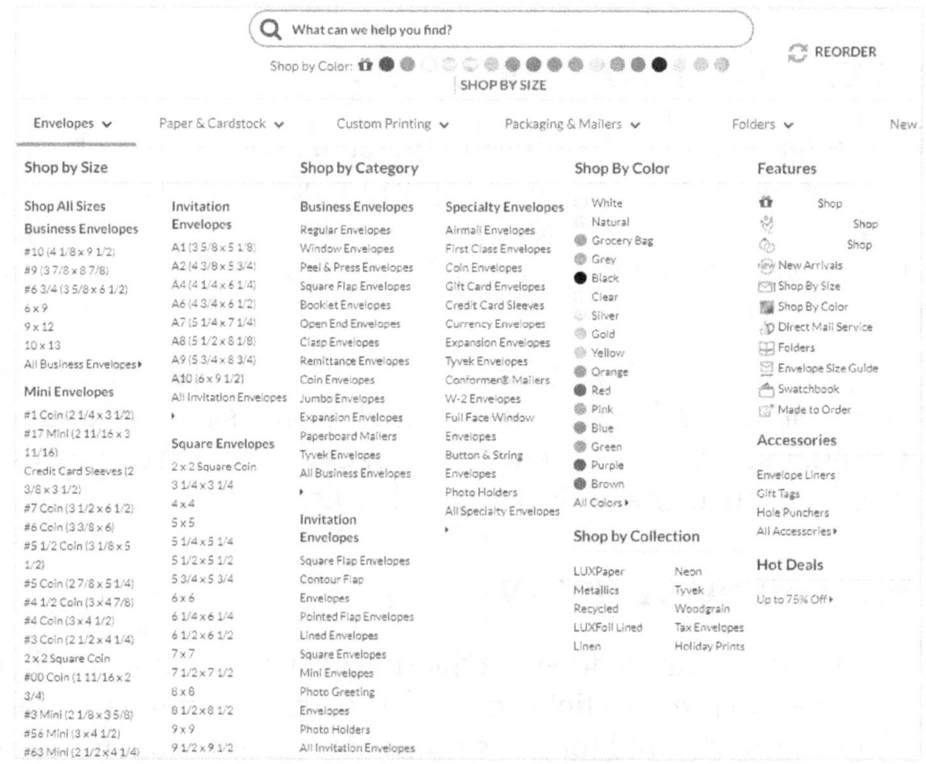

Figure 20 An extreme mega navigation example.

Manager takeaway: When we replaced a mega menu with conditional/navigation-by-context at a major bank, relevant financial terms rose materially within three months. The win came from concentrating links on priority pages, not from adding more links.

STRATEGIC NAVIGATION ALTERNATIVES

Better approaches exist that serve both users and search engines:

Conditional Navigation (Flat Structure)

Conditional navigation displays different menu options on pages based on users' location in the site hierarchy.

What is required (manager controls):

- Consistent top-level nav for orientation and brand.
- Section-level menus that keep users and crawlers inside the topic cluster.
- Mandatory breadcrumbs and on-page "related" modules to deepen within the topic, not jump laterally.

SEO advantages:

- Important pages receive concentrated link equity
- Topical relevance remains clear—loan pages primarily link to other loan pages
- Navigation reflects actual user context rather than showing everything everywhere

UX considerations:

- Requires more clicks than mega menus to reach deep pages
- Users must understand where they are in the site hierarchy
- Breadcrumbs become essential for orientation

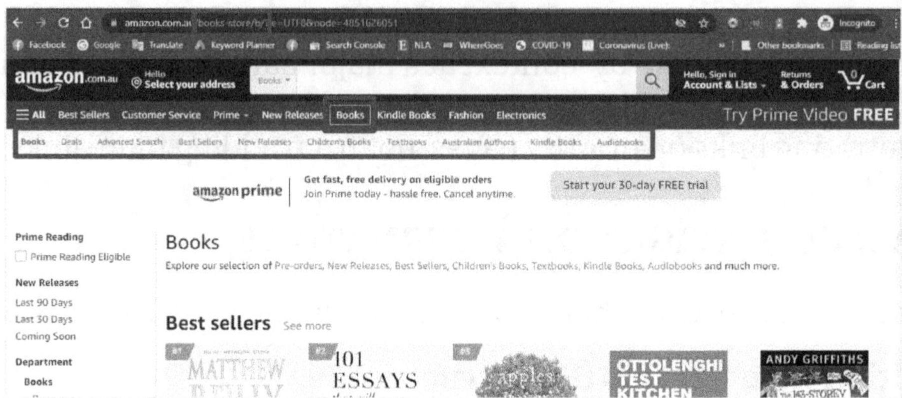

Figure 21 Amazon's flat navigation approach—showing minimal top-level categories that expand contextually, concentrating link equity while maintaining usability.

Internal link distribution affects topical authority when more than 60% of links come from global navigation; topical signals are diluted. Balance navigation links with contextual connections that concentrate authority within topic clusters.

Compromise Navigation

Sometimes, perfect flat navigation isn't feasible due to organizational politics, user research findings, or brand requirements. A compromise approach can work:

Hybrid model:

- Keep global navigation minimal (5-8 top-level items maximum)
- Add popular shortcuts in a small hover menu for convenience
- Use contextual navigation for topical depth
- Implement on-page modules for related content discovery

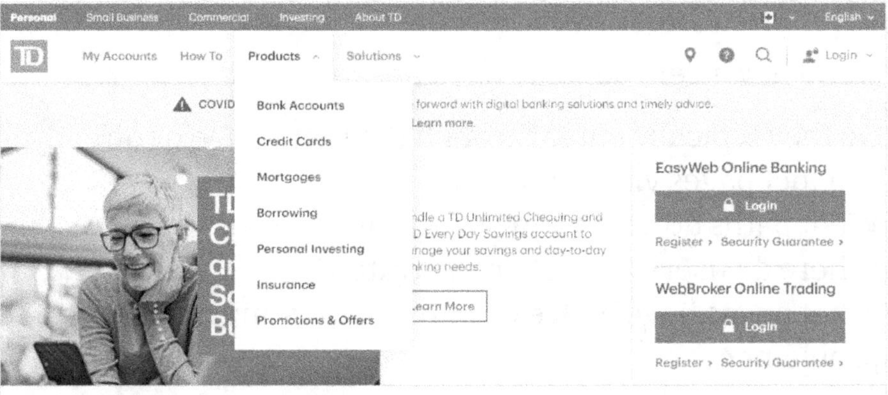

Figure 22 TD Bank uses a hybrid approach—major divisions in flat navigation, while popular destinations live in hoverable dropdowns. This balances UX convenience with SEO topical clarity.

The principle: Popular shortcuts may reside in a hover menu for user convenience, but equity-bearing links to key categories should appear in the flat primary navigation.

MAKING NAVIGATION DECISIONS

Use this framework when evaluating navigation changes:

Step 1: Identify Your Most Important Pages

Not all pages deserve equal navigation treatment. Identify:

- **Revenue-driving pages** - Products/services that generate the most revenue

- **High-traffic pages** - Content that attracts the most organic search traffic

- **Strategic priorities** - New initiatives requiring visibility

- **Conversion paths** - Pages that move users toward conversion

These pages should receive preferential navigation treatment.

Step 2: Map User Journeys

Understand how users actually navigate your site:

- Do they typically enter through the homepage or directly to product pages via search?
- What paths do converting users take?
- Where do users get lost or frustrated?
- What pages have high exit rates, suggesting navigation problems?

This data should inform navigation decisions more than stakeholder opinions.

Step 3: Evaluate Trade-offs

Every navigation decision involves trade-offs. Consider:

Mega menu trade-offs:

- Gain: Users reach any page in 1-2 clicks
- Cost: Diluted link equity, topical confusion, maintenance burden

Flat navigation trade-offs:

- Gain: Concentrated link equity, clear topical signals, easier maintenance
- Cost: More clicks required, users must understand hierarchy

Compromise navigation trade-offs:

- Gain: Balance between competing priorities
- Cost: Complexity in implementation and testing

Step 4: Governance and Measurement

No navigation change without:

- A defined hypothesis and success metrics (who owns which KPI)
- A baseline snapshot (index coverage, internal link concentration to target pages, path completion)
- A time-boxed review (2–4 weeks post-release) with a keep/iterate/rollback decision.

INTERNAL LINKS

Internal Linking Strategy Beyond Navigation

Navigation isn't the only way pages link to each other. Navigation decisions impact site architecture and should be considered during the technical planning phases outlined in Chapter 3.

A comprehensive internal linking strategy includes:

Contextual links within content - These are often more valuable than navigation links because they appear in a relevant topical context. A comprehensive article about home loans linking to specific loan products carries more topical weight than a navigation link.

Related content modules - "You might also like" or "Related articles" sections can guide users to relevant content while concentrating link equity within topic areas.

Breadcrumb navigation - Shows hierarchy, provides navigation utility, and enhances accessibility when marked up with schema.org BreadcrumbList and ARIA labels.

Footer links - Use sparingly. Footer links carry less weight than body content links and should focus on utility pages (privacy policy, contact, etc.) rather than recreating the navigation.

Balance link distribution strategically. As a rough guideline, aim for no more than half of total internal links to come from global navigation, with the remainder from contextual or in-content links. This concentrates authority within topic clusters rather than dispersing it evenly across the entire site.

Faceted Navigation Considerations

Some websites offer filtering options that let users refine the content displayed. For example, a car marketplace might allow users to filter by fuel type (electric, hybrid, gasoline), price range, year, and other attributes.

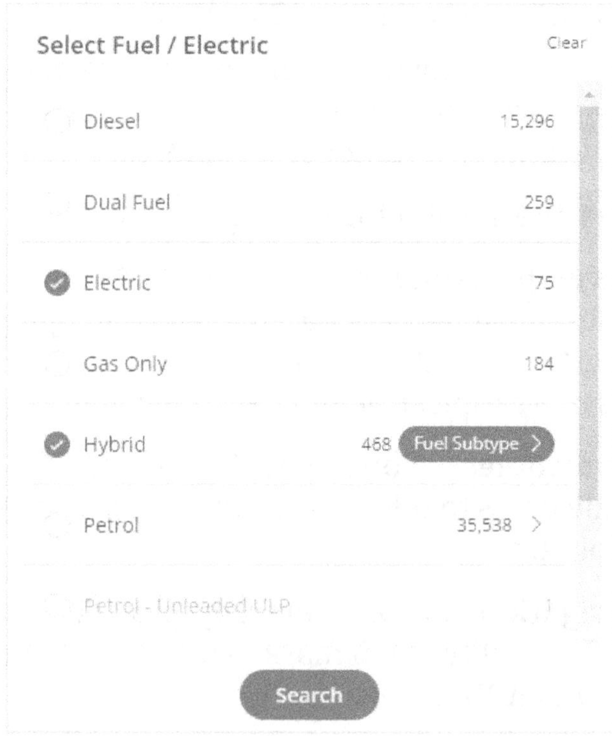

Figure 23 Facets create numerous URLs for very similar pages.

The SEO challenge: Each filter combination can create a unique URL. With ten filter options, you might have millions—or even quintillions—

of possible URL combinations. I know of a site that had ten quintillion URL permutations from faceted navigation. If Google tried to crawl that site completely, it would take longer than the universe has existed.

The problem: This wastes crawl budget – the finite crawl resources Googlebot allocates to your site within a given timeframe. Your fresh, valuable content might not get indexed because crawlers are stuck in an infinite loop of faceted navigation.

Review These Navigation Decisions:

- "How many unique URLs can our faceted navigation create?"
- "Have we implemented crawl controls to prevent search engines from crawling all combinations?"
- "Are we using canonical tags or robots meta tags to manage faceted navigation?"

Set policy before launch: name an owner, publish an allowlist of crawlable facet combinations, block the rest, and require a pre-launch crawl to verify indexable URLs match the allowlist. Post-launch, review Search Console coverage monthly to confirm controls hold.

More about Internal Links

Set distribution targets for internal links:

- Navigation links (menus, footers, breadcrumbs): aim ~30–40%
- Contextual links (in-content): aim ~50–60%
- Discovery modules ("Related"/"You might also like"): ~10–20%

Why this matters: Over-weighting navigation links dilutes topical signals; contextual links concentrate authority within topic clusters.

Questions to Ask Your Team

About distribution:

- "What percentage of our internal links come from navigation versus content?"
- "Do our most important pages have the most internal links?"

About strategy:

- "How do we ensure new content gets strategically linked from existing content?"
- "Do we have documented guidelines for internal linking in our content creation process?"

About maintenance:

- "How often do we audit for orphaned pages (pages with no internal links)?"
- "When we publish better content on a topic, do we update old internal links?"

Red Flags

- Important pages buried 5+ clicks from homepage
- Pages with zero internal links (orphaned content)
- Every page links back to the homepage in the body content
- Content sections that never link to each other (siloed)

What Your Team Should Handle

Your SEO or content team should:

- Develop specific internal linking guidelines
- Use tools (Screaming Frog, Ahrefs) to analyze link distribution
- Build topic clusters with pillar and supporting content
- Maintain quarterly internal linking audits

You don't need to run these analyses—you need to ensure they're happening.

MANAGER'S FRAMEWORK: INTERNAL LINKING HEALTH CHECK

When to Use This Assessment

Conduct this internal linking health check:

Annually: As a baseline assessment of link distribution. **After major content initiatives:** New content hubs, topic cluster development, and site section launches. **When diagnosing ranking issues:** Important pages not ranking despite quality content. **After site architecture changes:** Navigation restructuring, URL changes, major content migrations

Not routinely every quarter. Internal linking strategy doesn't require constant reassessment unless you're actively making changes.

For quarterly reviews, monitor:

- Are new important pages receiving adequate internal links?
- Have any strategic pages become orphaned?
- Is link equity concentrated on business priorities?

If answers are "yes, no, yes," your quarterly internal linking review is complete. If any answer is concerning, then use this framework to diagnose and fix issues.

Coverage (1-5): ___

- Important pages accessible in ≤3 clicks
- No critical orphaned pages
- Topic clusters properly linked

Is Our SEO Working?

Strategy (1-5): ___

- Team has documented guidelines
- New content gets strategically linked
- Links concentrate within topic areas

Maintenance (1-5): ___

- Regular audits conducted
- Links updated as content evolves
- Tools used to track distribution

Total: ___ / 15

- 11-15: Strong internal linking program
- 6-10: Gaps exist; prioritize documentation and audits
- Below 6: Internal linking needs strategic attention

COMMON NAVIGATION MISTAKES

Watch for these issues:

- **Orphaned pages** - Important pages with no internal links pointing to them. Search engines may never discover them.
- **Deep burial** - Critical pages requiring 5+ clicks from the homepage. Users won't find them, and they receive minimal link equity.
- **Inconsistent navigation** - Different templates showing different navigation make both users and search engines confused.
- **JavaScript-dependent navigation** — Primary navigation must be crawlable in the initial HTML. Make this a release gate: no launch if primary nav links aren't present and functional without client-side execution.

- **Generic anchor text** - Labels such as "click here" or "learn more" add little context. Use concise, descriptive text that matches the linked topic; this improves accessibility and relevance signals.

Measuring Navigation Effectiveness

Build a simple navigation dashboard with named owners:

- Index coverage of priority pages (Owner: SEO) — Target ≥95% indexed; investigate gaps weekly.
- Internal link concentration (Owner: Content/SEO) — Top pages should be top-linked; review monthly.
- Depth to conversion pages (Owner: UX) — Key revenue pages ≤3 clicks from entry; test quarterly.
- Path completion rate (Owner: Product/Analytics) — Monitor drop-offs after nav changes; act within 2 weeks.

Track navigation performance using the measurement framework established in Chapter 4.

Navigation and AI Search

AI-driven search systems increasingly assess site structure and internal-link patterns to infer topical authority. Well-organized navigation helps these systems map relationships between topics and identify priority content.

Manager's consideration: Expect more direct-to-page arrivals from AI/organic answers. Require landing templates that orient users without the homepage (prominent breadcrumbs, in-topic links, clear next steps) and track "entry-page to next in-topic click" as a KPI.

MANAGER'S FRAMEWORK: NAVIGATION EVALUATION

When to Use This Assessment

Use this navigation evaluation framework:

Before major navigation changes: Site redesigns, menu restructuring, information architecture changes. **Annually:** As part of a comprehensive SEO health assessment. **When diagnosing problems:** Conversion rates declining, high bounce rates on key pages, users can't find content. **After implementing changes,** 30-60 days post-launch to measure impact

Not routinely every quarter. Navigation doesn't change frequently enough to warrant a quarterly assessment.

For quarterly reviews, monitor:

- Any significant changes in bounce rate or exit rate patterns
- User feedback about findability
- Conversion path completion rates
- Orphaned page counts from crawl tools

If these indicators are stable, your quarterly navigation review is "no significant changes, metrics stable." If indicators show problems, then use this framework to diagnose root causes.

Link Equity Distribution (1-5):

- Most important pages have most internal links ___
- Navigation doesn't dominate internal linking (>60 percent) ___
- Topically related pages link primarily to each other ___
- No critical pages are orphaned ___

User Experience (1-5):

- Users can reach key pages in ≤3 clicks ___
- Navigation is consistent across templates ___
- Breadcrumbs provide orientation ___
- Mobile navigation works effectively ___

Technical Health (1-5):

- All navigation links work (no 404s) ___
- Navigation accessible without JavaScript ___
- Faceted navigation (if present) doesn't create crawl problems ___
- Important pages indexed in search engines ___

Strategic Alignment (1-5):

- Navigation highlights business priorities ___
- Revenue-driving pages receive prominent placement ___
- Navigation supports key conversion paths ___
- Changes are measured and evaluated ___

Total: ___ / 20

- **16-20:** Navigation serving SEO and business goals well
- **11-15:** Solid foundation with optimization opportunities
- **6-10:** Significant issues limiting SEO performance
- **Below 6:** Navigation requires a strategic overhaul

Action items based on score:

- **Below 10:** Audit navigation against business priorities; consider restructuring
- **10-15:** Optimize link distribution; test alternative approaches
- **Above 15:** Maintain and refine; focus on measuring impact

Chapter 9

USABILITY AND PERFORMANCE

Site performance affects user experience, conversion rates, and—to a lesser extent—search rankings. As a manager, you need to understand the business case for performance investment, set appropriate standards, and allocate resources effectively. You don't need to run Lighthouse tests yourself, but you should know what good performance looks like and what it's worth.

Performance is a critical technical foundation (Chapter 3) that requires ongoing monitoring through QA processes (Chapter 5).

THE BUSINESS CASE FOR PERFORMANCE

Performance matters because users abandon slow sites:

Google/Deloitte research found that improving load time by 0.1 seconds can boost conversion rates by 8 percent.

User behavior data shows:

- Bounce rate increases 32 percent as load time goes from 1s to 3s
- Bounce rate increases 90 percent as load time goes from 1s to 5s
- At 8 seconds, bounce rates exceed 100 percent increase

Figure 24 Three seconds represent the critical threshold—beyond this point, more than half of mobile users will abandon your site. Every additional second of delay compounds abandonment rates exponentially.

For a site with 100,000 monthly organic visitors:

- Current bounce rate: 40 percent
- Load time improvement from 5s to 2s
- Projected bounce rate: 25%
- 15,000 additional engaged visitors monthly
- At 2% conversion rate with a $100 average order value: $30,000 monthly revenue

Even conservative estimates show a strong ROI on performance investments.

WHAT MANAGERS NEED TO KNOW ABOUT CORE WEB VITALS

As mentioned in Chapter 3's technical foundations, Core Web Vitals represent Google's standardized approach to measuring user experience quality. While Chapter 3 established their role within the technical infrastructure, this chapter examines the business case for performance investment and the practical management of these metrics.

Google's Core Web Vitals measure three aspects of user experience. You don't need to memorize thresholds, but understand what they measure and why they matter:

LCP - How long until the largest visible element loads?

INP - How quickly pages respond to user interactions.

CLS - How much content moves around while loading?

Manager's perspective: These are user experience metrics first, ranking signals second. Google has indicated they're **not** strong direct ranking factors, but poor Core Web Vitals correlate with higher bounce rates, which definitely hurt performance. Don't sweat the small stuff here—an image that loads in 1.8 seconds rather than 1.6 seconds will not annoy the viewer; however, if it takes 20 seconds to load, it needs to be fixed.

SETTING PERFORMANCE STANDARDS

Work with your technical team to establish:

- Load time budgets for different page types (revenue-critical pages should be fastest)
- Core Web Vitals targets based on industry benchmarks and competitor performance

Is Our SEO Working?

- Release gates preventing launches that degrade performance
- Clear ownership for performance across templates and page types

Your engineering team will determine specific thresholds. Your role is to ensure:

- Standards exist and are documented
- No releases bypass performance review
- The performance owner has the authority to block launches that violate budgets
- Budget violations trigger investigation, not exceptions

Performance Investment Decisions

Decision rule for prioritizing performance work:

HEAVY investment is needed when:

- You're below budget on revenue-generating pages
- Competitors are measurably faster
- Performance directly impacts conversion or engagement metrics

Action: Fund a cross-functional sprint with clear ROI projections and success metrics.

MODERATE investment when:

- You're near budget but not critically underperforming
- Specific templates show performance gaps

Action: Prioritize high-leverage fixes on the highest-traffic templates first.

MAINTAIN the current state when:

- You're meeting or exceeding targets
- Performance is stable and monitored

Action: Put guardrails in CI/CD pipelines and monitor for regressions.

Common Performance Issues and Ownership

When performance degrades, ask these questions to the right teams:

Design/Content team: "Are we using optimized images and appropriate media formats?"

Marketing/Analytics team: "Which third-party scripts are essential vs. nice-to-have? Can we defer or remove non-essential tracking?"

Engineering team: "Is critical content rendering efficiently? Are we following performance best practices?"

IT/Infrastructure team: "Is our CDN configured optimally for our traffic patterns?"

Platform team: "Are we shipping unnecessary code or assets with our CMS/theme?"

Balancing Performance and Design

Set non-negotiables before creative work begins to avoid costly redesigns:

Design reviews must include performance validation:

- No launch approval without performance sign-off from technical owner
- UX/design teams must understand performance constraints before finalizing creative
- Performance budget verification is a required gate in the design process

Common design decisions with performance implications:

- Font selections (fewer font families and weights load faster)
- Media usage (video backgrounds, image-heavy layouts, animations)
- Interactive elements (can degrade user experience if poorly implemented)
- Third-party integrations (each added script impacts performance)

Manager responsibility: Require your technical team to provide design-friendly performance guidelines before creative work begins, not after designs are finalized. "We love this design, but it's too slow" is a failure of process, not design.

CONTENT DELIVERY NETWORKS (CDNS)

For websites serving global or distributed audiences, a CDN is essential infrastructure for acceptable performance.

Manager responsibilities:

- Ensure CDN is in place for non-local audiences
- Verify IT and SEO/marketing teams coordinate on performance validation
- Confirm monitoring covers global latency and user experience across regions
- Understand CDN costs and performance ROI

Leave to technical teams: CDN provider selection, configuration details, caching strategies, edge optimization specifics.

Red flag: If your technical team says "we don't need a CDN" for a site serving users across multiple countries or continents, get a second opinion.

MOBILE PERFORMANCE PRIORITY

Mobile performance must be validated with real-world conditions, not just lab tests on high-speed connections.

Manager requirements:

- Mobile testing is mandatory before launch, not optional
- Real device testing on typical mobile networks (not just office Wi-Fi)
- Field data from actual users is the success metric, not synthetic lab scores

Why this matters: Your office has fast Wi-Fi and recent computers. Your customers have varying device quality and network speeds. Test what they experience, not what you experience.

PERFORMANCE MONITORING AND ALERTS

Ensure your technical team maintains performance monitoring with:

- Clear ownership for each performance metric
- Automated alerts when performance degrades
- Defined response protocols (when to investigate, when to roll back changes)
- Regular reporting to business stakeholders

Your role as manager: Review performance trends in regular business reviews, not daily dashboard monitoring.

Questions to ask in reviews:

- Are we meeting our performance targets?
- Have recent launches degraded performance on key templates?
- What's blocking improvement on underperforming pages?
- Do we have the right people and tools to maintain performance standards?

What you don't do: Set specific alert thresholds, configure monitoring tools, or interpret raw performance metrics. Your team owns the technical details—you own the outcomes and accountability.

PERFORMANCE AND AI SEARCH

Manager takeaway: Performance is unlikely to be a standalone "AI ranking" factor, but fast, stable pages are easier to crawl, more engaging, and more citable. Optimize for users; AI benefits follow.

ACCORDIONS AND TABS FOR CONTENT MANAGEMENT

Collapsible content (accordions, tabs, expand/collapse sections) is a common UX pattern, but requires technical review to ensure search engines can access hidden content.

Manager responsibility: Establish a review process in which UX/design proposes collapsible content patterns and the technical/SEO teams validate that implementation won't harm discoverability.

Red flag: If designers implement collapsible content without a technical review, the content may be invisible to search engines and AI systems.

WHAT YOU DON'T NEED TO DO

You don't need to:

- Run Lighthouse, tweak bundlers, configure CDNs, or read waterfalls.

You DO need to:

- Set budgets and gates, fund the work, assign owners, and review outcomes against commercial targets.

MANAGER'S FRAMEWORK: PERFORMANCE INVESTMENT DECISION

Use this framework to evaluate performance investment proposals from your technical team.

Your role: Ensure your team provides these answers and commits to measurable outcomes. You don't need to know the technical thresholds—you need to ensure they exist and are realistic.

What to Ask Your Team

1. Current State Assessment

- What's our current performance on key revenue-generating pages?
- How do we compare to competitors and industry benchmarks?
- What's the business impact of current performance issues? (bounce rate, conversion impact, revenue at risk)

Your team should provide: Specific metrics with context, not just numbers. "Our mobile load time is 4.2 seconds, which is 40% slower than our top 3 competitors" is useful. "Our LCP is 3.8s" without context is not.

2. Cost Estimate

- Engineering/platform hours required
- Tool, infrastructure, or third-party service costs
- Ongoing maintenance costs (if applicable)
- Total investment (one-time + recurring)

Your responsibility: Ensure costs are realistic and include hidden work (testing, rollback planning, monitoring setup).

3. Expected Impact (with ranges, not false precision)

- Performance improvement targets (team provides specifics)
- Expected business impact:

  o Bounce rate improvement

  o Additional engaged sessions

  o Conversion rate lift

  o Revenue impact (conservative and optimistic scenarios)

Red flag: If your team provides only point estimates ("we'll improve by exactly 15%"), push for ranges that reflect uncertainty.

4. ROI Calculation: Your team should provide:

- Cost vs. revenue return ratio
- Payback period
- ROI percentage
- Comparison to alternative investments

Your job: Validate assumptions. Ask: "What has to be true for this ROI to be realistic?"

5. Success Gates and Rollback Plan. Before approving investment, ensure your team commits to:

- Specific success criteria (performance metrics and business metrics)
- Measurement timeline (typically 30-60 days post-launch)
- Rollback plan if targets aren't met
- Owner accountable for outcome

Example success criteria your team might propose:

- "Improve median mobile page load by at least 30% on top 10 revenue templates."
- "Increase mobile 'Good' Core Web Vitals pass rate from 62% to 80%."
- "Reduce bounce rate on product pages by 10 percentage points."
- "Generate $30K+ additional monthly revenue from improved engagement."

Decision Framework

Approve investment when:

- Business impact justifies cost (ROI > your hurdle rate)
- Team has a realistic plan with clear ownership
- Success criteria are measurable and committed to
- Rollback plan exists if targets are not met

Request revision when:

- ROI assumptions seem optimistic without evidence

- Success criteria are vague or unmeasurable
- No clear owner or rollback plan
- Cost estimate excludes obvious work

Reject when:

- ROI doesn't justify investment vs. alternatives
- Team can't articulate clear success criteria
- Higher-priority performance issues exist
- Proposal is "nice to have" vs. business-critical

Post-Investment Review Template

30-60 days after launch, your team should report:

Performance outcomes:

- Did we hit technical performance targets? (yes/no, with data)
- If not, why not? What's the corrective action?

Business outcomes:

- Did we achieve the projected business impact? (bounce rate, engagement, revenue)
- What was the actual ROI vs. the projected?

Lessons learned:

- What would we do differently next time?
- What should we prioritize next?

Your role: Hold the team accountable to commitments. If they consistently miss projections, adjust future approval criteria.

Chapter 10

ACCESSIBILITY - BUILDING INCLUSIVE DIGITAL EXPERIENCES

Web accessibility ensures that people with disabilities can perceive, understand, navigate, and interact with your website. Beyond being ethical and often legal, accessibility improves SEO, enhances user experience for everyone, and expands your potential audience.

The sections below cover accessibility requirements, how to build compliance into processes, and when to engage specialists.

ACCESSIBILITY CONCERNS FOR MANAGERS

Accessibility may seem separate from SEO, but the two share foundational principles and practical overlap.

Accessibility problems rarely show up as isolated defects. In practice, partial accessibility behaves exactly like inaccessibility: if a user cannot complete a critical task—such as account creation, product selection, or payment—using assistive technology, the entire experience fails, regardless of how many secondary pages pass formal checks. This is where many teams get misled by averages. Accessibility scores often improve on paper, while critical task flows quietly break. These failures typically arise from everyday changes: template tweaks, content updates, third-party scripts, or redesigns that alter the structure without being tested end-to-end. Managers typically address the problem only after complaints arise or conversion declines, by which time remediation is slower and more expensive. To ensure accessibility holds over time, it must be tested across real user journeys and revalidated whenever layouts, components, or forms change. Without that discipline, teams can ship frequent improvements while unintentionally blocking core interactions—and believe accessibility is largely "under control."

The Business Case

Legal risk is real. In 2024, U.S. state and federal courts saw more than 4,000 web-accessibility lawsuits filed against digital properties. Four major retailers in France were taken to court in 2026 for the inaccessibility of their online platforms and apps.

Market reach expands. Approximately 15-20 % of the global population lives with some form of disability (WHO estimate). Accessible websites help ensure you're not excluding this audience.

SEO benefits follow. Many accessibility best practices—such as proper heading structure, descriptive link text, and alt text for images—directly improve how search engines understand content.

User experience improves for everyone. Captions help users in noisy environments. Clear navigation helps multitasking. High-contrast text helps users read in bright sunlight. Accessibility features benefit all users.

AI systems benefit. Accessible HTML helps AI systems extract and understand content more reliably. Structured, semantic markup serves both screen readers and LLMs.

Brand reputation strengthens. Organizations that demonstrate a commitment to inclusion build stronger brand loyalty and attract talent who value these principles.

The SEO-Accessibility Overlap

Consider these overlapping requirements:

Accessibility Requirement	SEO Benefit
Alt text on images	Helps search engines understand image content
Proper heading hierarchy (H1, H2, H3)	Clarifies content structure for search engines
Descriptive link text	Provides context about link destinations
Semantic HTML	Helps search engines parse page structure
Skip navigation links	Signals clear site architecture
Transcripts for video/audio	Creates indexable text content
Fast page loading	Reduces bounce rate
Mobile-friendly design	Meets mobile-first indexing requirements

The key insight: You don't optimize for accessibility *and* SEO separately. Many optimizations serve both simultaneously.

UNDERSTANDING ACCESSIBILITY REQUIREMENTS

Accessibility guidelines provide concrete standards for implementation.

WCAG 2.2: The Current Standard

The current official standard is Web Content Accessibility Guidelines (WCAG) 2.2 (published 5 Oct 2023). WCAG 3.0 (formerly "Silver") is still in the working draft stage and not yet a finalized standard.

URL: https://www.w3.org/TR/WCAG22/

It is also available as an international standard in PDF format.

URL: https://www.iso.org/standard/91029.html

Three conformance levels exist:

Level A: Basic accessibility features. Minimum legal requirement in many jurisdictions, but insufficient for good accessibility.

Level AA: Enhanced accessibility. Target level for most organizations. Meets most legal requirements and serves most users well.

Level AAA: Highest accessibility. Difficult to achieve for entire sites. Often used selectively for specific content.

Manager's target: Aim for Level AA conformance across your site. This balances legal compliance, user needs, and implementation feasibility.

Pro Tip: Make a reasonable effort to address accessibility and keep records of it. If a lawsuit hits you, a court might agree that you made reasonable efforts to make adjustments as per your entity size.

The Four Principles (POUR)

WCAG organizes around four principles:

- **Perceivable:** Information and user interface components must be presentable to users in ways they can perceive.
- **Operable:** User interface components and navigation must be operable.

- **Understandable:** Information and operation of the user interface must be understandable.
- **Robust:** Content must be strong enough to be interpreted by a wide variety of user agents, including assistive technologies.

Common Accessibility Challenges

Real-world examples help illustrate requirements:

Visual impairments affect users who are blind, have low vision, or have color blindness.

Requirements:

- Screen reader compatibility (semantic HTML, proper Accessible Rich Internet Applications (ARIA) labels)
- Alt text for images providing equivalent information
- Sufficient color contrast (minimum 4.5:1 for normal text)
- Text that can be resized without breaking layout
- Content doesn't rely on color alone to convey meaning

Motor disabilities affect users with limited fine motor control, tremors, or paralysis.

Requirements:

- All functionality accessible via keyboard (no mouse required)
- Large click/tap targets (minimum 44x44 pixels)
- No time limits on interactions, or easy extensions
- Ability to cancel accidental activations

Cognitive disabilities include learning disabilities, attention disorders, or memory challenges.

Requirements:

- Clear, simple language

- Consistent navigation and layout
- Error prevention and clear error messages
- Ability to pause, stop, or hide moving content

Hearing impairments affect users who are deaf or hard of hearing.

Requirements:

- Captions for video content
- Transcripts for audio content
- Visual alternatives to audio cues

BUILDING ACCESSIBILITY INTO PROCESSES

Retrofitting accessibility is expensive and disruptive. Building it in from the start is cheaper and more effective. Accessibility should be integrated into QA processes (Chapter 5) and technical foundations (Chapter 3) from project inception.

Requirements and Planning Phase

Include accessibility in project briefs:

- "Site must meet WCAG 2.2 Level AA standards."
- Specify who is responsible for ensuring compliance
- Budget for accessibility testing and remediation

Conduct accessibility review of design mockups:

- Check color contrast before development begins
- Verify proposed interactions can be keyboard-operated
- Ensure heading hierarchy makes logical sense
- Flag potential issues early when changes are cheap

Choose accessible-friendly technologies:

- CMS platforms with good accessibility support

- Component libraries built with accessibility in mind
- Avoid plugins or frameworks with known accessibility issues

Development Phase

Train developers on accessibility basics:

- Semantic HTML usage
- ARIA labels when needed (but not overused)
- Keyboard navigation patterns
- Common pitfalls to avoid

Include accessibility in code reviews:

- Check for semantic HTML structure
- Verify form labels are properly associated
- Ensure keyboard navigation works
- Validate that interactive elements have proper ARIA roles

Implement automated testing:

- Tools like axe-core, Pa11y, or WAVE (Web Accessibility Evaluation tool) catch many issues
- Integrate into CI/CD pipeline
- Fix issues before they reach production

Testing and QA Phase

Include accessibility compliance metrics in your measurement framework as described in Chapter 4.

Automated testing catches ~30-40% of issues:

- Missing alt text
- Color contrast failures
- Missing form labels
- Improper heading structure

Manual testing catches the rest:

- Keyboard navigation completeness
- Screen reader experience quality
- Logical content flow
- Context-dependent issues automated tools can't assess

User testing with people with disabilities:

- Provides real-world validation
- Identifies issues that no testing tool catches
- Builds empathy within the organization

PRACTICAL ACCESSIBILITY IMPLEMENTATION

Moving from principles to practice, here are key implementation areas:

Images and Alt Text

All images on your site need appropriate alternative text for screen readers and AI systems.

What your team should implement:

Informative images (charts, diagrams, product photos): Descriptive text explaining what the image conveys, not just what it depicts.

- Good: "Bar chart showing Q3 sales increased 23% from Q2, reaching $4.2M"
- Bad: "sales chart" or "bar chart image."

Decorative images (dividers, background patterns, design elements): Marked so screen readers skip them entirely.

- Your team should document which images are purely decorative vs. informative
- Decorative images should not announce to screen readers

Functional images (icons used as buttons or links): Text describing the action, not the icon's appearance.

- Good: "Search" or "Close menu."
- Bad: "magnifying glass" or "X icon"

Complex images (infographics, detailed diagrams): Longer descriptions provided in surrounding text or on linked pages.

- Screen reader users need the same information that visual users get
- Don't rely solely on image alt text for complex information

How to verify:

Spot-check method:

1. Right-click any image on your site and "Inspect Element."

2. Look for alt text in the HTML

3. Read the alt text without seeing the image - does it convey the purpose?

4. Ask: "If I couldn't see this image, would this description tell me what I need to know?"

Red flags:

- Alt text that says "image," "photo," or "graphic" (describes medium, not content)
- Alt text matching the filename ("IMG_2847" or "hero-banner.jpg")
- Missing alt text on informative images
- Decorative images with unnecessary descriptions
- Icon buttons with descriptions like "blue arrow" instead of "Next page."

Questions to ask your team:

- "How do you determine which images are decorative vs. informative?"
- "Show me examples of good and bad alt text from our site."
- "What's your process for reviewing alt text before launch?"

Heading Structure

Proper heading hierarchy helps screen reader users navigate and helps search engines understand content organization.

What your team should implement:

Heading rules:

- Only one H1 per page (typically the page title)
- Never skip heading levels (don't jump from H2 to H4)
- Headings describe the section they introduce
- Heading levels are based on content structure, not visual appearance

Example structure for a product page:

- H1: Product name
- H2: Features (main section)

  o H3: Feature category 1

  o H3: Feature category 2

- H2: Specifications (main section)

  o H3: Technical specs

- o H3: Dimensions

How to verify:

Browser method:

1. Install a browser extension that shows heading structure (like HeadingsMap)

2. View the heading outline of your pages

3. Check: Does the outline make logical sense? Any skipped levels?

Screen reader test:

1. Use your keyboard to navigate headings only (screen readers have this feature)

2. Can you understand the page structure from headings alone?

3. Can you jump to the section you want?

Red flags:

- Multiple H1 tags on one page (confuses screen readers)
- Skipped heading levels (H2 → H4 with no H3 between)
- Headings chosen for visual size instead of structural hierarchy
- Pages with no headings at all
- Headings that don't describe their sections ("Click here" as a heading)

Common mistake: Designers choose H3 because it "looks better" than H2, breaking the structural hierarchy.

Questions to ask your team:

- "Show me the heading structure for our top 5 page templates."

- "How do you ensure designers don't break heading hierarchy for visual reasons?"
- "What happens when a designer wants a smaller heading - do they change the level or the CSS?"

Manager responsibility: Establish that heading levels are structural requirements, not designer preferences. Visual styling should be handled with CSS, not by changing heading levels.

Form Accessibility

Forms are critical to conversions, but often have accessibility issues that prevent users from completing purchases, sign-ups, or contact requests.

What your team should implement:

Required elements:

- Every input field has a properly associated label (not placeholder text as a substitute)
- Error messages are clear and associated with specific fields
- Required fields are indicated with text, not just color or asterisks
- Instructions provided before the form, not after submission
- Tab order follows logical sequence (top to bottom, left to right)
- Form can be completed using the keyboard alone

How to verify:

Keyboard-only test:

1. Put your mouse away

2. Try completing a form using only Tab, Shift+Tab, Enter, and arrow keys

3. Can you reach every field? Is the order logical?

4. Can you submit the form?

5. Can you read error messages when they appear?

Label association test:

1. Click on a label (like "Email Address")

2. Does the cursor move to the associated input field?

3. If not, the label isn't properly associated

Error message test:

1. Submit a form containing deliberate errors

2. Are error messages clear about what's wrong and how to fix it?

3. Are errors announced to screen readers (not just shown visually)?

4. Can you identify which fields have errors without seeing color?

Red flags:

- Placeholder text used instead of labels (placeholders disappear when typing)
- Required fields marked only with red asterisks or color
- Error messages that appear but aren't associated with specific fields
- Generic errors like "Form contains errors" without specifics
- Error messages only visible as color changes (red border)
- Tab order that jumps around illogically

- Submit button that can't be reached with the keyboard

Common accessibility failures in forms:

- "Email" placeholder instead of visible label
- Red border as only error indicator (invisible to screen readers and color-blind users)
- Multi-step forms that don't announce which step you're on
- CAPTCHA without an audio alternative
- Forms that reset when you make an error, losing all entered data

Questions to ask your team:

- "Show me a user completing our checkout form with keyboard only."
- "What happens if someone submits a form with an error - how do they know what's wrong?"
- "How do we indicate required fields to screen reader users?"
- "Can color-blind users identify which fields have errors?"

Business impact: Accessibility issues directly affect conversion rates. Users who can't complete forms abandon purchases, creating immediate revenue loss.

Manager responsibility: Test critical forms yourself using keyboard-only navigation. If you struggle, your customers struggle more.

Keyboard Navigation

All page functionality must be operable via keyboard alone.

Test: Try using your site with only the keyboard (no mouse):

- Tab key moves between interactive elements
- Enter/Space activates buttons and links
- Arrow keys work in drop-down menus
- Escape closes modals and menus
- Focus indicator is always visible

Common failures:

- Custom dropdowns that don't respond to keyboard
- Navigation menus and modals that trap focus (can't escape)
- Hidden skip links (should appear on keyboard focus)
- Invisible focus indicators
- Mega navigation menus with hundreds of choices take longer to escape

Color Contrast

Text must have sufficient contrast against the background for readability. Under WCAG 2.2/2.1 AA:

- Normal text: at least **4.5:1** contrast ratio
- Large text (18 pt/24px or bold 14pt/18.6px+): at least **3:1** contrast ratio
- User interface components and graphical objects: at least **3:1** contrast ratio

Tool: WebAIM (Web Accessibility In Mind) Contrast Checker (https://webaim.org/resources/contrastchecker/)

Common failures:

- Light gray text on a white background
- Buttons with insufficient contrast in the hover state
- Placeholder text too light to read

Video and Audio Accessibility

Multimedia content needs text alternatives.

Video requirements:

- Captions for all speech and important sounds
- Audio descriptions for important visual information
- Transcript providing full text equivalent

Audio requirements:

- Transcripts for podcasts and audio content

Benefits beyond accessibility:

- Captions help users in sound-sensitive environments
- Transcripts create indexable content for search engines
- Better user experience for non-native speakers

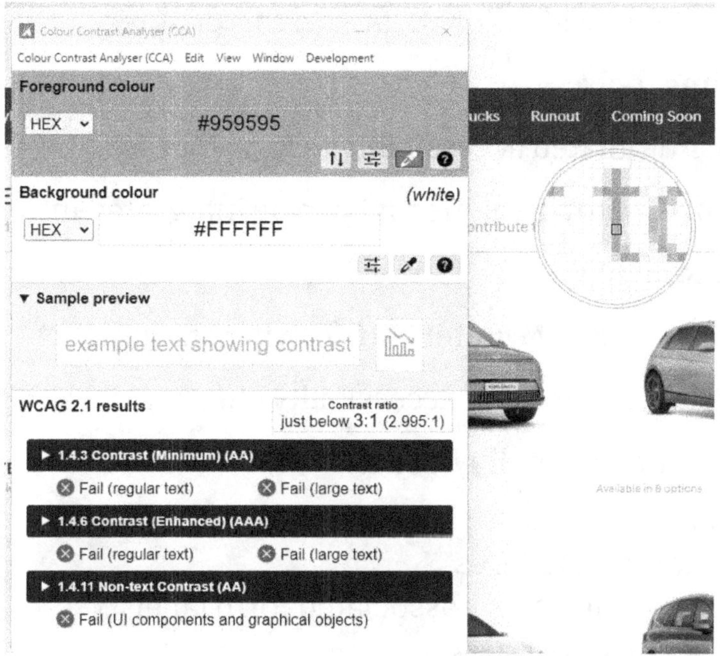

Figure 25 Colour Contrast Analyser (CCA) indicates that the gray font fails all WCAG 2.1 levels.

TESTING FOR ACCESSIBILITY

Comprehensive accessibility testing combines automated tools with manual evaluation.

Automated Testing Tools

Browser extensions:

- **axe DevTools** (Chrome/Firefox): Comprehensive automated checking

- **WAVE** (Chrome/Firefox/Edge): Visual feedback on accessibility issues

- **Lighthouse** (Chrome): Includes accessibility audits

- **CoPilot (Edge):** Mentioned later in this chapter.

Command-line tools:

- **Pa11y**: Automated accessibility testing for CI/CD pipelines
- **axe-core**: Testing engine that can be integrated into workflows

Online scanners:

- **WAVE by WebAIM**: Enter URL for an instant report
- **AChecker**: Free online accessibility checker

Automated tools typically detect:

- Missing alt text/alt attributes
- Color-contrast failures
- Missing or improperly associated form labels
- Some ARIA-role issues

Manual testing is still required for:

- Meaningful and accurate alt text/context
- Logical tab order and focus management
- Real screen-reader user-flow experience
- Context-sensitive usability issues and dynamic content

Manual Testing Methods

Keyboard-only navigation:

- Unplug your mouse
- Navigate the entire site using only the keyboard
- Verify all functionality works
- Check that the focus indicator is always visible

Screen reader testing:

- Narrator (Windows system, free): Basic screen reader
- NVDA (Windows, free): Most-used screen reader
- JAWS (Windows, paid): Professional-grade screen reader
- VoiceOver (Mac/iOS, built-in): Apple's screen reader
- TalkBack (Android, built-in): Google's screen reader

Learn basic screen reader commands:

- Not to become an expert, but to understand user experience
- Many online tutorials available
- Even 30 minutes reveals issues automated tools miss

Zoom and reflow testing:

- Increase browser zoom to 200 percent
- Verify content remains readable and usable
- Check that the layout doesn't break

AI-ASSISTED ACCESSIBILITY CHECKING WITH MICROSOFT EDGE AND COPILOT

AI tools are increasingly complementing traditional accessibility audits. In Microsoft Edge, Copilot can perform a quick compliance review of a live webpage — ideal for preliminary checks, governance audits, or training exercises.

Scenario: Auditing a Web Page for Accessibility Compliance (WCAG 2.2)

Step 1. Open the Web Page

Navigate to the page you want to audit in Microsoft Edge.

Step 2. Activate Copilot

Click the Copilot icon in the upper-right corner of Edge, or press Ctrl + Shift + . to open the sidebar.

Step 3. Ask for an Accessibility Review

Type a prompt such as:

- "Review this page for WCAG 2.2 accessibility issues."
- "Which images are missing alt text?"
- "Does this page use ARIA landmarks correctly?"

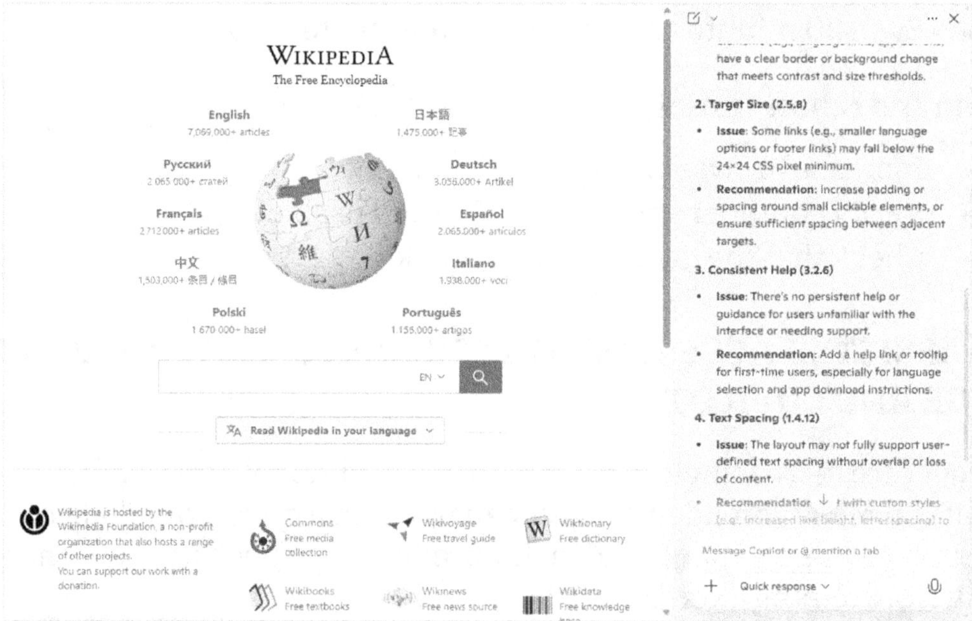

Figure 26 Bing Copilot is performing a live WCAG 2.2 review of Wikipedia's home page.

Step 4. Review the Findings

Copilot analyses the visible page and returns structured guidance, highlighting:

- Missing or meaningless alt text
- Insufficient color contrast
- Improper heading structure
- Unlabeled form elements or small tap targets
- Lack of persistent help or contextual guidance

You can ask follow-up questions or request a checklist summary mapped to WCAG success criteria.

This conversational workflow is useful for:

- Reviewing internal or external pages before launch
- Training non-technical authors
- Spot-auditing policy or compliance pages

Step 5. Document or Export Findings

Copy the AI-generated report into your documentation or accessibility tracker. Copilot can summarize issues or classify them by severity.

Governance Use Case

Because Edge runs Copilot in the browser, it can audit live pages without accessing code repositories—a valuable feature for managers verifying public-facing sites, PDFs, or dashboards.

Caution

Treat these results as directional insights, not as a formal WCAG conformance audit. Use Copilot for quick discovery and training, then validate findings with professional accessibility tools or human testers.

COMMON ACCESSIBILITY MISTAKES

Learn from others' errors:

- **Mistake 1: Relying entirely on automated tools.** Automated tools catch only ~30-40 percent of issues. They can't evaluate whether the alt text is meaningful or the tab order is logical.
- **Mistake 2: Using "accessibility overlays."** Third-party widgets that claim to make sites accessible with a single line of code don't work and can cause additional issues. Fix the underlying code instead.
- **Mistake 3: Hiding accessibility features.** Skip links that are permanently hidden or labels that are visually hidden but poorly implemented don't help users who need them.
- **Mistake 4: Treating accessibility as a final checkbox.** Accessibility is ongoing. New content, features, and third-party integrations can introduce issues.
- **Mistake 5: Ignoring mobile accessibility**. Mobile users have the same accessibility needs as desktop users. Touch targets must be large enough, text must be readable, and functionality must work without precise gestures.
- **Mistake 6: Overusing ARIA.** ARIA attributes can fix accessibility issues, but incorrect ARIA is worse than no ARIA. Use semantic HTML first; add ARIA only when needed.

ACCESSIBILITY STATEMENTS

Publishing an accessibility statement demonstrates commitment and provides users with the information they need.

What to Include

Commitment statement: Example: "We are committed to ensuring digital accessibility for people with disabilities. We continually improve the user experience for everyone and apply relevant accessibility standards."

Standards targeted: Example: "We aim to conform to WCAG 2.2 Level AA standards."

Known limitations: Be honest about areas not yet conforming. Example: "Some PDF documents on our site were created before our current accessibility standards and may not be fully accessible. We are working to remediate these documents."

Contact information: Provide a clear way for users to report accessibility issues. Include email, phone, and/or web form.

Date: Include when the statement was last updated and when the next review is planned.

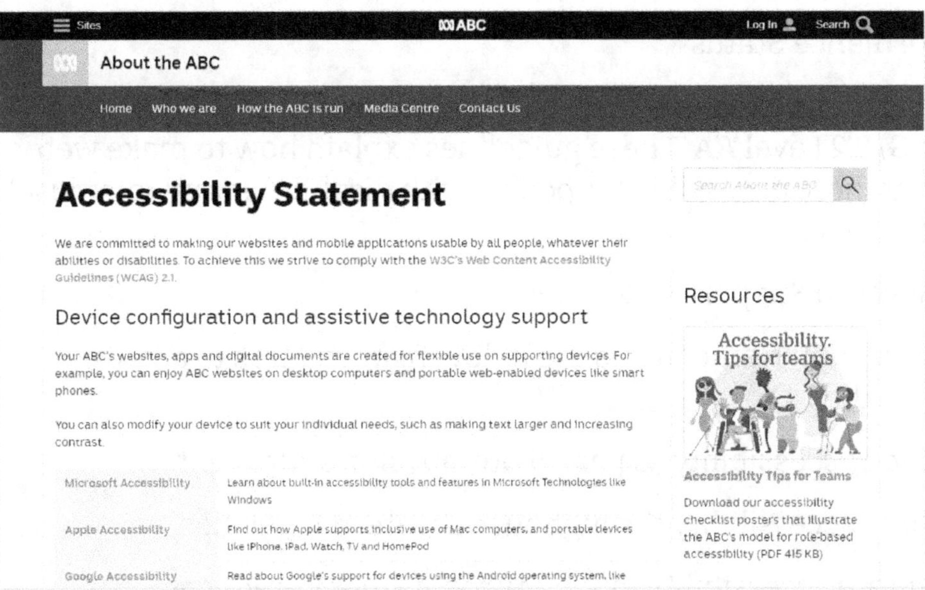

Figure 27 ABC's accessibility statement is linked from the footer navigation, demonstrating the organization's commitment to inclusive digital experiences and transparency regarding WCAG compliance.

Is Our SEO Working?

- https://about.abc.net.au/accessibility-statement/
- https://nda.ie/accessibility/accessibility-statement/

The W3C offers a handy tool to generate an Accessibility Statement if you do not have one.

URL: https://www.w3.org/WAI/planning/statements/

Sample Accessibility Statement

Accessibility Statement

Last updated: [Date]

[Organization Name] is committed to ensuring digital accessibility for people with disabilities. We continually improve the user experience for everyone and apply relevant accessibility standards.

Conformance Status

We aim to conform to the Web Content Accessibility Guidelines (WCAG) 2.2 Level AA. These guidelines explain how to make web content more accessible for people with disabilities and more usable for everyone.

Measures to Support Accessibility

[Organization Name] takes the following measures to ensure accessibility:

- Include accessibility as part of our mission statement

- Include accessibility throughout our internal policies

- Integrate accessibility into our procurement practices

- Provide continual accessibility training for our staff

- Assign clear accessibility goals and responsibilities

- Employ formal accessibility QA methods

Feedback

We welcome your feedback on the accessibility of [website name]. Please get in touch with us:

- Email: [email]

- Phone: [number]

- Address: [mailing address]

We aim to respond to accessibility feedback within [X] business days.

Known Limitations

Despite our efforts, some content may not yet be fully accessible. We are actively working to improve accessibility across our entire digital presence.

Current known limitations include:

- [List specific known issues]

Assessment Approach

[Organization Name] assessed the accessibility of [website name] through the following methods:

- Self-evaluation

- External evaluation by [organization/consultant name]

This statement was last reviewed on [date] and will be reviewed again by [date].

LEGAL AND REGULATORY LANDSCAPE

Accessibility laws vary by jurisdiction. Managers should understand the requirements in the markets they serve.

United States

- **ADA:** Applies to places of public accommodation. Courts increasingly interpret this to include websites.
- **Section 508:** Requires federal agencies and contractors to make electronic and information technology accessible.
- **State laws:** Some states (California, New York) have specific digital accessibility requirements beyond federal law.

European Union

- **The European Accessibility Act (EAA)** requires accessibility for products and services, including websites and mobile apps.
- **EN 301 549:** European standard referenced in procurement and compliance.

Other Jurisdictions

- **Canada:** Accessible Canada Act requires federally regulated organizations to identify and remove barriers.
- **UK:** Public Sector Bodies Accessibility Regulations require conformance to WCAG 2.1 AA.
- **Australia:** The Disability Discrimination Act prohibits discrimination, including digital accessibility barriers.

Manager's responsibility: Understand which laws apply to your organization. Consult legal counsel for specific compliance requirements.

ACCESSIBILITY AND AI

As AI systems increasingly mediate access to information, accessibility takes on new dimensions. Structured, semantic content benefits both screen readers and AI systems. Clear heading hierarchies help both assistive technologies and LLMs understand content organization, and alt text that helps blind users also helps AI systems understand visual content.

Accessible websites are often more machine-readable, which may help AI systems that analyze site content—though there's no publicly confirmed direct ranking benefit from accessibility alone. The principle: Optimization for human accessibility often aligns with optimization for AI understanding.

MANAGER'S FRAMEWORK: ACCESSIBILITY COMPLIANCE ROADMAP

Use this to plan accessibility improvements systematically:

Phase 1: Assessment (Weeks 1-4)

- Conduct automated scan of entire site
- Sample manual testing of key pages/journeys
- Engage a specialist for a comprehensive audit (optional)
- Document current state and gap analysis
- Prioritize issues by severity and impact

Phase 2: Foundation (Months 2-3)

- Fix critical issues (preventing access entirely)
- Implement keyboard navigation
- Address color contrast failures
- Add missing alt text
- Fix form label issues

Phase 3: Enhancement (Months 4-6)

- Improve heading structure site-wide
- Add skip navigation links

Is Our SEO Working?

- Create accessible alternatives for complex interactions
- Add captions/transcripts for multimedia
- Refine ARIA usage

Phase 4: Process Integration (Ongoing)

- Train all relevant teams
- Update design system with accessible patterns
- Integrate automated testing into CI/CD
- Establish a QA checklist, including accessibility
- Publish accessibility statement

Phase 5: Maintenance (Ongoing)

- Quarterly automated scans using WCAG 2.2-compliant tools (e.g., Axe Monitor, Siteimprove, or Accessibility Insights).
- Annual comprehensive audits conducted manually by certified accessibility specialists, following WCAG 2.2 and Section 508 Standards, evolution tracking (monitoring the W3C WAI Working Group's WCAG 3 draft progress). (where applicable).
- User feedback monitoring and response
- Ongoing team training

Accessibility improvements reduce legal exposure under ADA Title III and similar international statutes, while improving engagement metrics—an operational win as much as an ethical one.

Chapter 11

AN IDEAL SEO ECOSYSTEM

BUILDING ON GOVERNANCE AND ACCOUNTABILITY

Building on the governance principles established throughout this book, this chapter explores what an ideal SEO ecosystem looks like in practice—where roles, budgets, and processes align to sustain visibility performance. An effective SEO ecosystem is not accidental; it is designed through collaboration, foresight, and disciplined governance. Some of these topics are covered in detail elsewhere in this book set.

In a mature SEO ecosystem, authority is not produced by isolated pages or bursts of content activity; it emerges from **deliberately engineered systems**. High-performing organizations increasingly treat content the way they treat platforms or infrastructure: audited holistically, designed around intent and structure, internally connected by logic rather than convenience, and developed through repeatable workflows rather than creative improvisation. In this model, content hubs behave less like editorial collections and more like governed knowledge architectures—where clarity, consistency, and internal coherence reduce interpretive risk for search engines and AI systems alike. The managerial implication is subtle but critical: sustainable SEO performance is not the result of publishing more content, but of designing environments in which meaning can be reliably assembled, validated, and reused by machines at scale.

WHEN TO INVEST IN SEO

Startups

The best time to invest in SEO is before the first website is built. The next best time is when you realize what SEO can do for you. Startups often postpone SEO investment until revenue arrives, but that is like assembling a car before tuning its engine. Launching without search readiness stalls growth before scale.

Mature Organizations

Mature organizations face the opposite challenge. Legacy systems, entrenched silos, and governance inertia make it difficult to retrofit ideal SEO processes. Changing mindsets can be harder than rewriting code. Yet without structural reform, visibility stagnates, and competitors advance.

ATTITUDES TOWARD SEO

SEO is not a set-and-forget discipline; it is a continuous process embedded across content, development, UX, analytics, and governance.

Start at the C-Suite (Operational Ownership)

If you are not ready to appoint a single executive owner, the leadership team must still sponsor discoverability as a shared responsibility. Visible, recurring reinforcement from leadership ensures that search visibility is treated as a strategic, not a tactical, priority.

AN IDEAL SEO BUDGET

Principle

In an ideal world, the SEO budget aligns with the organic revenue it drives—just as paid search budgets align with paid revenue. If SEO delivers a large share of inbound sales, funding should reflect that contribution.

Real-World Challenges

In practice, SEO often competes for scraps, while paid channels expand more easily because their ROI is easier to calculate. That can underfund the very infrastructure that reduces Customer Acquisition Cost over time.

Hidden Costs

SEO's true costs extend beyond the team, tools, or agency fees. They include CMS constraints, tech debt, duplicated content pipelines, and cross-team coordination—costs that remain invisible until traffic drops.

Budget Formula (Pre-Budget Audit Required)

Begin with a thorough pre-budget audit and a signed strategy. Include: team salaries/overheads; agency retainers; tool subscriptions; content and UX for SEO; engineering and testing for SEO; and all gaps and risks identified in the audit.

SEO Salary Levels (Indicative)

Salaries depend on geographic location and other factors.

Role	USD	AUD	GBP
Junior SEO	35,000–50,000	50,000–70,000	20,000–30,000
Senior SEO Specialist	45,000–65,000	60,000–90,000	25,000–35,000
Senior Technical SEO	50,000–70,000	80,000–110,000	30,000–40,000

Role	USD	AUD	GBP
SEO Manager	65,000–100,000	120,000–150,000	40,000–50,000
SEO Director	100,000–250,000	140,000–180,000	50,000–60,000

Retain talent by rewarding impact and revenue protection, not parity with unrelated functions.

TAXATION AND INCENTIVES (COORDINATE WITH FINANCE)

Technical SEO work (e.g., original performance code or analytics automation) can qualify for R&D incentives in many jurisdictions. Ensure Finance evaluates eligibility and accurately records time.

SEO REPORTS

Purpose

Report impact and actions, not just data. Executives should see how SEO tasks link to business outcomes.

Preferred Contents

Organic traffic vs. other channels; organic conversions; key SEO wins and anomalies; progress against strategy; risks/governance issues needing attention.

Reporting by Exception

Automated dashboards are useful, but human-curated exception reporting drives faster action.

BUILDING THE RIGHT WAY

Only a new organization needs to build a website from scratch these days. To a lesser extent, some entities rebuild their websites when forced to replace the underlying technology, usually the content management system (CMS). Google will not care about your web server or CMS platform, but please make the effort to find out which ones are search-friendly out of the box or require less effort to make search-friendly.

Who Chooses the Core Technology?

To put it simply, the Website team does not choose the company's core technology. Most companies operate in either a .NET Framework or a Unix-like operating system (OS) environment, which dictates the other software needed to be interconnected. Sometimes a startup builds its initial offering on one OS or the other, and this will continue indefinitely. It would require a merger or acquisition with a larger company to change the OS. I have seen more than one OS used in a company, but that's in specialized situations, such as banking, where core services still run on legacy mainframe OSs.

The IT and Security teams also choose the core hardware environment, as they should.

Does the SEO Team Have a Say?

About the only area where the SEO team might have a say is the CMS (but I would not bet on it). As with most enterprise software, the high-end CMSs are sold to the C-suite. A low-end CMS might be perfect for SEO and cost much less to maintain, but your IT and Security teams are not too concerned with costs.

In large companies, the real issue for the SEO team is that a high-end CMS is not guaranteed to be search-friendly out of the box. Yes, you read that right. Your team will spend weeks, months, and even years getting the CMS to do "everything" to make it search-friendly. You won't believe how many hours your team will spend on this.

Out of the box, the CMS will enable you to lay out webpages and manage content assets. If you want to insert structured data (schema.org) tags, this is a custom add-on. This might take six months of consulting time and developer time. Your own IT team will not have anyone capable of working on this CMS, so you will hire contractors who specialize in this platform. You would be dealing with a "body shop", so the individuals who worked on your project last year might never work on your CMS again, so you will have to brief a new group of developers every time.

They say that time is money, and your company will spend a lot of it, but the time lost before you get all the SEO functionality and the consequent impact on lost revenue is impossible to measure.

DIGITAL ASSET MANAGEMENT (DAM)

In larger organizations where more than one team creates website content, particularly when external agencies do so, it is almost impossible to know where the digital assets are coming from, the rights attached to them, such as reuse, and where copies are stored. Images might be acquired in multiple formats, cropped, and used inconsistently.

A Digital Asset Management (DAM) solution is the answer. Of course, some commercial vendors offer DAMs, but I am referring to a DAM that your organization creates and manages. It should have the following characteristics:

- Defines a "digital asset" so that everyone concerned is left in no doubt about the purview of a DAM system.
- Places a high value on Accessibility factors. This will include color contrast, alternative text, captions, transcripts, and so on.

- Places a high value on website performance factors. Any content that could slow a page load requires a compelling reason to be in the DAM.
- Sets various parameters about the digital assets, such as file-naming conventions, file formats, maximum compressibility, web-safe colors, prohibited colors (for both Accessibility and brand reasons), watermarks, and more.
- Sets access policies for users of these assets, such as reuse only where permitted by the license.

PRODUCT INFORMATION MANAGEMENT (PIM)

What is Product Information Management (PIM)? PIM stands for Product Information Management. It stores product data and may include a Digital Asset Management (DAM) system. In other words, it contains product titles, descriptions, feature lists, images, variants, videos, prices - whatever attributes you can attach to a product. A PIM might offer these features:

- Data Modelling
- Data Quality Management
- Multichannel Publishing
- Digital Asset Management (DAM)
- Workflow Management
- Data Management
- App Integration
- Product Data Syndication
- Multi-Language Integration
- Product Feed Management
- Marketplace Software Integration
- Product Literature Integration

Companies that sell thousands of products/SKUs – say, a hardware store – might invest in a PIM solution. Nowadays, these are cloud-based, and the key question from your SEO team is whether they are SEO-friendly. Can you select which structured data tags to output with the product information? Do the pages include product schema, or do we need to merge them on our website via an API, assuming one is available? Do they include a DAM? If none of this is out of the box, what will the customization cost be? In my experience, enterprise software is deliberately minimal so that customization can be billed later.

The other question I would ask a PIM vendor concerns faceted search for the website's product catalog. Mentioned elsewhere in this book is the risk of generating zillions of pages if the facets generate an infinite number of permutations. A clothing brand, for instance, might have each dress in many colors and sizes. Can we control the number of permutations on the PIM side, or should we handle it on the website? It would be counterproductive if Google deemed the content thin and not worth indexing.

DIGITAL EXPERIENCE PLATFORMS

Digital Experience Platform (DXP) is a trendy label for technology that is probably also known by other labels, such as:

- Web Experience Management (WEM)
- Content Management System (CMS) platform
- Ecommerce platform
- Digital Asset Management (DAM) platform
- A/B Test platform
- Personalization platform
- Information management platform

Almost all DXPs can change a website's characteristics, yet it's unlikely that the in-house SEO's input was solicited before the platform was purchased. The platform vendors can do without awkward questions that could cost them the sale, so the sales process is carefully engineered to avoid this possibility. The selling points of the DXPs tend to be:

- Lead management
- Automation
- Multi-device delivery
- Customer engagement

There will be no mention of website traffic and how the DXP will impact it.

Standard builds, blocked sites, blocked protocols.

The Network Security team is typically not incentivized by sales, so they are unlikely to be sympathetic to SEO's needs if that would require changing their strict policies. They will block specific network protocols, ports, and web destinations. Some of those choices are made through a subscription to a third-party service that maintains a list of dubious websites.

Some companies have more than one "build" for staff computers (mix of specs and software). Most employees receive a standard build, while some teams with special needs may receive a computer with higher specifications or additional software.

One company chose to block access to Google Workspace (formerly G Suite), apparently to prevent employees from copying company information to a third-party repository beyond their control. They also restricted employees' access to certain social media and entertainment platforms. This was about network security, not about people using company time for private matters.

Under such strict IT security protocols, staff cannot install non-standard software on their own laptops or virtual machines.

Sometimes, even web browsers are muzzled. The security concern is valid, as the network security team cannot tolerate weak spots in its network.

Access Exceptions for the SEO Team

Some of these restrictions could be removed for SEO team members upon application. For example, at one location, the keyword register was kept in a Google Sheet so external content writers could access it. Still, they could not access a worksheet on the company's internal network.

Since certain SEO tools are available for free in Google Sheets, it makes sense to grant network access to Google Docs. For example, at one company, data from Google Search Console (GSC) was automatically downloaded each month because, at the time, GSC only allowed viewing the last 16 months of data. Although Google Sheets has many built-in functions similar to those in Microsoft Excel and other products, its Apps Script offers unique custom functions, such as fetching live data from the internet.

Another type of network block aims to prevent scrapers from copying all your content for misuse in overseas jurisdictions. This might be a service such as DataDome. The SEO team will find that many popular SEO tools are also blocked because they tend to fetch pages very rapidly, which is not typical human browsing behavior. A special code is issued to the SEO team for use in tools that accept it. Third-party web-based site analyzers may not be able to receive this code.

As remote work becomes more popular, many home IP addresses will need to be added to network allowlists.

"Independent" SEO Laptops

Some companies might grant "Local Admin" privileges (on Windows machines), so some software can be installed. However, the laptops carry the rest of the corporate "build" of software, and the data flows through the same internet pathway as the rest of the company.

Sometimes it is not worth arguing for security exceptions for the SEO team. I have been in companies where the SEO team purchased standard laptops on an expense account card, along with any software they needed. They could now install any web browser extensions they wanted without having to write justifications every time. We also obtained our own internet access, separate from the corporate network, so it was as good as using a personal computer at home. This was also useful for checking competitor websites without leaving the corporate IP address "fingerprints" in their website logs.

Getting a subscription to a Virtual Private Network (VPN) service is useful for checking the SERPs from different cities if you operate nationally or internationally. Again, this must be done from outside the corporate network, as the firewall will block IP address impersonation.

The disadvantage of network independence is that your SEO data on these laptops remains off-network, and you must transfer it to your networked computer. This may be a breach of company policy, so it is best to discuss the situation with the network security team and reach a mutually acceptable compromise.

WRITING EFFECTIVE TECHNICAL REQUESTS

SEO implementation velocity depends significantly on how well you communicate technical requirements. Even straightforward changes stall when requests lack clarity, context, or specificity that technical teams need to prioritize and execute work confidently.

A poorly structured ticket can make a fifteen-minute task appear complex and resource-intensive, pushing it into the backlog indefinitely. Meanwhile, urgent fixes that would immediately improve performance or visibility are on hold because the request failed to communicate priority effectively.

The Business Impact of Request Quality

Technical teams triage requests based on three factors: clarity of requirements, estimated effort, and business impact. When any of these elements is unclear, requests default to low priority regardless of their actual importance.

Consider a typical scenario: A critical redirect fix remains unimplemented for two months because the ticket states "fix redirects" without specifying which URLs or what the correct behavior should be. Schema markup improvements that would enable rich results remain in the backlog because the ticket assumed developers understood why "Article schema" matters. A simple robots.txt update to unlock 10,000 pages for indexing is estimated to take multiple days because the ticket didn't specify the required one-line change.

Each delayed implementation compounds opportunity cost. The gap between SEO strategy and execution often stems from communication quality rather than resource constraints.

Collaborative Scoping

Brief pre-ticket collaboration with technical teams dramatically improves both request quality and implementation success rates. A five-minute conversation before writing the ticket accomplishes more than multiple rounds of formal clarification later.

These conversations validate feasibility before you commit to an approach, surface implementation constraints that may require alternative solutions, establish a shared understanding of what success looks like, and build relationships that facilitate future technical collaboration.

Frame these conversations as collaborative problem-solving rather than requirements delivery. "We need to solve duplicate content issues on product pages—what's the most practical implementation approach given our current architecture?" invites better solutions than "We need canonical tags implemented exactly this way."

AI-Assisted Clarity Verification (Optional Pre-Check)

Before submitting technical requests, you can use an LLM as a quick pre-check to identify potential clarity issues. This is not a substitute for validation with your technical team, but it can help you catch obvious gaps before wasting developers' time.

How to use this approach:

Ask the AI to role-play as a developer unfamiliar with SEO and explain back what it thinks you're requesting.

Example prompt: "Act as a backend developer who has never worked with SEO. Read this technical request and respond with: (1) What specific changes you think I'm asking for, (2) Which parts are unclear or ambiguous, (3) What additional information you'd need to implement this, and (4) What could go wrong if you implement this as currently described."

What this can reveal:

- Technical terminology used without definition
- Scope boundaries that seemed clear to you but create confusion
- Missing examples that would make requirements concrete
- Unstated assumptions about platform, timing, or priority

Critical limitations and warnings:

AI cannot validate technical feasibility: Just because an AI understands your request doesn't mean it's technically possible or advisable. Your developers know your platform's constraints and limitations—AI doesn't.

Hallucination risk: LLMs can confidently explain their "understanding" of your request even when that understanding is fabricated or technically incorrect. Don't mistake confident AI responses for proof that your request is clear or correct.

Not a substitute for human review: This is a pre-check to catch obvious communication gaps, not a replacement for actually asking your developers, "Is this clear and feasible?"

False confidence danger: If the AI paraphrases your request well, that doesn't mean the request is actually clear or complete. AI can fill gaps with assumptions that mask missing information.

Responsible usage:

1. Use AI as a quick pre-check before sending requests

2. If AI identifies confusion, revise your request

3. **Still validate with actual developers** before assuming clarity

4. Never rely solely on AI feedback for technical accuracy

5. Recognize that AI responses are generated, not validated

When to skip this step entirely:

- If you have a good rapport with developers and can ask them directly
- For urgent requests (faster to submit and get human feedback)
- When a request involves platform-specific or proprietary systems, AI can't know

- If you're uncertain about technical accuracy (AI can't help validate that)

Better alternative: Build relationships in which developers feel comfortable saying, "I don't understand this," without judgment. Clear communication culture beats AI pre-checking.

Core Request Components

When your SEO team submits technical requests to developers, ensure these elements are included:

Business rationale: Connect the technical change to measurable outcomes.

- Weak: "This will improve page speed."
- Strong: "Pages currently load in 4.2 seconds; this change should reduce to under 3 seconds, which typically improves conversion by 5-7% based on our analytics."

Your role: Ensure requests explain WHY, not just WHAT. Developers prioritize work that shows business impact.

Defined scope: Explicitly state what is and isn't included.

- Weak: "Update meta descriptions on blog posts."
- Strong: "Update meta descriptions on the 25 blog posts published in Q3 that currently have duplicate descriptions."

Your role: Reject vague requests. If your team can't quantify scope, they haven't thought it through.

Verifiable completion criteria: Define how success will be measured.

- Weak: "Implemented correctly."

- Strong: "All 25 posts have unique meta descriptions between 150-160 characters, verified via site audit."

Your role: Ensure your team can objectively verify completion before marking work done.

Testing approach: How will the work be validated before launch?

- Includes: Which pages to check, what to verify, who validates
- Your role: Ensure QA responsibility is clear before work begins

Priority and timing: When is this needed and why?

- Weak: "ASAP."
- Strong: "Medium priority - reducing indexation inefficiency but not causing immediate ranking issues. Next two sprints if capacity permits."

Your role: Ensure your team prioritizes realistically and communicates timeline needs clearly.

Manager-Level Examples

Example 1: Vague Request (Your team submits this to you)

"We need to fix our site's pagination issues for SEO."

Why you should send this back:

- No business impact stated
- No scope defined (how many pages?)
- No completion criteria
- No timeline or priority

What to ask:

- "What's the business impact of not fixing this?"
- "How many pages are affected?"
- "How will we know when it's fixed correctly?"
- "Where does this rank in our current priorities?"

Example 2: Clear Request (Your team submits this - you approve)

Request: Fix pagination implementation on blog category pages

Business impact: 750 paginated URLs are diluting ranking signals for our 15 main blog category pages. Consolidating signals should improve rankings for these high-traffic pages, which drive 15% of our organic leads.

Scope: 15 blog category pages in /blog/ that use pagination (list attached)

Technical approach: [Your SEO team provides implementation details to developers - you don't need to review tag-by-tag specifications]

Success criteria:

- Each category page consolidates pagination signals correctly
- All pagination navigation still works normally
- Site audit confirms correct implementation across all 15 categories

Testing: SEO team will verify implementation on 3 sample pages, then audit all 15 pages before marking complete

Timeline: Medium priority - would like in the next two sprints if capacity permits

Owner: [SEO team member name]

Why do you approve this:

Is Our SEO Working?

- Business impact clear (15% of organic leads)
- Scope quantified (15 pages, 750 URLs)
- Success criteria measurable
- Testing approach defined
- Priority realistic
- Owner assigned

Example 3: What You Don't Need in Requests

You DON'T need to see:

- Specific HTML tags to be used (<link rel='canonical'>)
- Page-by-page technical specifications
- Implementation code snippets
- Detailed technical validation steps

You DO need to ensure:

- Business case is clear
- Scope is defined
- Success is measurable
- Owner is assigned
- Priority is realistic

Your job: Verify that the request is clear and justified; do not specify the technical implementation. That's why you hired SEO practitioners.

Implementation Accelerators

Several practices accelerate technical implementation:

Provide code examples when possible. If you need specific JSON-LD structured data, include the complete code rather than describing it. Developers can adapt working code more quickly than they can interpret requirements.

Reference existing implementations. "Implement breadcrumb schema as we have on product pages" is clearer than explaining breadcrumb schema from scratch.

Link to authoritative documentation. When requesting the implementation of a standardized feature, such as schema.org markup or Open Graph tags, link to the official documentation rather than explaining the specification.

Schema prioritization note: When requesting schema implementation, verify that the type remains beneficial (see Chapter 6). FAQ and HowTo schema were restricted/deprecated 2023-2025; focus technical requests on Product, Organization, Review, and LocalBusiness types.

Separate discovery from implementation tickets. If you're not certain about the best technical approach, create a discovery ticket first: "Research options for implementing pagination SEO." This will produce a recommendation that becomes input to the implementation ticket.

Keep tickets focused. One discrete change per ticket makes estimation easier, reduces implementation risk, and allows partial progress if capacity is limited.

Quality Metrics

Monitor indicators that reveal ticket quality:

Implementation cycle time from ticket creation to completion—well-written tickets move faster through the queue. Clarification request frequency—clear tickets require minimal back-and-forth before work begins. Rework rate—correctly specified requirements get implemented right the first time. Technical team feedback—periodic surveys asking technical teams to rate SEO ticket quality and clarity.

Improving ticket quality typically results in a 30-50 percent reduction in implementation time and a significant reduction in rework.

QUALITY FRAMEWORK (QA FOR SEO)

SEO QA Framework

Education across teams; internal metrics and alerts; continuous improvement. Include QA analysts in SEO checks within existing squads to institutionalize accountability.

Severity Categories

Critical—manual penalty;

Major—accidental deindexation;

Minor—duplicate titles/sitewide issues;

Cosmetic—alt/schema gaps (often de-prioritized, but not trivial).

KNOWLEDGE PRESERVATION

Use a wiki (e.g., Confluence) to capture migrations, audit results, penalty recoveries, tool configurations, and playbooks. Institutional memory prevents repeated losses.

REVIEWS AND RATINGS

Encourage genuine reviews on third-party sites (e.g., Google Business Profile). Never incentivize 5-star reviews where this is illegal. Authenticity is a visibility signal.

SITE REBUILDS AND AUDITS

Incremental Change

Prefer iterative releases over big-bang rebuilds. Pilot on a lower-risk property when possible and ensure SEO is engaged pre-decision, not post-launch.

Annual Full Audit + Mini-Audits After Changes

Conduct a comprehensive audit yearly and run mini-audits after any CMS/platform/infrastructure change, even if SEO was consulted earlier. (This guards against silent regressions.)

Typical Audit Checks

Crawl/indexability; performance; content and E-E-A-T; backlinks; structured data/social tags; accessibility; traffic analysis; local signals (if relevant); competitor baselines; "skeletons" long ignored.

Causation, Correlation, Caution

Some issues are deterministic (robots or cloaking). Most require hypothesis and replication across cases—avoid premature certainty.

Sample Post-Audit Project Plan

Summary	Rob	Ash	Luke	Sarah	Time Reqd
Alert server admin that we might need to upload some verification files to the root.	X				Done
Arrange admin access to WordPress. Either this or the above is essential.	X				Done
Arrange access to Google Ads account to Ash (for access to Kwd Planner)	X				
Update version of WordPress		X			Minimal
Check indexing in GSC		X			Minimal
Re-crawl site with added GSC credentials; Export data		X			See notes – 2d
Study competitors and devise keyword groups (for task below)		X			See notes – 2d
Seek inbound links – Continuous – Rob would need an mrpfd.com email.	X				
Build online Keyword Register		X			See notes – 1d
Create content plan, with catalog of pages, PDFs, images etc	X				
Rewrite Prod/Svcs pages (and update Kwd Register later)	X				
Help Mark and Rob with Navigation paths		X			See notes – 2d
Write redirects file				X	
Create imagery for new site				X	
Build new site			X		
Insert structured data tags		X			See notes – 5d
Improve meta descriptions and title tags		X			See notes – 4d
Add image Alt text		X			See notes - 2d
Exclude subdomains from indexing		X			See notes – 1d
TOTAL – Ash days (once off)					**19 days (7 before new site is built; 12 after new site is built**

Figure 28 Post-Audit Project Plan.

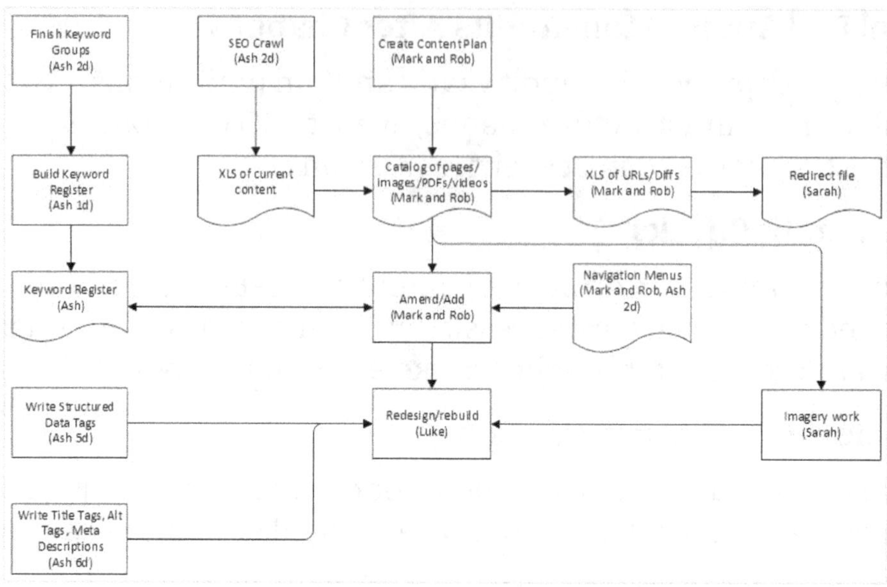

Figure 29 Post-Audit Implementation Workflow.

CONVERSION RATE OPTIMIZATION (CRO)

All conversion-focused organizations want to improve their website goals to drive Conversion Rate Optimization (CRO). CRO aims to increase the conversion rate, whether through form completions or committed sales. It is a continuous process of testing various ideas and designs, keeping only those that drive more conversions. It is important work, but it is not part of core SEO activities.

From the viewpoint of this book, there are two kinds of CRO:

- CRO that operates independently of SEO
- CRO that is collaborative, particularly with SEO

CRO that is performed without consulting SEO, or worse, rejecting inputs from SEO is a bad idea. I worked at a company where a "better converting" page design had a yellow heading on a white background. It failed color-contrast accessibility tests, but neither the CRO team nor our manager would change the heading color, and our manager failed to intervene. After all, why fiddle with a page that has been proven to increase conversions?

A collaborative approach works across all facets of business, and SEO is no different. In the scenario above, I successfully added an SEO team member to the CRO workflow. At least we were given a chance to speak up.

Split Testing for SEO

Here are some examples of collaborating with the SEO team to try some page alterations:

- Changing Title attributes
- Adding call-to-action interstitials
- Preventing Google from modifying Meta Descriptions
- Placing symbols in Titles and Meta Descriptions
- Adding introductory text to category pages
- Merging pages to reduce thin content

At first glance, such experiments are no-brainers and are attempted by many SEO teams, sometimes in response to sales pressure. The results might surprise you, and what works in one industry or for one audience might not in many others.

Collaborative, Consultative SEO Testing

I saw a highly collaborative product manager take the lead and consult with other stakeholders daily, including on SEO tests. This environment made the consultation process so transparent that no other teams raised objections, and their input was incorporated into the tests. Product teams should manage SEO testing.

A more formal way to collaborate is the RACI matrix:

- Responsible

Is Our SEO Working?

- Accountable
- Consulted
- Informed

It lists each task in the testing process and the teams that are responsible, accountable, consulted, or informed. Note that I used the word "teams," not "individuals," there. Such models sometimes use individuals in the matrix, implying that four people are enough to approve a test.

There are other decision-making models, and your company might already have a preferred one. There is no perfect approach, so do it as harmoniously as possible.

SEO tests can be classified into three types of changes to webpages:

- Transparent to users
- Visible to users
- Product functionality impacted

Changes to the page code are the usual case where an SEO-proposed change is tested transparently. This could be a set of structured data tags, or a change to the JavaScript code. Usually, there are no objections from other stakeholders unless a technical barrier exists.

Visible changes are those that a user can notice. These might be changes to the layout without altering the content, or to rectify a color contrast issue. By providing reference material to support the change request, the SEO team should find it easier to secure buy-in.

WIDER USE OF THE SEO TEAM

Leverage SEO research skills for M&A reconnaissance and competitor/product analysis. SEOs can uncover signals beyond the indexed web and synthesize them for decision-makers.

WHAT SUCCESS LOOKS LIKE

As processes mature, teams shift from reactive fixes to proactive improvements and new initiatives. This progression signals effective operational governance.

AI VISIBILITY IN THE IDEAL SEO ECOSYSTEM

In organizations with mature SEO ecosystems, AI visibility isn't treated as a separate initiative competing for resources. It's integrated into existing SEO operations, governance structures, and measurement frameworks. The approach reflects organizational maturity, competitive context, and resource reality.

How Mature Organizations Approach AI Visibility

Integrated, not isolated: AI visibility work happens within existing SEO workflows rather than requiring dedicated teams or parallel processes. The same people who optimize for traditional search extend their practice to include AI interpretability.

Governed, not ad hoc: AI visibility follows the same governance patterns as traditional SEO—documented standards, approval workflows, quality gates, and cross-functional coordination. Structured data policies cover both search rich results and AI citation. Content standards address both human readability and machine interpretability.

Measured systematically: AI visibility metrics integrate into existing reporting dashboards. The three-tier measurement framework (machine legibility, AI visibility, commercial impact) complements traditional SEO metrics rather than replacing them.

Resourced appropriately: Investment scales with category AI adoption rates and competitive maturity, not hype or fear. Organizations align their AI visibility capability development with strategic needs.

Capability Development Patterns by Organizational Maturity

Different organizations need different AI visibility approaches based on their overall SEO maturity.

Organizations at SEOGMM Level 1-2 (Ad Hoc / Emerging):

Reality: Basic SEO fundamentals aren't yet solid. Technical debt exists. Content quality varies. Governance is informal or nonexistent.

AI visibility approach: Defer systematic investment. Fix foundational SEO first.

Minimum viable actions:

- Ensure structured data validates (fix what's broken, don't expand coverage yet)
- Verify AI crawlers aren't accidentally blocked in robots.txt
- Spot-check quarterly that AI systems aren't severely misrepresenting your brand

Why: You can't build AI visibility on broken SEO foundations. Investing in AI-specific optimization when basic crawlability, content quality, or technical performance is poor is a waste of resources. Traditional SEO improvements (better content, cleaner structure, faster performance) naturally enhance AI interpretability.

Resource allocation: <5% of SEO effort on AI-specific work. Focus 95% on fundamentals.

Organizations at SEOGMM Level 3 (Structured / Embedded Controls):

Reality: SEO processes are documented and followed; the technical foundation is solid. Content standards exist. Measurement is systematic. Governance operates consistently.

AI visibility approach: Begin systematic capability-building with a minimum viable investment.

Typical 6-month development pattern:

Months 1-2: Eliminate technical contradictions

- Audit structured data across priority pages (top 50-100 by revenue/traffic)
- Fix validation errors and semantic inconsistencies
- Ensure cross-channel messaging consistency for core brand claims
- Integrate into existing technical SEO workflows (don't create a separate process)

Months 2-3: Enhance attribute completeness

- Add 5-10 explicit, machine-readable attributes to the top 20 offerings
- Work with product/service owners using the existing content development process
- Build attribute lists into standard content briefs
- Update content guidelines to require attribute completeness

Months 3-6: Build authority signals

- Secure 2-3 authoritative mentions in industry publications
- Use existing PR relationships and processes
- Focus on depth over volume (one quality placement beats ten directory listings)
- Track AI mention frequency quarterly (20-30 test queries × 3 platforms)

Integration points with existing SEO:

- Structured data work happens during regular technical audits, not separately
- Attribute enhancement happens during normal content refresh cycles
- Authority building uses existing PR workflows
- Measurement integrates into quarterly SEO reporting

Resource allocation: 15-20% of SEO effort on AI-specific enhancements. The work happens within existing processes, requiring coordination rather than separate capacity.

Expected outcome: AI mention frequency increases 30-50% over 6 months. Representation accuracy reaches 80%+. Branded search shows a 10-15% lift.

Organizations at SEOGMM Level 4-5 (Integrated / Predictive):

Reality: SEO is embedded across the organization. Cross-functional collaboration is natural. Continuous improvement operates systematically. Resources align with strategic priorities. Governance is proactive, not reactive.

AI visibility approach: Comprehensive capability development integrated across all SEO domains.

Typical 12-18 month evolution:

Phase 1 (Months 1-4): Technical and semantic excellence

- Comprehensive structured data implementation (80%+ coverage of strategic pages)
- Build a formal attribute taxonomy/schema defining all product/service characteristics
- Create brand knowledge graph documenting offerings, attributes, constraints, relationships

- Establish semantic consistency governance across all channels
- Integrate AI interpretability into technical SEO standards and QA processes

Phase 2 (Months 4-8): Agentic discovery readiness

- Identify all decision-making attributes in the category (customer decision trees, competitive differentiation)
- Express attributes in machine-readable formats across all offerings
- Create constraints and eligibility rules that AI agents can evaluate
- Build systematic FAQ content addressing "how to choose" queries (Note: Use clear HTML structure, not FAQ schema—see Chapter 6)
- Implement structured data for voice/agentic interfaces

Phase 3 (Months 6-10): Multimodal optimization (forward-looking)

- Audit imagery and video for attribute demonstration
- Standardize visual metadata (EXIF data, structured captions aligned with semantic taxonomy)
- Produce new assets designed for machine vision that are strategically important
- Connect visual and textual semantic layers
- Test multimodal discoverability quarterly

Phase 4 (Months 8-15): Authority and ecosystem presence

- Systematic PR strategy: 4-6 authoritative placements annually

- Create data-driven, citation-worthy content (original research, industry reports, unique datasets)
- Support authentic community participation in relevant forums and discussions
- Monitor brand mentions across all ecosystems (PR, social, reviews, Reddit, industry forums)
- Proactively correct inaccuracies and outdated information

Phase 5 (Months 12+): Cross-channel semantic governance

- Assign dedicated semantic governance owner (cross-functional role)
- Create a shared attribute dictionary defining standard terminology
- Implement quarterly consistency audits across all channels
- Establish approval workflow for content affecting AI interpretation
- Monitor AI representation quarterly and correct misalignments systematically

Integration with broader SEO ecosystem:

- Technical work extends existing infrastructure, doesn't replace it
- Content enhancements happen within established editorial workflows
- Multimodal optimization uses existing creative operations and DAM
- PR and authority building leverage existing communications relationships

- Governance follows established cross-functional collaboration patterns
- Measurement integrates into existing executive dashboards

Resource allocation: 30-40% of SEO effort explicitly addresses AI visibility, but much of this work also benefits traditional SEO (better-structured data improves rich results, clearer attributes improve conversion, and authority-building strengthens traditional rankings).

Expected outcome: AI mention frequency reaches 2-3× baseline. Competitive inclusion rate matches or exceeds traditional search share. Branded search growth outpaces the category. Documented customer discovery through AI systems.

Resource Allocation in the Ideal Ecosystem

The principle is that investment in AI visibility should be proportional to three factors:

1. **Category AI adoption rate:** What percentage of searches in your category show AI-generated answers? If <10%, AI visibility is a forward-looking investment. If >30%, it's a competitive necessity.
2. **Competitive AI maturity:** How systematically are competitors optimizing for AI? If you're early, you can move deliberately. If competitors are ahead, you need to close gaps quickly.
3. **Customer journey dependence:** Does AI discovery materially affect consideration sets? In some categories (B2B software research, travel planning, product comparisons), AI systems heavily influence what customers consider. In other areas (local services, emergency needs, habitual purchases), the impact is minimal.

Measurement approach: Assess these three factors quarterly. The importance of AI visibility changes as platforms evolve and user behavior shifts. What's optional in Q1 2026 might be critical by Q4 2026.

Budget guidance by organizational size:

Small organizations (<$10M revenue):

- Minimum viable approach: $10,000-$25,000 over 6 months
- Focus: Fix contradictions, add attributes to top offerings, secure 2-3 quality mentions
- Mostly internal capacity with selective external support for PR

Mid-sized organizations ($10M-$100M revenue):

- Integrated approach: $50,000-$150,000 over 12 months
- Focus: Systematic structured data, attribute completeness, authority building, cross-channel consistency
- Mix of internal capacity and specialized external support (technical SEO, PR, content)

Large organizations (>$100M revenue):

- Comprehensive approach: $150,000-$350,000 over 18 months
- Focus: Full capability development across all phases, dedicated governance, multimodal readiness
- Primarily internal capacity with strategic external expertise for specialized domains

Hidden costs to account for:

- Product/service owner time for attribute definition
- Cross-functional coordination (PR, product marketing, content, technical teams)

- Tools for AI visibility monitoring (emerging market, budget $5,000-$15,000 annually)
- Quarterly measurement and reporting (10-15 hours per quarter for manual testing until tools mature)

Success Indicators by Maturity Level

Level 3 organizations (Structured) should demonstrate:

- AI mention frequency for brand reaching 40-50% of test queries
- Representation accuracy exceeding 80%
- Structured data coverage of 60%+ on strategic pages
- Attribute completeness of 50%+ offerings with 8+ attributes
- Cross-channel consistency above 75%

Level 4-5 organizations (Integrated/Predictive) should demonstrate:

- AI mention frequency reaching 70%+ of test queries
- Representation accuracy consistently above 90%
- Competitive inclusion rate matching traditional search market share
- Structured data coverage exceeding 85%
- Attribute completeness above 75% with 10+ attributes
- Cross-channel consistency above 90%
- Documented customer discovery attribution to AI systems
- AI visibility integrated into executive dashboards alongside traditional metrics

When AI Visibility Doesn't Require Separate Investment

Some SEO improvements naturally enhance AI visibility without targeted effort:

Technical SEO excellence (fast loading, clean crawling, semantic HTML, proper rendering) makes content accessible to both traditional search and AI crawlers.

Content quality focus (clear explanations, specific examples, authoritative sources, structured organization) serves both human readers and machine interpretation.

Structured data implementation for rich results automatically provides signals that AI systems use to understand entities and extract attributes.

Authority-building through PR, thought leadership, and industry participation creates validation signals that both traditional search and AI systems weigh heavily.

User experience optimization (clear navigation, accessible design, fast performance) improves engagement metrics that influence both traditional rankings and AI confidence in recommending you.

In mature ecosystems, the question shifts from "should we invest in AI visibility?" to "are we doing SEO well enough that AI visibility naturally follows?"

Organizations at Level 4-5 maturity often find that 70-80% of AI visibility improvement comes from doing traditional SEO excellently, with only 20-30% requiring AI-specific enhancements.

The organizations that thrive in AI-mediated search will be those that integrate AI visibility into existing SEO excellence rather than treating it as a separate discipline requiring separate teams, budgets, and processes.

Chapter 12

RELEVANCE OF PAID SEARCH

Let's discard a persistent myth: paying for PPC ads—also known as Search Engine Marketing (SEM)—does not directly affect organic ranking algorithms. However, it can indirectly improve visibility and engagement signals. Search engines accept your ad budget, but the organic algorithm doesn't give you preferential treatment. Many businesses thrive without advertising, and some lack budgets.

Since late 2023, Google has tested co-locating ads with AI Overviews in Search Generative Experience (SGE) results. In early 2026, Performance Max and Search Ads 360 draw on Merchant Center feeds and Business Profile assets to enhance creative automation. Structured data markup on landing pages can support feed accuracy, but is not directly ingested into ad creation. This creates new opportunities for integration between SEO and paid search teams.

As a manager overseeing both channels or coordinating between them, understanding their relationship matters more than ever.

IS PPC/SEM RELEVANT TO SEO?

In a word: yes. While PPC and SEO serve different functions, they share a common goal—visibility in search results—and can be powerful allies when managed strategically. The keyword there is "relevant."

Shared Goal of Search Visibility

Both channels aim to increase your presence in SERPs. SEO earns organic placement through content quality, technical optimization, and authority signals. PPC buys paid placement through auction-based advertising. A dual strategy helps you occupy more SERP real estate. Google and Microsoft have published studies (e.g., Google Ads incrementality studies and Microsoft Advertising research) showing that a combined paid + organic presence can raise total click volume by ~20–30 percent. However, the exact lift varies by brand and query.

When users see your brand in both the paid ad section and the organic results, they perceive greater credibility and authority. Even if they don't click your ad, seeing it reinforces brand awareness before they click your organic listing.

PPC Data Informs SEO Strategy Rapidly

One of PPC's most significant values to SEO managers is the rapid feedback it provides. PPC campaigns generate immediate data on keyword performance—which search terms actually drive clicks and conversions, which ones look promising in keyword research but fail to convert, and what cost-per-acquisition you can expect from different keyword categories.

This data becomes invaluable for SEO prioritization. Before investing months in ranking for a keyword, you can test it through PPC for a few weeks. If it converts well, double down on organic efforts. If it attracts clicks but not conversions, you've avoided wasting SEO resources on a dead end.

A/B testing in paid ads also reveals which headlines, descriptions, and landing page approaches resonate with audiences. You can test five different headlines in PPC, identify the winner within days, then incorporate that winning messaging into your organic content. These de-risk major content investments and eliminate guesswork.

Example of a SaaS company: They ran ads with five different headlines and three landing page layouts promoting their tradespeople CRM product. After collecting data on thousands of impressions, the team identified a headline-layout combination that achieved 40 percent higher CTR than alternatives. They then rolled that winning combination into their organic pages, resulting in a 28 percent increase in organic conversions over the next quarter. Without PPC testing, they might have spent months building organic rankings around messaging that underperformed.

Speed vs. Longevity: Complementary Timelines

PPC can deliver traffic almost immediately once campaigns are approved. This makes it ideal for new product launches, time-sensitive promotions, seasonal campaigns, and testing new markets before committing to long-term SEO investment.

SEO, by contrast, is a long-term play. Building rankings takes months, but once established, they generate sustained traffic without ongoing per-click costs. The investment compounds over time—content created today can drive traffic for years.

Strategic implication: Use PPC to generate immediate visibility while SEO builds. For new pages not yet ranking, PPC bridges the visibility gap. As organic rankings improve, you can gradually reduce PPC spend on those terms and reallocate budget to new priorities. This creates a sustainable cycle in which paid and organic work together rather than compete for funding.

THE SEO—PPC COLLABORATION FRAMEWORK

To maximize value, treat SEO and PPC as complementary workstreams rather than isolated disciplines. A simple collaboration framework helps:

Regular Communication Cadence

Monthly joint strategy meetings align priorities between teams. Discuss: What keywords are we targeting? Where do we have organic momentum to reduce PPC dependence? Where is PPC discovering opportunities that SEO should prioritize? What changes in the search landscape (algorithm updates, competitor moves) affect both channels?

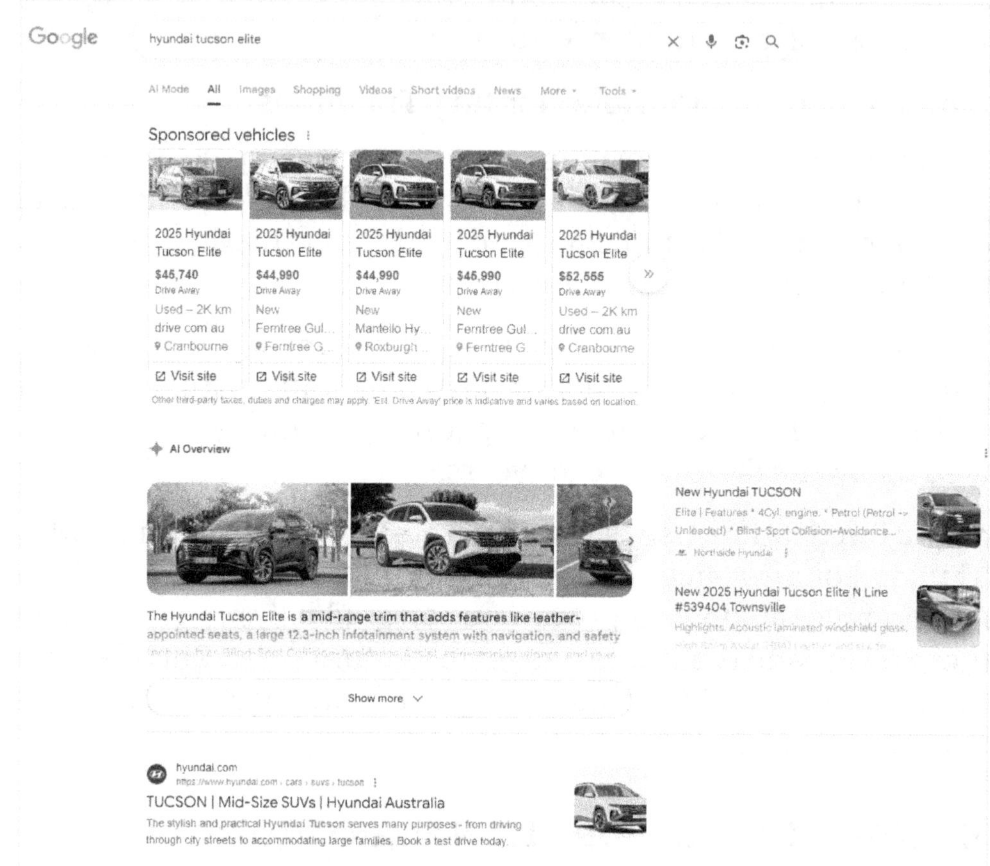

Figure 30 PPC ads at the top despite the brand ranking high organically.

Weekly performance check-ins share tactical insights and coordinate content or ad tests. These shorter sessions keep both teams informed without creating meeting overhead. They work best as 15–30-minute syncs focusing on actionable information: "PPC found keyword X converts 3x better than expected—should SEO prioritize it?" or

"Organic rankings improved for Y category—can we reduce PPC spend there?"

Shared KPIs and Metrics

For governance policies on shared metrics and cross-team accountability, see Book 3, *AI Visibility Playbook,* Chapter 7.

Workflow Alignment and Testing Integration

Use PPC to quickly test headlines, descriptions, landing pages, and new keywords. Once paid campaigns reveal what works, apply those insights to slower-moving organic SEO.

Use high-performing organic content to inform paid campaigns. Pages that rank well organically demonstrate Google's view that they satisfy user intent. These pages often make excellent paid landing pages with proven conversion potential. Their headlines and value propositions, validated through organic performance, can inform ad copy.

Pro Tip: If you use a product page as an ad landing page, be sure to notify the PPC team of any changes.

Coordinate keyword strategy. Identify where each channel plays the primary role: High-commercial-intent transactional keywords often work best for PPC in the short term (immediate revenue), while SEO builds long-term presence. Informational query content typically focuses on organic, with potential paid support during launches. Branded terms require both channels—organic for trust, paid for competitive protection against rivals bidding on your brand name.

IMPROVING SEO CONTENT THROUGH PPC TESTING

PPC serves as an excellent testing ground for content decisions before committing to SEO investments.

Example from a B2B software company: Before creating a comprehensive guide on "enterprise resource planning software selection," they tested interest through PPC ads. Three different angles were tested: cost-savings emphasis, integration-capabilities focus, and scalability messaging. The scalability angle achieved a 2.5x higher conversion rate than others.

Armed with this data, the SEO team created their comprehensive guide emphasizing scalability, confident that they were addressing the angle that resonated most with their target audience. The guide achieved strong rankings within four months and became their highest-converting organic resource.

The principle: By treating PPC as a rapid feedback mechanism, you de-risk major SEO content investments and avoid the months-long lag in discovering what works.

BUDGET ALLOCATION CONSIDERATIONS

As you balance SEO and PPC budgets, several principles apply:

Short-Term vs. Long-Term Investment

PPC excels at immediate visibility, product launches, seasonal campaigns, and time-sensitive promotions. You turn it on, you get traffic. When you turn it off, traffic stops.

SEO compounds value over time but requires patience and consistent investment. Initial results are slow to appear, but once established, they generate traffic without per-click costs. Content created today drives traffic for years if maintained properly.

There's no universal budget split. Some organizations allocate 70-90 percent to PPC, 10-30 percent to SEO fundamentals, while others reverse this ratio. The proper allocation depends on your business model, competitive landscape, and growth stage.

Market Maturity Considerations

Use competitive intelligence frameworks (Chapter 2) to inform optimal budget allocation between paid and organic search investments.

Competitive markets may demand higher PPC spending early to establish a presence while SEO builds authority. In these situations, paid visibility provides immediate revenue while organic investments mature.

Less competitive markets might warrant a heavier SEO investment, as you can achieve strong rankings more quickly, with PPC providing supplemental visibility for strategic terms.

New brands often require a heavier PPC allocation initially because they lack domain authority and content depth to achieve strong organic performance. As brand awareness grows and the content library expands, the ratio can shift toward organic.

Flexible Reallocation Based on Performance

The key is fluid reallocation—use data to shift investment as the landscape evolves. When organic rankings improve for high-value terms, consider reducing PPC spend on those keywords and reallocating the budget to new priorities. When competitors increase PPC aggression, you may need to defend with increased paid investment. When algorithm updates impact organic visibility, PPC can fill gaps while you adapt.

From my experience: One retail client started with an 80/20 split between PPC and SEO. After 18 months of consistent SEO investment, organic traffic accounted for 60% of total search traffic. We gradually reduced PPC spend from 80 percent to 40 percent of search budget, maintaining revenue while dramatically reducing cost-per-acquisition. The PPC spend that remained focused on competitive brand protection and high-value product categories where organic competition was intense.

BRANDED SEARCH PROTECTION

Competitors may legally bid on your brand terms. Google Ads policies allow competitors to bid on trademarked terms, provided their ad copy does not infringe on or mislead consumers. Enforcement focuses on ad copy use, not on keyword bidding. Running ads on your own brand name helps ensure you control the top of the screen—even if you already rank #1 organically.

Why branded PPC matters even with #1 organic ranking:

AI Overviews and expanded SERP modules can push organic results below the visible fold on desktop and mobile devices. Your #1 organic ranking might appear below the fold if multiple paid ads and an AI Overview appear above it. Paid ads ensure premium visibility regardless of SERP layout changes.

Competitors bidding on your brand create confusion. When users search for your brand name and see competitor ads, some click them instead of your organic listing. Your branded PPC ad pushes competitors lower and captures clicks that might otherwise go to rivals.

Cost is typically low. Branded searches have high Quality Scores (Google recognizes strong relevance between your brand name and your ads), resulting in low cost-per-click. The investment to protect your brand is often surprisingly affordable.

Exception: If you have absolute organic dominance, strong brand recognition, and competitors aren't bidding on your brand, you might skip branded PPC. Monitor monthly—if competitors start bidding, respond quickly.

SHARED METRICS AND TOOLS

Google Ads, Search Console, and GA4 integration via Google Ads Data Manager (2024 release) provides the most complete cross-channel reporting. Unified tracking provides a complete view of user journeys that span both channels:

- **Example journey:** A user clicks a PPC ad for "CRM for tradespeople" (first touchpoint). A few days later, they search "best CRM for electricians" and click your organic blog post (second touchpoint). They download a brochure or book a call, which is the conversion (third touchpoint).
- **With siloed tracking,** PPC might get credit under last-click attribution, or organic might, depending on the attribution model. Neither reflects reality—both channels contributed to the conversion.
- **With integrated tracking and multi-channel attribution,** both channels receive appropriate credit for their role in the conversion. GA4 Data-Driven Attribution (DDA) models assign fractional credit across touchpoints using machine-learning trained on your property's historical conversion data, provided sufficient volume exists for model training.
- **Manager's responsibility:** Ensure your analytics implementation tracks users across both channels and that your attribution model reflects multi-touch reality. Last-click attribution systematically undervalues channels that drive awareness and consideration.

Integrate PPC metrics with your SEO measurement framework (Chapter 4) using data-driven attribution to understand the full value of search channels.

PPC AND SEO IN THE AI AGE

AI Overviews in Search and 'AI Organized Results Page' experiments in 2026 are reshaping user behavior. When AI delivers a summarized answer at the top of the SERP, fewer users click through—reducing the impact of high rankings and sometimes lowering ad click-through rates as well.

Strategic responses:

- Monitor where AI Overviews appear in SERPs—industry tracking (e.g., SERP API, BrightEdge data) estimates roughly 20–25 % of English-language queries show AI Overviews as of early 2026, but coverage fluctuates by topic and region. Identify which of your target keywords show AI features and adjust expectations accordingly.
- **Target long-tail, transactional, or complex queries** less likely to trigger AI summaries. Simple factual questions are increasingly answered directly by AI, but complex decision-making queries still drive clicks.
- **Optimize structured data** to ensure your content can be surfaced in AI Overviews and related ad placements. Structured data (Schema.org markup and LLMs.txt accessibility directives) *may* help AI systems parse and attribute content more effectively for AI Overviews or summaries. However, inclusion is not guaranteed, and the criteria are not public.
- **Adjust PPC strategy** toward high-intent keywords or segments where AI is less dominant. Transactional queries ("buy X," "X near me," "X price") still prominently display traditional ad placements.
- **Regularly review impression share, CTR trends, and ad placement performance** whenever Google rolls out AI changes

in your sector. The landscape shifts quickly—what works today might need adjustment in three months.

- **Coordinate AI response across both channels.** If organic visibility suffers from AI Overviews, PPC can compensate. If PPC costs increase due to AI-driven inventory reductions, organic optimization becomes more valuable. Don't optimize channels in isolation when the competitive landscape affects both.

COMMON INTEGRATION MISTAKES

Several patterns prevent effective SEO—PPC collaboration:

- **Mistake 1: Siloed teams with conflicting incentives.** When the SEO team is measured only on organic traffic and the PPC team only on paid conversions, teams will optimize locally rather than globally. They might target the same keywords without coordination, bid against each other for resources, or fail to share valuable insights.
  Fix: Establish shared goals and a regular cadence for collaboration. Measure both teams partly on combined search performance.
- **Mistake 2: Assuming PPC "steals" from organic.** Some managers worry that buying ads for terms they rank for organically wastes money—" We'd get those clicks anyway." Google Ads incrementality studies (2018–2024) have reported that combined paid and organic listings deliver an incremental lift of 50%-120%, depending on brand and category.
  Fix: Test incrementality. Pause branded PPC for two weeks and measure whether organic clicks increase to compensate. Usually, they don't fully compensate, proving that paid ads generate net-new traffic.

- **Mistake 3: Never testing assumptions.** Both channels benefit from experimentation, yet many organizations run the same strategy quarter after quarter without testing alternatives.
  Fix: Allocate 10-20 percent of the budget to testing. Try new keyword categories, ad formats, landing page variants, or budget allocations. Measure results rigorously. Scale what works, cut what doesn't. One test I ran at a few workplaces was to stop PPC ads for a month on a given product line where we ranked #1 organically. The finding was always to keep the PPC ads.
- **Mistake 4: Attribution myopia.** Relying solely on last-click attribution systematically undervalues awareness-building channels (typically SEO) and overvalues bottom-funnel conversions (typically PPC).
  Fix: Use DDA or, at a minimum, position-based attribution that credits both first and last touches.

KEY TAKEAWAYS FOR MANAGERS

Paid and organic search work best as complementary channels when they share a strategy and data integration.

Strategic Principles

Use PPC for speed and testing; use SEO for compounding long-term value. Neither is "better"—they serve different strategic purposes. Integrate measurement and attribution to understand how channels work together rather than in isolation, and establish collaboration cadence and shared metrics to align teams around total search performance rather than channel-specific vanity metrics.

Test assumptions regularly across both channels—what worked last year might be suboptimal now. Monitor AI's impact across both channels and adjust strategies in coordination rather than in silos.

Budget flexibly based on performance data, competitive dynamics, and strategic priorities—not rigid percentages.

As a manager orchestrating SEO and PPC together, your leadership in creating collaboration frameworks will determine whether your brand gains or loses visibility as AI reshapes the search landscape. Organizations that maintain channel silos will fall behind those that treat search holistically.

Chapter 13

STAYING CURRENT WITH SEO

Google reports making thousands of improvements to Search each year (including ranking changes, quality updates, and feature tweaks), per Google Search Liaison. New platforms emerge—such as AI-powered search assistants —that reshape how users find information. User behavior shifts. Tactics that worked last year become ineffective or harmful. For managers, the challenge isn't mastering every detail—it's knowing enough to make informed decisions and ask the right questions.

This chapter addresses a paradox: you must stay current without drowning in information. The solution lies in systematic learning approaches, quality filters, and clear boundaries between what you and your team need to know.

THE LEARNING PARADOX: MORE INFORMATION, LESS CLARITY

SEO information has exploded in volume while declining in average quality. Anyone can publish SEO advice online. Much of it is wrong, outdated, or context-specific, masquerading as universal truth.

The modern SEO information landscape looks like this:

- Official documentation from search engines—Google Search Central, Microsoft Bing Webmaster Guidelines, and Yandex Documentation—provides authoritative guidance but often lags tactical developments. Google's Search Central documentation answers many questions but leaves many ambiguous.

- Industry publications such as Search Engine Journal, Search Engine Land, Moz, and Search Engine Roundtable that aggregate news and analysis with good quality control and expert contributors.
- Independent practitioners sharing insights on blogs, Twitter/X, LinkedIn, and newsletters. Quality varies enormously from genuine experts sharing hard-won knowledge to self-promoters repeating conventional wisdom.
- Social media discussions on platforms like Twitter/X, LinkedIn, and Reddit, where valuable insights mix with speculation, misinformation, and algorithmic bait.
- Conference presentations at events like Pubcon, SMX, and BrightonSEO, where practitioners share case studies and strategies, though results often aren't replicable across different contexts.
- Academic research that provides rigorous analysis but typically lags real-world practice by months or years.
- Tool vendor content that often mixes genuine education with product marketing, requiring critical evaluation.

The manager's challenge isn't finding information—it's filtering signal from noise while allocating reasonable time to professional development.

What Managers Must Know vs. What Teams Must Know

Clear boundaries prevent managers from drowning in practitioner-level details while ensuring they understand enough to make informed decisions.

Managers Must Know:

- **Strategic implications of industry changes.** When Google announces a new AI Overview feature that may reduce click-through rates, managers need to understand the business impact, not the technical implementation details.

- **Enough to evaluate team or agency work.** Can you distinguish good SEO from bad? Do you recognize when someone is following outdated tactics or taking unnecessary risks?
- **How to ask the right questions.** What questions expose whether your team truly understands what they're doing versus just following a checklist?
- **Enough to advocate for SEO resources.** Can you make a business case for SEO investments to executives who don't understand it?
- **Principles that remain constant despite tactical changes.** Core concepts like relevance, authority, and user experience persist even as specific tactics evolve.
- **Red flags that indicate problems.** What signals suggest your SEO program is heading in the wrong direction before severe damage occurs?

Practitioner Teams Must Know:

- **Detailed SEO implementation tactics.** How exactly to implement structured data, configure redirects, optimize crawl budget, and execute hundreds of other specific tasks.
- **Advanced tool-specific features and workflows.** Mastering Screaming Frog, Google Search Console, various analytics platforms, and other specialized tools.
- **Technical troubleshooting.** Diagnosing why pages aren't indexing, why rankings dropped, or why crawl errors persist.
- **Latest tactics trends and experiments.** Whether a new approach discussed in the community actually works or is hype.

- **Granular competitive intelligence.** What specific tactics do competitors use, and are they worth replicating?

This division of labor allows managers to stay strategically informed without becoming tactical practitioners.

BUILDING YOUR LEARNING SYSTEM

Effective professional development requires systems, not just consuming random information.

The Three-Tier Information Diet

Tier 1: Essential Daily Awareness (15 minutes/day)

- Subscribe to 2-3 high-quality aggregators that curate SEO news. These act as filters, surfacing the most important developments while screening out noise.
- Recommended starting points include Search Engine Roundtable (by Barry Schwartz) for daily updates, SEOFOMO (by Aleyda Solis) for curated weekly highlights, and the Google Search Central Blog for official announcements.
- Skim headlines in your chosen aggregators each morning. Read full articles only when headlines indicate something affects your organization directly.
- Set up Google Alerts for your company name plus "SEO" or your industry plus "search rankings" to catch relevant discussions early.

Pro Tip: Follow prominent SEOs on platforms like LinkedIn to see which articles they forward—this often saves me time.

Tier 2: Weekly Deep Dives (60-90 minutes/week)

- Choose one day weekly for deeper learning. Friday afternoons work well—time for reflection before the weekend.
- Read 2-3 substantial articles, watching for strategic implications rather than tactics. Ask yourself: "How does this affect our business? Should I raise this with our team or agency?"
- Review your own SEO performance data. Are metrics moving as expected? Do recent industry changes explain any anomalies?
- Check a few key competitors. Have they made significant changes to their sites? Launched new content initiatives?
- Scan LinkedIn or Twitter for conversations among practitioners you respect. What topics are generating discussion and debate?

Tier 3: Quarterly Strategic Learning (1-2 days/quarter)

- Attend one virtual or in-person SEO or digital-marketing event per quarter; most major conferences (Pubcon, BrightonSEO, SMX) now offer virtual streams. Even if only one session provides actionable insights, that justifies the time investment.
- Read a book or take an online course on SEO management, digital marketing strategy, or adjacent topics like analytics or UX.
- Conduct a personal knowledge audit: What came up in recent months that you didn't understand? What skills do you need to develop?
- Meet with peers from other companies for informal knowledge sharing. What are they struggling with? What have they learned?

QUALITY FILTERS: EVALUATING SEO INFORMATION

Not all SEO advice deserves equal weight. Apply these filters:

- **Consider the source's credibility.** Does this person have a track record of accurate insights? Have they worked on sites at scale, or only small projects? Do other respected practitioners reference them?
- **Look for evidence, not assertions.** Claims such as "keyword density should be 2-3 percent" require data to support them. Assertions without evidence deserve skepticism.
- **Evaluate generalizability.** A tactic that worked for one e-commerce site may not work for B2B service businesses. Context matters.
- **Check recency.** SEO advice from 2020 might be outdated. Check publication dates and assess whether the recommendations still apply.
- **Detect conflicts of interest.** Is this guidance genuinely helpful, or is it designed to sell services or tools? Not all vendor content is biased, but consider the motivations behind it.
- **Verify with multiple sources.** If one person claims something, they might be wrong. If five respected practitioners independently reach similar conclusions, pay attention.
- **Test against your own experience.** Does this advice align with what you've observed working in your organization? Contradictions deserve investigation.

Red Flags in SEO Advice

Certain claims should trigger immediate skepticism:

- **"Guaranteed rankings" promise.** No one can guarantee specific rankings. Search algorithms are complex, competitive, and constantly changing. Anyone promising "#1 for keyword X in 30 days" is either lying or planning risky tactics.

- **Secrets or tricks that search engines hate.** Legitimate SEO tactics aren't secret—they're openly discussed. Claims of "loopholes" or "tricks Google doesn't want you to know" usually describe tactics that violate guidelines.
- **Universal best practices without context.** Almost no SEO tactic works universally. Advice that doesn't acknowledge trade-offs or context-dependency oversimplifies reality.
- **Outdated tactics presented as current.** Keyword stuffing, exact-match anchor text at scale, article spinning, and other tactics from the 2000s still get recommended. These approaches cause more harm than good.
- **Over-emphasis on any single factor.** SEO involves hundreds of signals. Anyone claiming "just do X and you'll rank" misunderstands how search works.
- **Catastrophizing minor changes.** Not every Google update is the end of the world. Beware voices that turn every announcement into a crisis.
- **Tool worship.** Tools provide data, not answers. Advice that amounts to "just use tool X" without strategic thinking isn't advice.

LEARNING FROM CONFERENCES AND EVENTS

Conferences offer concentrated learning and networking but require intentional participation to justify costs.

Choosing Events

Evaluate conferences on these dimensions:

- **Speaker quality.** Do they feature practitioners with real-world experience, or those who are constantly on the speaker circuit? Review past agendas to assess quality. Check their LinkedIn profile.
- **Audience relevance.** Is this conference for practitioners, managers, or executives? Attending the wrong event wastes time.
- **Content depth.** Some conferences offer tactical deep dives. Others provide strategic overviews. Match depth to your needs.
- **Format.** Single-track conferences ensure everyone hears the same agenda. Multi-track events offer more choice but dilute networking.
- **Size.** Intimate events (50-100 people) enable meaningful connections. Large events (1,000+ people) offer more content but less personal interaction.
- **Location and timing.** Can you justify the travel time and cost? Does timing conflict with critical business periods?
- **Established conferences worth considering** include Pubcon for technical SEO depth and practitioner networking, brightonSEO for broad content with optional workshops, SMX for comprehensive search marketing, including PPC, and Content Marketing World for strategic SEO and content marketing.
- **Regional meetups and smaller events.** They often deliver a higher ROI than major conferences. A local meetup costs nothing, requires no travel, and connects you with practitioners facing similar challenges in your market.

- **So-called "tax-deductible holidays"** describe SEO conferences held in exotic locations overseas — a tongue-in-cheek industry term rather than a formal category.

Maximizing Conference Value

Before attending:

- Review the agenda and identify which sessions address current challenges or strategic questions you're facing.
- Research speakers whose sessions you plan to attend. What's their expertise? Have they written anything you should read first?
- Set specific learning objectives. "Learn three new things" is vague. "Understand how to evaluate AI's impact on content strategy" is a specific goal.
- Schedule meetings with other attendees, vendors you're considering, or speakers whose work you respect.

During the conference:

- Take notes on insights, not facts. Capture "This changes how we should think about X" rather than trying to transcribe entire presentations. Most speakers share their slide decks.
- Ask questions in sessions, but make them specific to your context. "How would this apply to a B2B SaaS company?" gets better answers than generic questions.
- Network strategically during breaks and social events. Other managers face similar challenges and may have solved problems you're encountering.
- Skip, or walk out of sessions that aren't delivering your expectations. You paid for flexibility—use it. A productive hallway conversation may be worth more than a mediocre session.

- Visit vendor booths selectively. Do you really need their branded swag? Most vendors want to schedule sales calls, but some genuinely educate and offer useful tools or resources.

After the conference:

- Write a summary within 48 hours while your memory is fresh. What are the 3-5 key takeaways? What should you do differently?
- Share insights with your team. A 30-minute team meeting sharing conference highlights multiplies the value of your attendance.
- Follow up with valuable contacts made. Connect on LinkedIn, schedule calls with people who offered help, or share resources you discussed.
- Implement at least one thing learned. Conferences that don't change your behavior weren't worth attending.

SEO PODCASTS: SELECTIVE LISTENING

Dozens of SEO podcasts exist, from well-produced interview shows to solo commentary recordings. Quality varies enormously. The best podcasts bring genuine expertise and diverse perspectives. They work well for commute-learning or exercise time. The worst are thinly-veiled product pitches or repetitive regurgitation of industry news you've already read. Evaluate podcasts by checking: Does the host ask probing questions or just softball their guests? Do episodes provide actionable insights or just surface-level commentary? Is the production quality professional enough to respect your time?

Sample 2-3 episodes before subscribing. If a podcast hasn't taught you something useful after three episodes, unsubscribe ruthlessly. Your attention is finite—save it for sources that actually inform decisions rather than fill airtime. Some managers avoid podcasts entirely, preferring written content they can skim and revisit. That's legitimate—podcasts demand linear attention that written content doesn't. Choose the format that fits your learning style, not what's trendy.

Pro Tip: Use AI tools (e.g., ChatGPT for browsing, Claude for summarization, or podcast summary tools) before committing to full episodes—this helps you pre-screen whether the content is worth your listening time.

BUILDING A PROFESSIONAL NETWORK

Your professional network is the most valuable learning resource you have. Other managers understand your challenges better than bloggers and speakers can.

Finding Your Peer Group

- **LinkedIn groups** focused on SEO management or your industry often facilitate discussions and questions. Quality varies, but well-moderated groups provide value.
- **Slack communities** like The SEO Community or Tech SEO Connect offer ongoing conversations with practitioners. These can be overwhelming due to volume, but they enable real-time discussions.
- **Private mastermind groups** of 5-8 managers who meet regularly to discuss challenges provide the deepest value. You might form one organically with managers you meet at conferences or through mutual connections.

Giving to Get

The best networks are reciprocal—to receive help, you must give it. Share what you learn at conferences, in social media platforms, or from experiments; others benefit from your experience and remember your generosity when you need help. Introduce people who should know each other, as facilitating valuable connections builds social capital. Answer questions honestly when others face challenges you've solved.

Admit what you don't know. Vulnerability builds trust and often leads to helpful suggestions you wouldn't receive if you pretended expertise. And respect confidentiality—what's shared in the network stays in the network unless explicitly allowed otherwise.

STRUCTURED LEARNING: COURSES AND CERTIFICATIONS

Formal education in SEO ranges from free introductory courses to expensive certifications. Choose based on your goals and learning style.

Recommended Free Resources

- **Google Search Central Documentation** provides authoritative guidance on Google's perspective. Start with "SEO Starter Guide" and "Search Essentials."
  URL: https://developers.google.com/search/docs
- **Google's GA4 training resources** cover the only supported Google Analytics version since July 2023, covering implementation, analysis, and reporting that support SEO measurement.
  URL: https://support.google.com/analytics/answer/15068052
- **LearningSEO** is a repository of SEO learning resources curated by Aleyda Solis.
  URL: https://learningseo.io/
- **Ahrefs Academy** offers free courses on various SEO topics with high production quality, though naturally featuring their tools.
  URL: https://ahrefs.com/academy

- **Semrush Academy** similarly provides free education with tool-focused examples, but covers fundamental concepts well. URL: https://www.semrush.com/academy/

Paid Training Worth Considering

- **University programs** like UC San Diego Extension offer multi-week digital marketing programs including SEO modules. This is best for structured learning and recognized credentials.
- **Industry-specific training,** for example, for developers or publishers, addresses niche needs that generic courses don't cover.

Certification Value and Limits

SEO certifications have debatable value. I once owned a company that issued such certifications nearly fifteen years ago, but I would not do it now. SEO is so broad that it is impossible to offer anything beyond a basic certification.

Google Search Console certification costs nothing and serves as a basic validation of knowledge. Certifications from established training companies such as Moz or Semrush demonstrate a commitment to learning. But certifications don't replace experience—they supplement it.

Treat certifications as structured learning opportunities rather than credential-collecting. The learning matters more than the certificate.

UNLEARNING: THE HARDER PART OF PROFESSIONAL DEVELOPMENT

Staying current requires not just learning new information but unlearning outdated practices.

Common Outdated Beliefs Still Circulating

- **"Keyword density should be X percent"** – This was never officially true, and modern algorithms focus on semantic meaning and relevance rather than word repetition.
- **"You need exactly 300 words minimum per page"** – Content length should serve user needs, not arbitrary minimums. Some topics require 3,000 words; others, 100.
- **"Meta keywords tag matters"** – Major search engines stopped using the meta keywords tag by 2009 (Google never used it; Bing officially ignored it from 2009 onward). It's harmless but pointless.
- **"You must use exact-match keywords in anchor text"** – Over-optimization of anchor text looks manipulative. Natural, varied anchor text performs better.
- **"H1 tags are the most important ranking factor"** – Heading tags help structure content, but aren't uniquely powerful. Obsessing over them misses the forest for the trees.
- **"Google penalties are common"** – Manual penalties are rare and typically target egregious violations. Most ranking drops result from algorithm changes or competitive dynamics, not penalties.
- **"PageRank is dead"** – The public toolbar is gone, but link-based authority remains a major ranking signal. The concept persists even if the specific metric isn't visible.
- **"SEO is dead"** – this is more of an annual in-joke among practitioners when a significant challenge to traditional SEO is unveiled.

Recognizing When to Unlearn

How do you know when a practice you've always followed is outdated?

- When multiple respected sources independently say it's no longer effective, pay attention. One person might be wrong, but consensus signals change.
- When your own experiments contradict conventional wisdom, trust your data if it's statistically significant.
- When official documentation explicitly contradicts a practice, update your understanding. Google occasionally clarifies that widely-believed tactics don't actually work.
- When tactics feel increasingly mechanical or divorced from user value, question whether they're still relevant. SEO increasingly rewards user-focused optimization over technical manipulation.

Time Management for Professional Development

The biggest obstacle to staying current is finding time. Here's how to protect it:

Calendar Blocking

- Schedule learning time as recurring calendar appointments. Treat them as seriously as meetings.
- Friday afternoons (60-90 minutes) work well for many managers. The week is winding down, making it easier to focus on learning rather than urgent operational tasks.
- Block 4-6 hours quarterly for deeper learning—reading a book, taking an online course, or attending a virtual conference.

Learning in Found Time

- Consume audio content during commutes or exercise. Podcasts such as "Search Engine Journal Show," "Majestic Podcasts," and "EDGE of the Web" turn otherwise unproductive time into learning opportunities.
- Read saved articles during waiting time. Tools like Instapaper or Pocket let you save articles for later reading during unexpected downtime.
- Watch conference session recordings at 1.5x speed. You can consume 90 minutes of content in 60 minutes without losing comprehension.

Team-Based Learning

- Distribute learning across your team. Have different team members attend different conference sessions or follow different information sources, then share key insights in team meetings.
- Establish monthly lunch-and-learns where team members present topics they've researched. This spreads learning while developing presentation skills.
- Create a shared reading list where team members recommend articles or resources worth the team's time.

EVALUATING YOUR SEO KNOWLEDGE GAPS

Periodically audit what you don't know to identify strategic learning priorities.

Knowledge Self-Assessment

Rate your confidence (1-5 scale) in these areas:

Strategic understanding:

- Business case for SEO investment
- SEO's role in the overall marketing mix
- Competitive positioning and differentiation
- Resource allocation and prioritization

Technical concepts:

- How search engines crawl and index content
- Site architecture and information design
- Performance and Core Web Vitals
- Structured data and schema markup

Content and optimization:

- Keyword research and search intent
- Content strategy and planning
- On-page optimization fundamentals
- Content quality evaluation

Analytics and measurement:

- Google Analytics interpretation
- Search Console analysis
- Attribution models
- ROI calculation for SEO

Team and vendor management:

- Evaluating agency proposals
- Managing in-house teams

Is Our SEO Working?

- QA processes
- Stakeholder communication

Industry trends:

- AI impact on search
- Algorithm update implications
- Emerging platforms and opportunities
- Regulatory changes affecting SEO

Areas scoring 1-2 indicate knowledge gaps that warrant attention. Areas scoring 4-5 may need only occasional updates to stay current.

Feedback from Your Team

Ask your team where they would like you to have more knowledge. They may diplomatically avoid mentioning gaps, so frame it constructively: "What should I learn more about to support you better?"

Tip: Book 2, *Accidental SEO Manager*, is perfect for this purpose.

Typical responses include requests to understand technical constraints better, appreciate the complexity of certain tasks, or recognize the time required for quality work.

Feedback from Stakeholders

When executives or other stakeholders ask questions you can't answer confidently, note those as learning priorities.

If you're frequently explaining the same basic concepts to stakeholders, it's a signal that you need stronger frameworks or analogies to communicate SEO effectively.

Red Flags That You're Falling Behind

Sure signs that indicate you're not keeping pace with industry changes:

- **Your team references concepts or tactics you haven't heard of.** Occasional unknowns are fine, but consistent confusion suggests a knowledge gap.
- **Stakeholders ask about industry news you weren't aware of.** If others in your organization are more informed about SEO developments than you are, adjust your information sources.
- **Your strategic recommendations feel increasingly tactical.** When you can't distinguish between important strategic shifts and minor tactical adjustments, you've lost perspective.
- **You're still talking about things that mattered five years ago.** References to Penguin penalties or Authorship markup indicate outdated concerns—Penguin has been part of Google's core algorithm since 2016, and Authorship markup ended in 2014.
- **Your team seems frustrated by your questions or suggestions.** If they're repeatedly explaining why your ideas won't work, you may be out of touch with current practice.
- **You can't evaluate vendor pitches confidently.** If every agency proposal sounds equally plausible or implausible, you lack the knowledge to distinguish good from bad.

BUILDING A LEARNING CULTURE

Your own SEO learning matters less than establishing systems that keep the entire organization up to date. Establish learning systems alongside the QA processes (Chapter 5) and measurement frameworks (Chapter 4) that define your organization's SEO maturity.

Knowledge Sharing Rituals

- **Weekly team huddles** (15-30 minutes) where each person shares one thing they learned or tried that week. Brief and regular beats long and sporadic.

- **Monthly deep dives** where one team member presents research on a topic, competitive analysis, or experimental results. Rotate presenters to develop everyone's skills.
- **Quarterly reviews** of significant industry changes, algorithm updates, and strategic implications. These connect day-to-day work to the broader context.
- **Internal wiki or documentation** that captures institutional knowledge. When someone solves a problem, document it so others can benefit from it.

Encouraging Experimentation

- Allocate 10-20 percent of team time to experimentation and learning. Google's famous "20 percent time" principle applies to SEO—innovation requires slack in the system.
- Create safe environments for sharing failed experiments. Teams that only share successes stop experimenting.
- Celebrate learning as much as results. "We tried X and learned it doesn't work for us" is valuable knowledge, even if traffic didn't increase.

External Connections

- Encourage team members to attend conferences, participate in online communities, and build professional networks.
- Some managers fear that external networking will lead to team members leaving for other opportunities. The opposite is often true—employees who feel invested in and connected to the industry are more engaged and loyal.
- Budget for conference attendance, training courses, and tool subscriptions that support professional development.

AI IMPLICATIONS FOR STAYING CURRENT

AI is both changing what you need to know and creating new learning tools such as ChatGPT Search and Gemini Learn.

What AI Changes About SEO Learning

- **Information synthesis** becomes more important than information collection. AI can summarize hundreds of sources; your value lies in interpreting implications and making decisions.
- **Tactical knowledge becomes less differentiated.** When AI can implement standard SEO tactics, managers add value through strategy and judgment, not tactical expertise.
- **Learning accelerates** because AI can tutor you on specific topics, answer questions in real-time, and provide examples tailored to your context.
- **Misinformation risk increases** because AI can generate confident-sounding but incorrect SEO advice at scale. Critical evaluation skills become more important.

Using AI for Professional Development

- **Custom tutoring:** Ask Gemini, ChatGPT, or Copilot to explain concepts you don't understand, asking follow-up questions until clarity emerges.
- **Scenario analysis:** Pose hypothetical situations to AI and analyze its recommendations critically. This builds judgment even when AI's specific advice may be flawed.
- **Content summarization:** Use AI to summarize long articles, videos, research papers, or conference session transcripts, then read full versions of what seems most relevant.

Is Our SEO Working?

- **Knowledge testing:** Ask AI to quiz you on SEO concepts or generate case studies to analyze.

Pro Tip: Remember that AI knowledge bases have cutoff dates (often two years ago for major models) and may omit recent SEO developments. Verify important claims against current sources.

MANAGER'S FRAMEWORK: PERSONAL LEARNING PLAN

Use this template to structure your ongoing professional development:

Current Quarter Learning Goals:

- [Specific knowledge or skill to develop]
- [Specific knowledge or skill to develop]
- [Specific knowledge or skill to develop]

Information Sources (Daily/Weekly):

- Daily aggregator: [Which service/newsletter]
- Weekly reading time: [When blocked on calendar]
- Key sources followed: [List 3-5 blogs, newsletters, or people]

Deep Learning (Quarterly):

- Conference or event: [Which event, when]
- Course or book: [What you'll complete]
- Peer learning: [Meetup, mastermind, or connections to develop]

Knowledge Gaps to Address:

- [Specific area where understanding is weak]
- [Learning resources or approaches for each]
- [Timeline for improvement]

Unlearning Checklist:

- Reviewed practices against current best practices
- Identified outdated beliefs to discard
- Updated team documentation accordingly

Evaluation:

- How will you measure whether learning efforts are effective?
- What would indicate you're staying current successfully?
- What would signal you're falling behind?

Review Schedule:

- Monthly check-in on learning progress
- Quarterly assessment of knowledge gaps
- Annual comprehensive review of the learning system

Note on frequency: Set learning goals quarterly, but don't treat this as a quarterly fill-out-the-template exercise. The template is designed to help you structure your approach at the outset. After that:

- **Monthly:** Quick check—am I making progress on learning goals?
- **Quarterly:** Refresh goals for next quarter based on business priorities
- **Annually:** Comprehensive review of learning system effectiveness

In most quarters, your learning review is either "still progressing on Q2 goals, will continue," or "completed X, shifting to Y for Q3." Extensive template completion happens annually, not quarterly.

LEARNING AND PROFESSIONAL DEVELOPMENT

Professional development policies—including learning cadence and resource allocation—are detailed in Book3, Chapter 10: *AI Visibility Playbook*.

Chapter 14

YOUR 90-DAY IMPLEMENTATION ROADMAP

You've read about GEO, competitive intelligence, QA, technical foundations, and dozens of other topics. Now what?

This 90-day roadmap turns frameworks into action. Whether you're new to managing SEO or refining an established program, these first 90 days set your trajectory.

BEFORE YOU BEGIN: TAKING STOCK

Organizational SEO Maturity Assessment

Rate your organization honestly (1=just starting, 5=highly mature):

- Strategic alignment (1-5): __
- Technical foundation (1-5): __
- Content capability (1-5): __
- Team capacity (1-5): __
- Measurement maturity (1-5): __
- Governance processes (1-5): __
- Total score: __ / 30

Interpretation:

- 24-30: Mature program; focus on optimization
- 17-23: Solid foundation; strengthen weak areas
- 10-16: Building phase; establish fundamentals
- Below 10: Start with basics and quick wins

- Below 23? Consider engaging an external consultant or agency for the first 90 days to establish frameworks, train your team, and accelerate progress. A fresh perspective and expertise can compress learning curves.

Resource Reality Check

Document honestly:

- Annual SEO budget: $____
- Team size: ____ people (FTE + contractors)
- Your time available: ____ hours/week
- Executive support level: High / Medium / Low
- Technical capability: Quick / Moderate / Slow

Limited resources? Prioritize ruthlessly. Do three things well rather than ten things poorly. External support on a project-by-project basis can help fill gaps.

Governance Maturity Context

The activities in this 90-day roadmap build governance foundations that will be assessed through frameworks like:

SEOGMM (SEO Governance Maturity Model) - Evaluates how effectively your organization governs SEO across people, process, technology, and accountability (covered in *AI Visibility Playbook*, Chapter 5)

LVMM (Local Visibility Maturity Model) - For organizations with multiple physical locations (covered in *AI Visibility Playbook*, Appendix C)

IVMM (International Visibility Maturity Model) - For organizations operating across multiple countries/languages (covered in *AI Visibility Playbook*, Appendix D)

Why this matters now: The processes, documentation, and workflows you establish in these 90 days become the evidence base for future governance assessments. By documenting ownership, standards, and workflows properly from the start, you're building toward SEOGMM Level 2-3 maturity without additional work later.

Key principle: Don't build processes to "pass assessment"—build processes that reflect good governance, and the assessment will naturally reflect that maturity.

DAYS 1-30: QUICK WINS AND ASSESSMENT

Week 1: Orientation and Access

Secure essential access:

- Google Analytics 4 (GA4 — the only supported Google Analytics version since July 2023) and Search Console
- SEO tools (Ahrefs, Semrush, etc.)
- CMS and internal systems

Meet individually with team members:

- Understand roles and current work
- Identify immediate concerns
- Ask: "What should I know that I haven't asked?"

Establish meeting cadences:

- Weekly team sync
- Bi-weekly stakeholder updates
- Monthly executive briefing

Week 2: Performance Baseline

Document current state:

- Organic sessions (12-month trend)
- Top 10 keyword rankings
- Conversion rate from organic
- Revenue contribution (if trackable)
- Establish baseline metrics using the measurement framework from Chapter 4.

Run initial technical audit:

- Full site crawl (Screaming Frog, Sitebulb, or JetOctopus)
- Search Console error review
- Core Web Vitals assessment (INP replaced FID as the interaction metric in March 2024)
- Critical issues identified: [Document]

Technical Health Scorecard

Technical health monitoring is established and protected through the QA processes described in Chapter 5.

Use this quarter to assess technical foundations:

Indexation Health (1-5):

- >90 percent of important pages indexed __
- Minimal crawl errors in Search Console __
- Sitemaps submitted and processed __
- No significant indexation drops __

Performance (1-5):

- Core Web Vitals meet "Good" thresholds __
- Mobile page speed competitive __

- No significant performance regressions __

Code Quality (1-5):

- No critical HTML validation errors __
- Semantic heading structure __
- Clean, maintainable codebase __

Infrastructure (1-5):

- HTTPS implemented correctly __
- Valid SSL certificate __
- Proper redirect handling __
- Canonical tags used appropriately __

Mobile Experience (1-5):

- Responsive design implemented __
- Mobile-desktop content parity __
- Mobile UX validated via Lighthouse and field data (CrUX) __

Structured Data (1-5):

- Appropriate schema types implemented __
- Validates without errors __
- Coverage across important page types __

Total Score: __ / 30

- **24-30:** Excellent technical foundation. Focus on maintenance and optimization.
- **18-23:** Solid foundation with some gaps. Address specific weak areas.
- **12-17:** Significant technical debt. Prioritize the improvement plan.

Below 12: Critical issues likely affecting performance. Urgent action needed

Benchmark complete: You now know where you stand.

Week 3: Quick Win Identification

Find low-hanging fruit from:

Search Console:

- Pages ranking 11-20 (small optimization could push to page 1)
- High-impression, low-click pages (metadata improvement)
- Easy-to-fix crawl errors

Site review:

- Missing/duplicate title tags or meta descriptions
- Orphaned pages (no internal links)
- Broken links
- Missing image alt text
- Slow-loading pages with obvious fixes

Prioritize top 3-5 opportunities:

- Implementable within two weeks
- High probability of positive impact
- Low resource requirement
- Visible results to stakeholders

Week 4: Execute and Report

Implement 2-3 quick wins:

- Assign resources
- Define success metrics
- Track implementation

Map stakeholders:

- Marketing leadership (expectations)
- Product/development (processes)
- Content team (capabilities)
- IT/technical (requirements)
- Legal/compliance (constraints)

Create a 30-day assessment:

- Current baseline
- Quick wins are in progress
- Major opportunities are identified
- Critical risks are flagged
- Initial recommendations made

Present to Stakeholders by the end of Week 4.

Are you struggling to identify quick wins or concerned about priorities? This is an ideal time to bring in a consultant for a focused assessment. A day or two of external expertise can identify opportunities your team is too close to see.

DAYS 31-60: FOUNDATION-BUILDING

Week 5-6: Process Development

Establish SEO governance:

- Define what requires SEO review
- Document approval workflow
- Create review request template
- Communicate to stakeholders

Is Our SEO Working?

For the full governance framework—including approval workflows, oversight roles, and escalation paths—see Book 3, Chapter 5 of the *AI Visibility Playbook*.

This roadmap focuses on execution timing; Book 3 defines the policies that maintain consistency across teams and markets.

Implement QA:

- Pre-launch checklist for your organization
- QA roles and responsibilities
- Testing environments
- Monitoring and alerts
- Implement the QA framework from Chapter 5, adapting it to your organization's maturity level and resources.

Set up reporting:

- Identify NSM
- Define supporting KPIs
- Create executive dashboard
- Schedule reporting cadence

Week 7: Competitive Intelligence

Conduct competitive analysis (using Chapter 2 framework):

- Identify 3-5 key SEO competitors
- Analyze keyword visibility gaps
- Assess content strategies
- Review technical implementations
- Evaluate backlink profiles
- Test AI visibility (ChatGPT with browsing, Google Gemini's web results, and Perplexity (Profiles)
- Conduct this analysis using the framework detailed in Chapter 2.

Document findings:

- Our competitive position
- Strengths to defend
- Vulnerabilities to address
- Opportunities to exploit

Set up ongoing monitoring:

- Rank tracking
- Backlink alerts
- Competitor content monitoring

Week 8: Strategic Planning

Conduct a strategy workshop (2-4 hours with stakeholders):

- Review business objectives (next 12 months)
- Map SEO opportunities to objectives
- Identify resource requirements
- Prioritize initiatives
- Build consensus

Output: 12-Month SEO Roadmap

Q1-Q4 priorities: Each quarter: 2-3 major initiatives with owner, timeline, and success metrics

Get the roadmap approved:

- Team review
- Stakeholder feedback incorporated
- Executive sign-off
- Resources committed

Is Our SEO Working?

Prepare budget proposal (if needed):

- Tool subscriptions started/renewed
- Agency/contractor support
- Content creation (if external)
- Training and development
- Total investment and expected ROI

Roadmap feels overwhelming or lacks expertise? Many organizations engage agencies or consultants specifically for strategic planning. They bring industry benchmarks, competitive intelligence, and patterns from similar companies that inform better decisions.

DAYS 61-90: MOMENTUM AND SCALE

Week 9-10: Launch Strategic Initiatives

Begin 2-3 major initiatives:

For each:

- Clear objective
- Assigned owner
- Defined timeline
- Success metrics
- Status tracking
- Blocker identification

Build a knowledge base:

- Internal wiki created/enhanced
- SEO standards documented
- Process documentation complete
- Training materials developed

Week 11: Team Development

Assess capabilities:

- Individual strengths
- Development areas
- Skill gaps vs. needs
- Training opportunities

Provide development:

- Conference attendance planned
- Online courses assigned
- Mentoring relationships
- Career discussions

Build culture:

- Team rituals (lunch & learns)
- Win celebration process
- Knowledge sharing
- Psychological safety

Week 12: Review and Refine

Conduct 90-day retrospective:

What went well:

- [Achievement and why]
- [Achievement and why]

What didn't go as planned:

- [Challenge and why]
- [Challenge and why]

Is Our SEO Working?

What we learned:

- [Insight and implications]
- [Insight and implications]

What we should change:

- [Adjustment and rationale]
- [Adjustment and rationale]

Update stakeholders comprehensively:

- Achievements in 90 days
- Challenges and responses
- Strategic plan for next quarter
- Resource needs

Refine processes:

- Update documentation
- Adjust templates
- Implement improvements

Set goals for the next 90 days.

SUCCESS METRICS FOR 90-DAY PERIOD

Quantitative:

- Traffic: Baseline → Target → Actual
- Top 10 rankings: Baseline → Target → Actual
- Technical issues resolved: Target → Actual
- Quick wins delivered: Target → Actual

Qualitative:

- Stakeholder relationships (1-5): Beginning __ → End __
- Team confidence (1-5): Beginning __ → End __
- SEO organizational visibility (1-5): Beginning __ → End __
- Foundation for scale: Yes / Partially / No

Deliverables completed:

- 30-day assessment ☐
- 12-month roadmap ☐
- Reporting template ☐
- Governance framework ☐
- QA processes ☐
- Quick wins executed ☐
- Training materials ☐
- Executive presentation ☐

COMMON 90-DAY CHALLENGES

- **Too many priorities:** Limit work in progress. Complete three things thoroughly rather than starting ten.
- **Stakeholder resistance:** Build relationships before needing favors. Frame SEO in terms of their goals.
- **Analysis paralysis:** Set decision deadlines. Imperfect action beats perfect planning.
- **Quick wins don't materialize:** Ensure correct measurement and allow 4-6 weeks for impact.
- **Team pushback:** Involve the team in decisions. Listen to concerns—they know constraints you don't.
- **Executive disengagement:** Make updates shorter, action-oriented. Lead with business impact.

- **Persistent issues or lack of progress?** External consultants excel at breaking through organizational inertia. They bring fresh perspective, executive credibility, and experience from similar situations. Consider a focused engagement to unstick blocked initiatives.

BEYOND 90 DAYS: SUSTAINING MOMENTUM

Avoiding Assessment Overload

This book contains multiple assessment frameworks and scorecards. They exist to help you diagnose problems and evaluate initiatives—not to create quarterly paperwork burdens.

Do not run all frameworks quarterly. That path leads to assessment fatigue, a box-checking mentality, and managers spending more time on framework scoring than on managing SEO.

Monthly Dashboard Review (30-60 minutes): Review automated dashboards covering:

- Traffic, rankings, conversions vs. goals
- Technical health alerts (Search Console errors, Core Web Vitals)
- Competitive rank tracking for strategic keywords
- Any custom business metrics (leads, revenue, etc.)

Action when dashboards show problems: Use the relevant framework from this book to diagnose the issue. Competitive position declining? Run Chapter 2's competitive analysis. Are technical errors increasing? Use Chapter 3's technical scorecard. Dashboards tell you **what** needs attention; frameworks help you understand **why** and **what to do**.

Quarterly Integrated SEO Business Review (4-6 hours): Consolidate all SEO dimensions into ONE quarterly review:

Part 1: Business Performance (2 hours)

- Performance vs. quarterly goals (Chapter 4 measurement framework)
- Competitive position summary (Chapter 2—but only detailed analysis if position changed significantly)
- AI visibility trends (Chapter 4 AI scorecard—track trends, don't score every dimension)
- Attribution to business outcomes (revenue, leads, pipeline)

Part 2: Operational Health (1-2 hours)

- Technical health summary (Chapter 3—review dashboard trends, use scorecard only if concerns exist)
- QA effectiveness (Chapter 5—incidents prevented, issues caught, process improvements)
- Structured data coverage trends (Chapter 6—track %, don't re-score readiness)
- Navigation/UX flags requiring attention (Chapter 8)

Part 3: Team & Capability (30-60 minutes)

- Learning progress against quarterly plan (Chapter 13)
- Process improvements implemented
- Resource adequacy assessment
- Stakeholder relationship health

Part 4: Strategic Planning (1-2 hours)

- Next quarter objectives and key results
- Resource allocation decisions
- Major initiatives to launch/continue/stop

- Stakeholder communication plan

Output: One executive summary document covering all dimensions, decisions made, and next quarter priorities.

Annual Deep Assessment (1-2 days): Once per year, conduct a comprehensive evaluation:

- Full competitive analysis (Chapter 2 complete framework)
- Technical audit (Chapter 3 complete scorecard)
- Structured data readiness assessment (Chapter 6 complete framework)
- Navigation architecture evaluation (Chapter 8)
- International/local capabilities if applicable (Chapter 7)
- Team skill assessment and development planning

This becomes your strategic planning foundation and baseline for the coming year.

When to Use Individual Frameworks

The detailed frameworks in this book are diagnostic tools. Use them when:

Chapter 2 Competitive Framework: Competitive position changes unexpectedly, entering a new market, before major content strategy decisions

Chapter 3 Technical Scorecard: Technical health dashboards show concerning trends, before/after migrations, and annual deep assessment

Chapter 4 Measurement Framework: Building a new measurement approach, dashboards show attribution problems, switching analytics platforms

Chapter 6 Structured Data Framework: Implementing schema for the first time, rich results not appearing as expected, annual coverage review

Chapter 8 Navigation Scorecard: Site redesign, conversion paths underperforming, major UX changes planned

The principle: Frameworks are for diagnosis and decision-making, not compliance. Use them when you need insights, not because the calendar says so.

Red Flags of Assessment Overload

You're doing too much assessment if:

- You spend more time scoring frameworks than implementing improvements
- Team views assessments as bureaucracy rather than a useful diagnosis
- Quarterly reviews take longer than 6 hours
- Same scores repeat quarter after quarter with no change
- Assessments don't lead to decisions or actions

Fix: Reduce assessment frequency, consolidate related assessments, automate what's measurable, and only deep-dive dimensions showing problems.

Quarterly Planning Cycle

Week 1: Review and Reflect

- Conduct integrated quarterly review (see "Avoiding Assessment Overload" above)
- Review results against quarterly goals
- Identify what worked, what didn't, and why

- Update competitive intelligence only if the position changed significantly
- Document key learnings

Week 2: Plan and Prioritize

- Set next quarter objectives aligned with annual goals
- Prioritize 2-3 major initiatives (not 10)
- Allocate resources (time, budget, people)
- Identify dependencies and risks
- Get stakeholder alignment

Weeks 3-12: Execute and Monitor

- Implement planned initiatives
- Monitor monthly dashboards
- Course-correct as needed
- Communicate progress to stakeholders

Week 13: Prepare for Next Cycle

- Complete any in-flight work that can be finished
- Document status of ongoing initiatives
- Prepare quarterly review materials
- Begin next quarter planning

Key principle: Most of your time should be spent executing, not assessing. Reserve deep assessment for when you need strategic insight, not calendar compliance.

Annual Strategic Refresh

Once yearly, assess:

- Business alignment (strategy shifts?)
- Competitive landscape (new threats/opportunities?)
- Capability audit (team skills, process fitness)
- Technology assessment (tech stack helping or hindering SEO automation and AI integration?)

CRISIS MANAGEMENT: WHEN THINGS GO WRONG

Traffic Drop Response Protocol

Immediate (First 24 hours):

- Confirm drop is real (not tracking issue)
- Check Search Console for manual actions
- Review recent site changes
- "Check for ranking-related notices on the Google Search Status Dashboard and monitor reliable volatility trackers (e.g., Semrush Sensor, MozCast).

Verify the site is accessible to both users and search engine bots (HTTP 200 responses and no DNS failures).

Short-term (Week 1):

- Technical audit. Cover the technical foundations outlined in Chapter 3 during this audit.
- Compare competitor performance
- Analyze which pages/keywords declined
- Interview the team about changes
- Document timeline

Medium-term (Weeks 2-4):

- Develop a hypothesis about the cause
- Implement remediation
- Monitor recovery
- Communicate status
- Document learnings

Do NOT:

- Make changes without understanding the cause
- Try multiple fixes simultaneously
- Hide problems from stakeholders

Escalate to executives when:

- Business impact severe ($\approx$ 20 %+ revenue or traffic decline persisting > 48 hours)
- Recovery requires significant resources
- External factors are involved (legal, security)
- Timeline to resolution is long (3+ months)

Disaster Recovery Awareness

When a traffic or ranking crisis is caused by infrastructure or data loss, the issue shifts from analysis to restoration. Managers should understand whether the organization's **disaster recovery plan (DRP)** covers web servers, CMS backups, and search visibility dependencies.

What to Confirm

- Backups exist and are tested for CMS, DNS, and structured data.
- Recovery time targets align with business expectations.
- Rollback procedures and contact chains are documented.
- SEO and analytics teams are included in recovery drills.

Governance Connection

A working DRP is a visible part of governance maturity.

Even when IT leads the technical response, marketing and SEO leaders should know who declares recovery complete—and when to communicate that the site and data are stable again.

Bring solutions along with problems:

- Present the situation clearly
- Explain probable causes
- Propose options with trade-offs
- Recommend specific action
- Request specific decisions/resources

Major crisis or rapid decline? This is when agencies and consultants prove their value. They've seen similar situations, know recovery patterns, and can diagnose quickly. Time matters in crisis—leverage expertise to accelerate recovery.

CUSTOMIZING THIS ROADMAP

Mature Organizations (Score 24+)

- Compress timeline
- Focus on optimization and innovation
- Expand scope to new channels/markets

Early-stage Organizations (Score below 16)

- Extend key phases (take full 30 days for assessment)
- Focus on basics before advanced tactics
- Build credibility through visible quick wins
- Consider: a 90-day consulting engagement to establish frameworks

Is Our SEO Working?

Resource-constrained

- Reduce parallel workstreams
- Leverage free tools
- Focus on high-leverage activities
- Consider: Project-based consultant support for critical initiatives

In Crisis

- Start with diagnosis and stabilization
- Communicate frequently
- Strongly consider expert help for crisis diagnosis—specialist agencies can triage within 24–48 hours and prevent compounding loss.

MEASURING ROADMAP SUCCESS

Leading Indicators (Visible Early)

- QA catching issues pre-launch
- Stakeholder requests following processes
- Reduced friction getting things done

Lagging Indicators (Visible Later)

- Traffic and rankings trending positively
- Conversions and revenue growing
- SEO included in strategic planning

Ultimate Success Measure

At 90 days, can you clearly articulate what's working, what's not, why, and what you'll do next?

- **If yes:** Foundation for sustainable success established.

- **If no:** Invest more in measurement and analysis—or bring in an external perspective to identify gaps.

YOUR NEXT STEPS RIGHT NOW

In the Next 24 Hours

- Complete an organizational maturity assessment
- Schedule a 30-day check-in meeting
- Block time on calendar for next 90 days

In the Next Week

- Conduct a resource reality check
- Identify the top 3 quick-win opportunities
- Schedule stakeholder meetings
- If score below 16 or in crisis: Research consultants/agencies for potential engagement

In the Next Month

- Execute at least one quick win
- Complete performance baseline
- Begin competitive intelligence
- Present 30-day assessment

THE MANAGER'S MINDSET

You'll constantly balance competing tensions: strategy versus tactics (understand tactics to evaluate work, but stay strategic); patience versus urgency (SEO takes time, but that's not an excuse for inaction); data versus intuition (let data inform decisions, but act on incomplete information when needed); collaboration versus advocacy (build relationships, but push back when decisions harm SEO); stability versus innovation (protect what works while exploring opportunities);

Is Our SEO Working?

and learning versus doing (stay current, but implementation matters more than knowledge).

THE QUESTION THAT STARTED THIS BOOK

"Is our SEO working?"

By now, you understand this isn't a simple yes/no question. SEO works when:

- It contributes meaningfully to business objectives
- Processes catch problems before they cause harm
- The team has clarity on priorities and why they matter
- Resources align with opportunities
- Measurement reveals truth, not just metrics
- Stakeholders understand SEO's role and value
- Continuous improvement is the norm

If those conditions exist, your SEO is working—regardless of whether traffic is up or down this month.

Your job is to create and maintain those conditions. This 90-day roadmap is your starting point.

BEYOND THIS BOOK

This volume focused on measurement, auditing, and evaluation—answering "Is our SEO working?" through frameworks and systematic analysis.

The first book, *Managing SEO,* serves as a concise strategic overview for busy managers, unifying the series' themes without duplicating the detailed material in each book.

The second book in this series, *Accidental SEO Manager*, covers foundational management concepts. If you haven't read it, that's your logical next step.

The third book, *AI Visibility Playbook*, addresses how organizations adapt visibility governance for an AI-influenced world—critical as LLMs reshape search behavior.

The fifth book, *The C-Suite Blind Spot: Winning in Organic Search with Good Governance*, makes the executive case for SEO as strategic infrastructure. Please share it with your leadership team.

But before reaching for another book, implement what you've learned here. Knowledge without application is entertainment, not education.

Build something. Then come back and tell us how it went.

INDEX

Web Content Accessibility Guidelines, 222
zero-click, 20